MISUSE C
A Handbook

D1633290

Keith S. Bovey
Solicitor, Glasgow

Butterworths
and
The Law Society of Scotland
London and Edinburgh
1986

United Kingdom
Butterworth & Co (Publishers) Ltd,
88 Kingsway, London WC2B 6AB
61A North Castle Street, Edinburgh EH2 3LJ

Australia
Butterworths Pty Ltd,
Sydney, Melbourne, Brisbane,
Adelaide, Perth, Canberra and Hobart

Canada
Butterworths. A division of Reed Inc,
Toronto and Vancouver

New Zealand
Butterworths of New Zealand Ltd,
Wellington and Auckland

Singapore
Butterworth & Co (Asia) Pte Ltd,
Singapore

South Africa
Butterworth Publishers (Pty) Ltd,
Durban and Pretoria

USA
Butterworth Legal Publishers,
St Paul, Minnesota, Seattle, Washington,
Boston, Massachusetts, Austin, Texas
and D & S Publishers,
Clearwater, Florida

ISBN 0 406 10390 9

Typeset in Scotland by
Macdonald Printers (Edinburgh) Ltd
Printed by Biddles Ltd, Guildford, Surrey

CONTENTS

Contents

TABLE OF CASES

vii

PREFACE

In describing this small work as a handbook for lawyers, I have in mind particularly the busy solicitor with a drugs case to defend in the morning and the papers, but few law books, at home the evening before. It is for this reason that I have allowed it to become a casebook and I hope that practitioners will find that the extensive quotations from judgments enable them to use these precedents, at least in the preparation of cases, without recourse to the reports but with confidence that the authorities are fairly represented by the excerpts reproduced here. Also, in some smaller courts, the library might not take in all the series of reports represented in this collection. If, therefore, prosecutors and judges find the compilation useful, I will be equally pleased. Readers are offered the assurance that the excerpts from decided cases have been chosen with care and are complete and not condensed.

For help with the glossary, I am indebted to Dr David Pollock. For expert and extremely patient typing I have to thank Ms Karen Shields and Ms Edith McNab. Mr David Fletcher, the publishers' consultant, and his colleague Riet Cannell have been the soul of kindness to a tyro author. I record my thanks also to Sheriff James P. Murphy for encouragement throughout and to Sheriff John S. Boyle, former Convener of the Law Society of Scotland Publications Committee, who first suggested the book and then kept me up to writing it.

Keith S. Bovey
June 1986

STOP PRESS

Whilst this book was in the final stages of production the Drug Trafficking Offences Act 1986 received the Royal Assent on 8th July 1986. It has been possible to summarise and discuss the new section 9A, which relates to the supplying of articles for the preparation or administration of controlled drugs, in Chapter 10, and to outline the new provisions relating to confiscation and other orders in England and Wales in Chapter 14. It has not been possible to reproduce these statutory amendments and additions in the Appendices.

INTRODUCTION

The Misuse of Drugs Act 1971

A statute of no great length or apparent complexity, of a largely codifying character, and little amended in twelve years, might suggest that the legal, as distinct from the medical or sociological, interest in the misuse of drugs could be described in a short space. But this has not proved to be so. Owing partly to inherent difficulties in defining the legal concept of possession, and partly to the ingenuity of accused persons in attempting to avoid the Act's penal sanctions, a considerable body of case-law has accumulated in the lifetime of the statute, while other cases decided under its predecessors have retained their authority as precedents.

The Misuse of Drugs Act 1971 (c 38) was passed on 27th May 1971 and its principal provisions came into operation on 1st July 1973 by virtue of the Misuse of Drugs Act 1971 (Commencement No 2) Order 1973 (SI 1973 No 795). The long title is 'An Act to make new provision with respect to dangerous or otherwise harmful drugs and related matters, and for purposes connected therewith'. The use of the word 'dangerous' may be so as to provide continuity with previous statutes, several of which were entitled 'Dangerous Drugs Act'. Those still in force (of 1965 and 1967) at the passing of the 1971 Act were repealed in their entirety (section 39 and Schedule 6). The phrase 'dangerous drugs' had been statutory for fifty years and to this day the lockfast drugs cabinet in pharmacies is known colloquially as the 'DD' cabinet, often to the pharmacists and their staff as well as to housebreakers whose target it is. The phrase is also necessary in order to indicate that the statute is an 'enactment for the time being in force relating to dangerous drugs' in terms of the Extradition Act 1932.

Lawyers now use the term 'controlled drugs' introduced by, and defined in, the Act. 'Dangerous or otherwise harmful drugs', however, appears not only in the long title but in section 32, which provides: 'The Secretary of State may conduct or assist in conducting research into any matter relating to the misuse of dangerous or otherwise harmful drugs.' The words used in the section are not defined and the clear intention is to authorise research over a wide field, including new drugs. At any rate, whatever 'dangerous or otherwise harmful drugs' may be, they are not the same as 'controlled drugs', which are defined in the Act (sections 2 and 37(1) and Schedule 2). The word 'misuse' in the short title harks back to the predecessor of 1964. It is defined in section 37(2) as the taking of a drug by a human being by way of any form of self-administration, whether or not involving assistance by another. Strangely enough, there is only

1

one penal provision in the Act which relates to misuse as so defined. This is found in section 9, whereby 'it is an offence for a person to smoke or otherwise use prepared opium'. On the principle of *expressio unius est exclusio alterius*, neither the smoking nor any other use of cannabis or cannabis resin, nor the taking of any other controlled drug, is an offence. Nor is any amount of misuse:

'Drug addiction is not a crime' (*Ramsay* v *HM Advocate* 1984 SCCR 409 per Lord Emslie, Lord Justice-General, at p 410).

Whether, and if so how, a person could 'smoke or otherwise use' a drug without being in possession of it and thus be in breach of section 5 of the Act is, of course, another matter: see *R* v *King* [1978] Crim L R 228 and cf, *R* v *Moore* [1979] Crim L R 789. The question is not, however, without significance. Suppose a blood or urine sample reveals that a controlled drug has been ingested, *quid juris*? No charge of consuming it is available to a prosecutor under the Act and a charge of possession may fail if the characteristics of the substance are changed by its ingestion: *Hambleton* v *Callinan and Others* [1968] 2 QB 427. Whether a court would draw the inference of earlier possession from evidence of ingestion and/or excretion is no doubt a matter of individual circumstances, and a problem for the draftsman of an indictment or complaint. Instances have occurred of police officers attempting to make a suspect regurgitate a substance. Proof of possession of a substance in such circumstances might not present evidential difficulties: see, eg, *R* v *Young* [1984] 1 WLR 654: 'The evidence clearly established that the appellant did have some lysergide which he swallowed as the police approached and some was found in the vomit which he was induced to produce.'

A further underlining of the omission to make the misuse of any drug an offence *per se*, with the exception of opium, is provided by section 8 which creates an offence, able to be committed only by occupiers and managers of premises, of permitting certain activities to take place on their premises. The activities are the smoking of cannabis, cannabis resin or prepared opium, but not the taking of any other controlled drug. It is thus more than theoretically possible for a roomful, or more, of people to indulge in the smoking of cannabis and only a non-smoking occupier or manager to be convicted as a result. And neither self-administration nor assisting in that act gives ground for prosecution.

The Act's forty sections are in eight unnumbered groups followed by six Schedules. The Lord Justice-Clerk found significance in the groupings when dismissing the usability heresy:

'Different subject matters are dealt with under different headings throughout the Act. For instance section 1 under reference to Schedule 1, and section 10 deal with the misuse of drugs. Section 5 is in a group of sections headed "Restrictions relating to controlled drugs, etc". There is nothing in this group of sections relating to the use or misuse of drugs from which an inference of "usable" in relation to section 5(1) can be drawn' (*Keane* v *Gallacher* 1980 J C 77 per Lord Wheatley, Lord Justice-Clerk, at p 82).

The predominant purposes of the Act from the penal standpoint are the prohibition and punishment of importation, exportation, production, supply and possession of controlled drugs. The prohibition of cultivation of cannabis (section 6), though not repealed, has become superfluous since the redefinition of cannabis by section 52 of the Criminal Law Act 1977. As that provision made the whole of the cannabis plant into a controlled drug, there is no longer a case for distinguishing the production of it from the production of any other controlled drug, and most prosecutors now charge cultivation under section 4.

CHAPTER 1

Sections 1 and 32; and Schedule 1

Section 1 of the Act constitutes the Advisory Council on the Misuse of Drugs, not 'some well-meaning people' as they have been dismissively referred to from the Supreme Court bench, but a body having the duty of keeping the situation under review and advising the government accordingly. The situation with which the Council is concerned is that of drugs of abuse, but it is not enough for such drugs to be dangerous or even lethal unless the harmful effects of misusing them are such as to 'constitute a social problem'. By definition, the Council's remit is not limited to controlled drugs, but is wide enough to enable it to recommend new drugs for control. No such power of recommendation is specifically conferred on the Council in section 1, but in section 2 the Secretary of State is restricted from laying a draft Order in Council, adding or subtracting drugs, before Parliament until 'after consultation with or on the recommendation of the Advisory Council'. It must therefore be inferred that the Council's duty of advising Ministers 'on measures which in the opinion of the Council ought to be taken for restricting the availability of a drug' includes the duty of recommending additions to or deletions from the lists of controlled drugs. The importance of these provisions lies in the flexibility which they provide, taken in conjunction with the powers conferred on the Secretary of State by section 2.

It may be, of course, that the Secretary of State will remain deaf to the Council. Its report of January 1979 recommending that cannabis and cannabis resin should be tranferred to Class C was not acted upon: see Parliamentary Debates, Vol 960, No 34, columns 579-583, 15th January 1979. The 'Secretary of State' is the Home Secretary.

Defence lawyers and sentencers also have a vested interest in the duty of the Advisory Council to advise the government on measures 'for securing the provision of proper facilities and services for the treatment, rehabilitation and after-care of persons affected by the misuse of drugs'. Here again a channel is provided whereby change may be brought about in response to perceived conditions. No doubt financial constraints will be invoked to temper demands, but the framework remains. The Council's remit extends also to advising the government on measures of public education and research.

The Council is to consist of not fewer than twenty persons, including persons with experience of the social problems connected with the misuse of drugs and persons from relevant professions. Why it should be mandatory to include a vet and a dentist may be a matter for speculation. It is not mandatory to include lawyers of any description, though they are not positively excluded. A simple constitution for the Advisory Council forms Schedule 1 to the Act.

Section 32 gives power to the Secretary of State to engage in research, and here the object of the research is the misuse of the 'dangerous or otherwise harmful drugs' of the long title, not only controlled drugs.

CHAPTER 2

Section 2—Controlled Drugs

Section 2(1) specifies the 'controlled drugs' by reference to Schedule 2, which is in four parts. Parts I, II and III contain lists of controlled drugs, known respectively as 'Class A drugs', 'Class B drugs' and 'Class C drugs'.

Class A drugs number 108, Class B eighteen (nineteen if cannabis and cannabis resin are counted separately) and Class C seven. The listings are alphabetical. The majority of the entries, even in the smaller classes, are quite unknown and even unimaginable to the average lawyer. Class A holds the record for obscurity with entries like '4-Phenylpiperidine-4-carboxylic acid ethyl ester' and 'Dihydrocodeinone O-carboxymethyloxime'. Such exotic inclusions need not be daunting as they are seldom if ever encountered in court. The British National Formulary (1985), describing controlled drugs, picks out only eleven from Class A, eight from Class B and four from Class C for mention. The Misuse of Drugs (Notification of and Supply to Addicts) Regulations 1973 list only thirteen, all Class A drugs.

Part IV provides definitions of expressions used in the Schedule, including one, 'opium poppy', which appears for the first time in Part IV itself, the remainder being entries in Part I (Class A drugs). These definitions are not exhaustive of the definitions provided by the Act of controlled drugs, as the definitions of cannabis, cannabis resin and prepared opium appear in the Interpretation section, section 37(1), as amended in the case of cannabis by the Criminal Law Act 1977, section 52.

Apart from common knowledge of the relative harmfulness, when misused, of some Class A drugs and some Class B drugs, the inference may be drawn from the punishments provided by Schedule 4 that the classes are in descending order of harmfulness. That said, it is apparent that such broad classification is a very blunt instrument, productive of anomalies. Thus the most addictive drug in general circulation, diamorphine, is in the same class as hallucinogens such as lysergide and psilocin (the product of Mexican magic mushrooms). Similarly, in Class B the amphetamines and cannabis products rub shoulders, though by no means equally mischievous. Experience shows that sentencers are aware that cannabis and cannabis resin are Class B drugs but are sometimes unaware, do not ask and are not told of the class to which, eg, amphetamine belongs. Defence lawyers ought to state the class in question if the prosecution, as sometimes happens, has neither specified it in the charge nor alluded to it in submissions. The maximum punishments for contraventions of sections 4(2), 4(3), 5(3) and 8, both summary and solemn, are the same for Class A and Class B drugs. The sentencer is thus given almost no guidance as to the relative harmfulness of misusing the substances in Classes A and B, either within each class or between the classes. Since it is of great importance that an offender should not be sentenced on the basis of judicial knowledge which may be seriously defective, it is desirable for prosecution and defence to present agreed facts to assist the judge in cases where no expert testimony as to the nature of the drugs in question has been heard.

The remainder of section 2 contains the provisions whereby substances may be added to the lists of controlled drugs, or removed. No specific power of reclassification is given, but it can be inferred from the power to add to and delete from 'any of' the lists. The power extends to emptying a class, and starting it up again. Redefining a drug is also competent, by virtue of section 2(3). Each House of Parliament has to approve, by resolution, any draft Order in Council containing amendments. Nothing of the sort can proceed unless the Advisory Council initiates it, or at least is consulted.

CHAPTER 3

Sections 3 and 20—Smuggling

Section 3(1) prohibits (*a*) the importation and (*b*) the exportation of a controlled drug. Section 3(2) exempts such activities if done under licence, or any controlled drug excepted by Regulations.

Unlike sections 4, 5 and 6, the prohibition of these activities in subsection 1 is not made an offence by a subsequent subsection. It is left to the Customs and Excise Management Act 1979 to create the relevant offences. Such offences have been held, for the purpose of deciding whether the consent of the Commissioners of Customs and Excise is required for the institution of proceedings, to have been 'created by the combined effect' of section 3 of the Misuse of Drugs Act and the relevant section of the Customs and Excise Act 1952 (now the 1979 Act). Although such an offence could be correctly described or charged as arising under either Act it could not be said to arise under one to the exclusion of the other: *R* v *Whitehead* [1982] 3 WLR 543. The offences are:

(*a*) unshipping, landing or unloading goods with respect to the importation or exportation of which these prohibitions are in force, or assisting or being concerned in doing so (by section 50(2)(*a*));

(*b*) removing from their place of importation or from such places as wharfs and customs sheds any such goods (by section 50(2)(*b*));

(*c*) importing or being concerned in importing any such goods, whether or not they are unloaded, with intent to evade the prohibitions (by section 50(3));

(*d*) being concerned in the exportation, or shipment as stores, of any such goods, with intent to evade the prohibitions (by section 68(2));

(*e*) knowingly acquiring possession of such goods with intent to evade the prohibitions (by section 170(1)(*a*));

(*f*) being knowingly concerned in carrying, removing, depositing, harbouring, keeping, concealing or in any manner dealing with such goods, with intent to evade the prohibitions (by section 170(1)(*b*)); and

(*g*) being knowingly concerned in any fraudulent evasion or attempt at evasion of the prohibitions (by section 170(2)(*b*)).

These offences are, in colloquial terms, smuggling, whether into or out of the country.

The penalties for these offences are those specified in the sections respectively, specially increased by subsections (5), (4) and (4) of sections 50, 68 and 170, respectively, and Schedule 1 when the smuggled goods are controlled drugs, as follows:

Goods	Summary	Indictment
Goods other than controlled drugs	Fine of £1,000 or three times the value of the goods, whichever is the greater, or six months or both.	Fine or two years or both.
Class A drugs or Class B drugs		Fine or fourteen years or both.
Class C drugs	Fine of £500 or three times the value of the goods, whichever is the greater, or three months or both.	Fine or five years or both.

The considerable overlapping of the offences prescribed both within section 50 and section 170 and between the sections presents prosecutors with a choice which in practice is invariably exercised in favour of proceeding under section 170(2)(*b*). The preference for the catch-all has nothing to do with sentence, as the sections are identical in that respect.

The value to be placed on the word 'knowingly' has been the subject of judicial decision:

'The word "knowingly" in the section in question is concerned with knowing that a fraudulent evasion of a prohibition in respect of goods is taking place' (*R* v *Hussain* [1969] 2 QB 567 per Lord Widgery at p 572).

In that case, the defendant was charged with being knowingly concerned in a fraudulent evasion of the prohibition on importation of cannabis, contrary to section 304(*b*) of the Customs and Excise Act 1952, the predecessor of the Customs and Excise Management Act 1979. The appeal was based on an alleged misdirection whereby the trial judge told the jury that they would convict if they were satisfied that the defendant was co-operating with the 'smugglers' in what he must have known was an operation of smuggling or getting prohibited goods into the country and that it did not matter if he did not know precisely the nature of the goods. Dismissing the appeal, the Court of Appeal held:

'It is, of course, essential that he should know that the goods which are being imported are goods subject to a prohibition. It is essential he should know that the operation with which he is concerning himself is an operation designed to evade that prohibition and evade it fraudulently. But it is not necessary that he should know the precise category of the goods the importation of which has been prohibited' (ibid).

It does matter, however, if the defendant's knowledge is defective in another respect, namely, while not knowing the precise nature of the goods being imported, he believes them to be goods which are not in fact subject to a prohibition, although he mistakenly thinks that they are.

'He is to be judged against the facts as he believed them to be. Had this indeed been currency and not cannabis, no offence would have been committed. Does it make any difference that the appellant thought wrongly that by clandestinely importing currency he was committing an offence? Mr Aylwin strongly submits that it does. He suggests that a man in this situation has to be judged according to the total mistake that he has made, both the mistake with regard to the fact of what he was carrying and also mistake of law as to the effect of carrying that substance. We think that that submission is wrong. It no doubt made his actions morally reprehensible. It did not, in our judgment, turn what he, for the purpose of argument, believed to be the importation of currency into the commission of a criminal offence. His views on the law as to the importation of currency were to that extent, in our judgment, irrelevant' (*R v Taaffe* [1983] 1 WLR 627 per Lord Lane CJ at p 631).

Where actings which take place beyond the jurisdiction of the court are in furtherance of the fraudulent evasion of the prohibition on importation, criminal liability is incurred by the person so participating.

'The basis of this appeal is that the jury may have believed that the only part played by the appellant in this business was his handling of the goods abroad for the purposes of their being transmitted to this country and that on that basis the conviction cannot stand because the appellant was charged with the others that on February 17, 1973, he was knowingly concerned in the fraudulent evasion of the restriction on importation. It is said that, if he did nothing relevant on that day and if what he did do earlier was not done in England, then he was wrongly convicted. Mr Parker for the appellant relied on the proposition that in general an act committed abroad cannot be the subject of criminal proceedings in this country' (*R v Wall* (1974) 59 Cr App R 58 per Lord Justice Cairns at p 60).

'We do not see why taking part in the dispatch of drugs from abroad to England with a view to evading the restriction on import should not be punishable here as being concerned in such evasion of restriction on import into the United Kingdom' (ibid at p 61).

The participation can commence after, even long after, the actual importation, and need not be at or near the place of importation.

'What is said, to put Mr Lloyd-Eley's principal point in a sentence, is that on the true construction of that section nothing happened sufficiently near to the actual moment of the importation of the cannabis with which this case is concerned on February 6, 1971, either in time or in place to render any of these appellants liable to conviction for an offence against that section, and therefore *a fortiori* to conviction for conspiracy to acquire possession of the goods with intent to evade the prohibition upon their importation' (*R v*

Ardalan and Others (1972) 56 Cr App R 320 per Lord Justice Roskill at p 325).

'It was pointed out to Mr Lloyd-Eley during the argument by MacKenna J that, if his suggested construction of the section were right, it produced a very curious result. If nothing that happened after the import of the prohibited goods could ever be an offence, the question naturally arises—w'iat is the point of putting the crucial words into the section and making the acquisition of possession an offence, if acquiring possession at any time after importation cannot on the true construction of the section be an offence? I venture to think that that question has only got to be asked for the answer to become manifest. If once, as Mr Lloyd-Eley was ultimately constrained to accept under some pressure from the Court, there can be an offence committed at some point of time and at some place after importation (for example, acquisition at or near the airport), it is difficult to see why there should be any limit to that point of time or place provided always, of course, that the goods the subject-matter of the charge are goods which are the subject of a prohibition or restriction upon importation and the acquisition is done knowingly and with intent to evade that prohibition or restriction' (ibid at p 326).

The offence of fraudulent evasion of the prohibition on importation is committed even if there is no intention that the goods should remain in the United Kingdom, but rather that they should be in the United Kingdom only in transit, and even if the goods remain in a customs area between unloading and reloading. Indeed this set of circumstances incurs liability for both importation into and exportation from the United Kingdom.

'It is to be observed that sections 44 and 45 [of the Customs and Excise Act 1952] are concerned with the improper importation of goods, and provide by section 44 for the forfeiture of goods improperly imported, and by section 45 for penalties for persons improperly importing. It seems quite clear that the Act contemplates that goods can be imported before they are either landed from a ship or unloaded from an aircraft. If, as we think, section 79 is not concerned only with budgetary matters, it is plain that goods entering the country by air are imported before they are unloaded, as are goods brought by sea before they are landed. In a fasciculus of sections dealing with the improper importation of goods, whether by evading the payment of duty on customed goods, or the prohibition upon the importing of prohibited goods, it would be strange indeed for Parliament to have excluded from the various categories of "goods imported" a category of "goods unloaded" without such an intention being precisely indicated. We cannot think that section 44(*b*) and section 45(1)(*b*) should be construed in the way contended for by Mr Payton, namely, as indicating that there can be a category of goods which are simply "unloaded" and not "imported" when they are taken off an aircraft at, eg, Heathrow and held in a Customs area until reloaded for onward transmission outside the country. It is sufficient to say that in this case we have no doubt that the cannabis in question was imported when the aircraft bringing it landed at Heathrow, and was exported when it was placed on board the BOAC aircraft and that it is quite irrelevant to the question of importation that it remained between unloading and reloading in a Customs area' (*R* v *Smith (Donald)* (1973) 57 Cr App R 737 per Lord Justice Edmund Davies at p 747).

So wide is the catch-all that it is effective to convict a person of being concerned in the fraudulent evasion of the prohibition on importation, notwithstanding that there is no evidence of his involvement with the actual act of importation.

'In any charge under section 170(1) the offence can be committed after importation is completed and by a person who may not have been connected with the importation. As section 170(2) is intended to widen the scope of section 170(1) it must follow that it cannot be construed as applying only to those engaged upon the initial illegal importation' (*R* v *Neal and Others* (1983) 77 Cr App R 283 per Lord Justice Griffiths at p 289).

It is not clear why a prosecutor should peril his case on a 'smuggling' charge when possession with intent to supply carries the same penalties, and the judgment in *Neal* proceeds to endorse

'the importance of the prosecution leading evidence to establish the necessary intention to evade the prohibition and that it is not sufficient to rely solely on the presumptions and a mere act of dealing. An act of dealing in a drug may or may not reveal an intention to evade the prohibition according to the circumstances in which it takes place. If no more can be proved than that a piece of cannabis changed hands in Piccadilly Circus, no doubt it would be foolish of the prosecution to proceed under this section of the Customs and Excise Management Act 1979, for it would be far-fetched to suggest that the real intent of such a transaction is to evade the prohibition on the import of cannabis' (ibid).

The 'presumptions' referred to are those specified in section 154(2) of the Customs and Excise Management Act 1979, the successor of section 290(2) of the Customs and Excise Act 1952. However, a prosecutor can go too far and if he makes no attempt to demonstrate a connection between any particular dealing with a controlled drug and some act of importation he can rely on losing his case.

'What happened at the trial of these two appellants was that ample evidence was led which the jury, by their verdict, must be taken to have accepted, that they had both been concerned in dealing with the prohibited drug cocaine. But no evidence was led, from start to finish, in the presentation of the prosecution's case, to show that that cocaine had ever been imported into this country, still less to show the circumstances in which such importation had taken place.

'There ensued, at the conclusion of the case for the prosecution, an argument between counsel, before the learned judge, as to whether there was any case to go to the jury. The submissions by counsel then acting on behalf of the two appellants to the effect that the absence of evidence of any importation of the cocaine dealt with meant that there was no case fit to be left to the jury under section 304(*a*) were met by Mr Finney (appearing for the Crown) by two distinct arguments.

'The first argument was an argument on the true construction of section 304(*a*) itself, and was to this effect: if it is shown that a particular substance is the subject-matter of a prohibition on its importation, then any person found in this country dealing with that substance is *ipso facto* dealing with the substance in circumstances in which there has been an evasion of the prohibition on importation and from which the jury can infer an intent to evade that prohibition.

'The second, and alternative, submission made, in support of the contention that there was a case to go to the jury, was that, even if it were necessary to show that the goods had in fact been imported, contrary to the initial submission, nevertheless the terms of section 290(2) of the Customs and Excise Act 1952 were such as to cast upon the defendant the onus of showing, either that the goods had not been imported at all, or that, if so, they had been lawfully imported, and that, on the footing of those two presumptions casting an onus on the defendant, the material before the Court was sufficient for the judge to invite the jury to infer that there had been an intention, on the part of the appellants, to evade the relevant prohibition on importation.

'The learned judge in fact upheld both arguments. He came to the conclusion that there was an evasion of the prohibition on importation of any goods, whenever goods of that description were dealt with in this country. The argument put to him, which he accepted, was that, for example, the growing of cannabis plants in a back garden in this country would be an evasion of the prohibition on the importation of cannabis; or a manufacture of the drug LSD in this country would be an evasion of the prohibition on the importation of that drug.

'In this Court (quite rightly, in the view which the Court takes), Mr Finney has resiled from and abandoned that argument. He recognises that in order that there should be an evasion of a prohibition, it must be shown that the prohibited act has been committed, and that there can be no evasion of a prohibition on importation unless a prohibited importation has taken place.

'The learned judge, having accepted the first submission on behalf of the Crown, proceeded to direct the jury that it was, in the circumstances of this case, quite immaterial whether the cocaine with which the two appellants had dealt had ever been imported or not. He so directed the jury in terms, and directed them, in effect, that the very fact of a dealing with cocaine coupled with the undoubted circumstance that the importation of cocaine is prohibited by statute, was sufficient to entitle the jury to infer—indeed he rather suggested to them that they could not avoid inferring from those facts once proved—an intent on the part of the appellants to evade the relevant prohibition on importation. Having reached that point, we are quite satisfied that, on that ground alone, these appeals must be allowed' (*R* v *Watts and Another* (1979) 70 Cr App R 187 per Lord Justice Bridge at p 190).

Nor should a prosecutor think to shift the onus of proof of importation on to a person accused under section 170(2)(*b*) by invoking section 152(2), the successor of section 290(2) of the 1952 Act.

'The Court, however, does not propose to let the matter rest at that point and to dispose of the appeals solely on that ground, because we have gone on to hear the interesting arguments addressed to us by Mr Finney, on the effect of section 290 of the Customs and Excise Act 1952 in relation to a prosecution for an offence under section 304(*a*) or, for that matter, 304(*b*) of that statute. The particular provisions of section 290 which are said to be material are all contained within subsection (2). I read the subsection only in so far as it is material for present purposes: "Where in any proceedings relating to customs or excise any question arises as to the place from which any goods have been brought or as to whether or not (*c*) any goods have been lawfully imported or lawfully unloaded from any ship or aircraft, then, where those proceedings are brought by or against the Commissioners, a law officer of the Crown or an officer, or against any other person in respect of anything purporting to have been done in pursuance of any power or duty conferred or imposed on him by or under the customs or excise Acts, the burden of proof shall lie upon the other party to the proceedings." The submission that is made is that those provisions have the effect, in proceedings under section 304, of casting on the defendant, wherever an issue arises, the burden of proof that goods were not imported—if there is an issue as to whether they were imported or not—and also of showing, if they were imported, that the importation was lawful and not unlawful.

'Clearly Mr Finney is right in saying that if an issue arises as to whether a particular proved importation was lawful or unlawful, the onus of proof of that issue is cast on the defendant by section 290(2)(*c*). The Court feels grave doubt as to whether the opening words of subsection (2) ("Where any question arises as to the place from which any goods have been brought") are words apt to refer to an issue as to whether goods have been imported or not. We think it more probable that those words are directed to an issue, which may arise in determining at what rate import duty is to be levied, as to the country from which the imported goods have originated. But setting those doubts aside, and assuming for the purpose of the argument that both the presumptions which Mr Finney claims cast an onus on the defendant (namely, a presumption that goods have been imported and a presumption that they have been unlawfully imported) do arise, we go on to consider whether those presumptions by themselves can ever be sufficient to justify a prosecution for an offence under section 304, where there is nothing other than the presumptions to connect the activities of the defendant with the presumed importation. In this connection it is important to bear in mind the decision of this Court in 1972 in *Ardalan and Others* [1972] 1 WLR 463; [1972] 2 All ER 257; [1972] Crim LR 370; (1972) 56 Cr App R 320. It is very clearly established by that authority that it is immaterial for the purpose of a prosecution under section 304(*a*) that the dealing, which is the *actus reus* of the offence, may have been separated by a long distance, both in point of time and place, from the relevant importation of the goods, whether they be prohibited goods or uncustomed goods, into this country. But does it follow from that, that in establishing an intent to evade a prohibition on the importation of goods, it is sufficient for the Crown simply to rely on the presumptions which, for this purpose, we are assuming to be established by section 290(2)? In our judgment it clearly does not.

'It seems to us quite clear that, on the true construction of section 304(*a*), in order to establish that any particular dealing with goods was done with intent to evade the relevant prohibition on importation, the onus on the Crown to prove that intent must involve establishing a link or nexus between the *actus reus* of the offence and some prohibited importation. Merely to establish that there has been a dealing with the prohibited goods, and that by virtue of the presumptions they are presumed at some time in the indefinite past to have been unlawfully imported, would not, in our judgment, ever justify, without anything further, inviting a jury to conclude that the evidence established an intent to evade the prohibition on importation' (ibid at p 191).

Watts has a sting in its tail:

'We want to say in very clear terms that if it has been the practice hitherto of the authorities responsible for such prosecutions to prosecute under section 304(*a*) where they are unable to establish a link between any prohibited importation and the dealing which is the *actus reus* of the offence which they charge against a defendant, that has been an erroneous practice and is one which should be discontinued' (ibid at p 192).

Just as the offence of being 'knowingly concerned' in the evasion of the prohibition on importation can be committed by one coming on the scene long after the act of importation, so a person whose actings come to an end before the importation takes place incurs full liability.

'Mr Mansfield relied upon the applicant's assertion that she had changed her mind immediately on leaving Accra and on the facts that she did not collect her suitcases in Paris, that she tore up the baggage tags on arrival at Heathrow and that she did not seek to claim her suitcases. He submitted that whether one referred to "withdrawal" or "abandonment" or "lack of *mens rea*" as the necessary ingredient of the defence, assistance was to be obtained from such cases as *Croft* (1944) 29 Cr App R 169; [1944] KB 295 and *Becerra and Cooper* (1976) 62 Cr App R 212. These cases are concerned with accomplices and secondary parties to crime, not with the principal offender, and in the view of this court are not of assistance to test the submission which is made. It is our view that the correct approach is to analyse the offence itself, but before turning to consider the wording of the section as a whole, it is valuable to look at decided cases and to see what assistance can be derived from them.

'The following propositions are supported by decisions of this Court. First, that the importation takes place when the aircraft bringing the goods lands at an airport in this country, see *Smith (Donald)* (1973) 57 Cr App R 737, 748; [1973] QB 924, 935G. Secondly, acts done abroad in order to further the fraudulent evasion of a restriction on importation into this country are punishable under this section, see *Wall (Geoffrey)* (1974) 59 Cr App R 58, 61; [1974] 1 WLR 930, 934C.

'For guilt to be established the importation must, of course, result as a consequence, if only in part, of the activity of the accused. If, for example, in the present case the applicant had taken her two suitcases off the carousel at Charles de Gaulle airport in Paris, removed all the luggage tags, placed the suitcases in a left luggage compartment and thrown the key of that compartment into the Seine, and then subsequently, in a general emergency, all left luggage compartments had been opened, a well-known English travel label had been found on her suitcase and those suitcases had been sent to the Travel Agents' agency, care of Customs and Excise at Heathrow, then that undoubted importation would not be the relevant one for the purposes of a charge against the applicant. We have already set out the wording of the relevant section and where the allegation concerns cannabis, the offence is, to be knowingly concerned in the fraudulent evasion (or attempt at evasion) of the prohibition on the importation of cannabis. Put more shortly, it is to be knowingly concerned in the fraudulent importation (or attempt at importation) of cannabis.

'Although the importation takes place at one precise moment—when the aircraft lands—a person who is concerned in the importation may play his part before or after that moment. Commonly, the person responsible for despatching the prohibited drugs to England acts fraudulently and so does the person who removes them from the airport at which they have arrived. Each is guilty. *Wall (supra)* is an example of the former and *Green* (1975) 62 Cr App R 74; [1976] QB 985 of the latter.

'There is no doubt, that, putting aside the question of duress, as we have done, the applicant had a guilty mind when at Accra she booked her luggage to London. By that act, she brought about the importation through the instrumentation of innocent agents. In this way, she caused the airline to label it to London, and the labels were responsible for the authorities in Paris sending it on to London.

'What is suggested is that she should not be convicted unless her guilty state of mind subsisted at the time of importation. We see no reason to construe the Act in this way. If a guilty mind at the time of importation is an essential, the man recruited to collect the package which has already arrived and which he knows contains prohibited drugs commits no offence. What matters is the state of mind at the time the relevant acts are done, ie, at the time the defendant is concerned in bringing about the importation' (*R* v *Jakeman* (1983) 76 Cr App R 223 per Mr Justice Wood at p 227).

An agreement to sell cannabis after importation is sufficiently close to the importation to warrant conviction of being knowingly concerned in the fraudulent evasion of the prohibition. In the case of Mr Harold Leon Williams, the admitted facts were that shortly after Christmas 1969 the appellant met an Indian named Habei Singh at a gaming club in Earl's Court, London. That Indian asked the appellant if he had contacts for selling 'stuff', clearly thereby referring to cannabis. The appellant at first put him off, but they met again a week later when another Indian, Abbas Singh, was present. Habei said he was going back to India and could send on 'samples'. He asked the appellant for his address. The appellant then gave the address of the house of a niece, Miss Reid, at Northolt and the name 'Harry Wragg', a name by which he was wont to go. The Indian said that the first sample would be small; that he was to get rid of it through his contacts; and that Abbas would meet him later. It was arranged that the Indian would write a letter before sending the samples. The appellant thereupon told the niece and a Mr Willoughby with whom she lived, that a letter would shortly be arriving for him at that address in the name of Harry Wragg. Thereafter Mr Willoughby did find an air-mail letter addressed to Wragg, and not realising that that was the appellant's pseudonym, he opened and read it, and having read it, he decided that he would not tell the appellant about it in the hope that the appellant would stop using his address for such a purpose. Accordingly, when the appellant called later, he was told that no letter had arrived. In due course, on 29th April 1970, customs officers examined a parcel addressed to 'H. Wragg' at the niece's address at Northolt, which apparently had come from Bombay. In it were three tins containing quantities of cannabis resin. Thereupon the customs officers reconstituted the parcel, substituting clay for the resin, and delivered it to the niece's address. Two customs officers kept watch on the house and called on Miss Reid and Mr Willoughby, and were told that the parcel addressed to H. Wragg, which they knew was the appellant's pseudonym, had been taken in.

'The submission was made that on those facts the offence had not been made out. The same point has been taken in this Court, and the way in which it is put, as the Court understand it, is that an agreement to sell cannabis after it had been imported into this country was not a sufficiently close act to the actual importation to constitute his being concerned in a fraudulent evasion of the restriction. The Court is, with all respect to Mr Shier, unable to understand his argument. It may well be that this was a joint enterprise to import, in which case there could be no doubt about it, but even if it is looked upon as an agreement on the one side to import, and on the other to sell, it seems to this Court that undoubtedly what the appellant was doing was sufficiently close to make him knowingly concerned in the importation' (*R* v *Williams* (1971) 55 Cr App R 275 per Lord Parker CJ at p 277).

The word 'fraudulent' in section 170(2) has been judicially defined:

'It seems to us to be a misinterpretation of Parliament's intention, and a path to absurdity, to make guilt depend on whether a customs officer is met and deceived on the one hand, or simply intentionally avoided on the other.

'In the result we have come to the conclusion that the presence of the word "fraudulent" in section 170(2) of the Customs and Excise Management Act 1979 has the effect that, in prosecutions under that provision for fraudulent evasion or attempted evasion of a prohibition or restriction with respect to goods or duty chargeable thereon, the prosecution must prove fraudulent conduct in the sense of dishonest conduct deliberately intended to evade the prohibition or restriction with respect to, or the duty chargeable on, goods as the case may be. There is no necessity for the prosecution to prove acts of deceit practised on a customs officer in his presence' (*Attorney-General's Reference (No 1 of 1981)* [1982] 1 QB 848 per Lord Lane CJ at p 856).

Section 20 creates the offence of assisting in or inducing the commission abroad of an offence punishable under a corresponding law. The actings of the accused must be in the United Kingdom. The offence punishable abroad need not correspond precisely or at all with offences created by the Act. For example, 'use' is one of the activities the control or regulation of which is envisaged by the foreign law. The expression 'corresponding law' is defined in section 36.

In *R* v *Vickers* (1975) 61 Cr App R 48 the appellant had agreed in England and elsewhere with another person that the appellant would acquire a truck, load it with speaker cabinets and transport them to Italy, knowing that thereafter cannabis would be fitted into the cabinets and shipped to the United States in contravention of US legislation corresponding to the UK's prohibition on importation.

'In our view Parliament chose the plain English phrase "assist in the commission of" so as to leave to a jury the opportunity of exercising a commonsense judgment upon the facts of a particular case. As Lord Reid said in *Cozens* v *Brutus* (1972) 56 Cr App R 799; [1973] AC 854, 861, the meaning of plain English words is a question of fact, not law—though the proper construction of a statute is a question of law. That is why in our judgment these admitted facts disclosed a case to go to the jury. Mr Blom-Cooper's argument was designed to impose a narrow, and we think artificially narrow, meaning upon the word "assist". Borrowing from the vocabulary of the law relating to attempts, he sought to say that it must be more proximate to the illegal importation than was the case on the admitted facts. To prove "assisting in the commission" of an illegal importation into the United States of America one must, he submitted, find acts directly concerned with the actual importation, for example, preparing a bill of lading, or loading the cannabis into an aeroplane bound for New York, or filling the containers with the drug' (*R* v *Vickers* (1975) 61 Cr App R 48 per Lord Justice Scarman at p 53).

In *R* v *Evans* (1976) 64 Cr App R 237 the same result flowed from circumstances which were similar except for the fact that the accused was himself the smuggler. It was held that although his actings in the United Kingdom consisted of nothing more than going to the English airport and flying to Brussels, there was sufficient evidence of assisting in the commission of the illegal importation of the drugs which he then ferried from Belgium to Canada.

Section 28 defences do not apply to section 3 offences.

CHAPTER 4

Sections 4 and 6

Section 4 prescribes six offences in relation to controlled drugs. These are:

   (i) to produce (by section 4(2)(*a*));
  (ii) to be concerned in the production (by section 4(2)(*b*));
 (iii) to supply (by section 4(3)(*a*));
  (iv) to offer to supply (by section 4(3)(*a*));
   (v) to be concerned in the supplying (by section 4(3)(*b*));
  (vi) to be concerned in the making of an offer to supply (by section 4(3)(*c*)).

The words 'produce' and 'production' are defined in section 37(1) in such a way as to include cultivation, a provision relevant to only a small minority of controlled drugs, specifically coca leaf, opium, poppy-straw and cannabis. All the others are products of the laboratory either by extraction from naturally occurring substances, or by synthesis. Of the naturally occurring substances, only cannabis can readily be grown in the temperate zones.

'Supplying' includes distributing (section 37(1)) and this definition is important in making clear the fact that there is no commercial element essential to the activity. Thus, to pass on gratuitously, or to share, a controlled drug or to act as a carrier thereof, or to take charge of and give up a deposit of any such drug, places the actor in the distributive chain and makes a supplier of him. What is the position, however, where a number of users pool resources to buy a joint supply and one of them is caught? Is he guilty of supplying the others in the consortium or have they not already supplied themselves? Section 37(3) provides that, for the purposes of the Act, 'the things which a person has in his possession shall be taken to include any thing subject to his control which is in the custody of another'. It appears from that that a depositary of a common supply does not 'supply' the shares belonging to the others in a consortium, but rather that they are already in possession of their respective shares. It is less clear that he will not be 'concerned in the supplying of such a drug to another', ie, by the supplier to the consortium and hence to each member of it other than himself. If he were, the consequences would be likely to be the same for him, as there is no distinction between principals and ancillaries in the matter of sentence (Schedule 4).

The argument against supply by a depositary has however been described as recondite, and rejected, in the Court of Appeal in England. In *R* v *Buckley* the appellant and another man determined to buy cannabis resin in bulk and thereafter each to take his share. They pooled their money but only the appellant met the supplier, handed over the money and received the cannabis resin. He then split it in the agreed proportions with the other man.

'"Supplying includes distributing". Whatever else Buckley may or may not have been doing when he divided up the cannabis and gave three-quarters of a pound to Gilchrist and kept the other quarter pound for himself, he was without any shadow of a doubt—it seems to us—distributing the cannabis' (*R v Buckley* (1979) 69 Cr App R 371 per Lord Justice Geoffrey Lane at p 373).

From this it appears that what passes from a supplier is possession, while what passes from a distributor is mere custody but that both are struck at by section 4(3)(*a*). A prosecutor who takes this view will not feel the necessity of invoking section 4(3)(*b*) in such circumstances. The dictum of Lord Parker CJ in *R v Mills* [1963] 1 QB 522 that 'supply' must denote the passing of possession from one person to another, though quoted from time to time in drugs cases, is clearly inapplicable to the extended meaning of 'supplying' in the Misuse of Drugs Act. The case in question was concerned with the supplying of instruments to procure an abortion, and the definition was laid down in the absence of a statutory one.

A person administering a possessor's own drug is not supplying it to him.

'If B has obtained in some way the possession of the heroin and all that A is doing is to assist him in injecting that heroin into B, then A is not supplying heroin' (*R v Harris* [1968] 1 WLR 769 per Lord Parker CJ at p 771).

Ms Harris's conviction was quashed. Mr Fowler ('B' of the Lord Chief Justice's illustration) was convicted of unlawful possession. Ms Harris was not charged with possession. Had she been so, *quid juris*? At first glance, as she had actual custody, the knowledge of what she had, and sufficient control over it at least to administer it to Mr Fowler, or give it back to him, she was in possession of it. Further, as her possession was not for her own use but with intent to hand it over to Mr Fowler (by way of administration), she must be guilty of possession with intent to supply it to another, contrary to section 5(3). But if by doing so she would not have been guilty of supplying it, and the Appeal Court found it

'quite impossible as a matter of ordinary common sense and law to say that a person administering heroin in those circumstances was supplying the heroin' (ibid)

it would be highly anomalous if she were to be convicted of possession with intent to do what she could not, in law, do. Does this lead to the inescapable conclusion that she was guilty of 'simple' possession? Since the ratio of the judgment was that the possession was Fowler's, it seems not. We thus arrive at a species of intromitting with a controlled drug which, although having the superficial attributes of possession, is not so in law. It is similar to, but not identical with, the 'fleeting contact' which was held to fall short of possession in *Mackay* v *Hogg (infra)*. Ms Harris's contact with the heroin was not, however, fleeting. What the cases have in common, it is submitted, is an absence of the *animus possidendi*. The defences provided by section 5(4) and section 28 are inapplicable. Another possibility is that Ms Harris and Fowler had joint possession.

For 'produce' and 'supply', there must be a controlled drug, but not so for 'offer to supply'. In *HM Advocate* v *Ferreira and Others* the accused were in possession of beeswax and were charged with offering to supply cannabis. In the course of his charge to the jury, the presiding sheriff said:

'If an offer was made to supply cannabis and this harmless fake was presented, it would still be an offence under this statute, because the offence is to make the offer. The rogue may have no cannabis at all, it would still be an offence if he offered to supply a controlled drug' (*HM Advocate* v *Ferreira and Others*, Unreported, Glasgow Sheriff Court, 2nd April 1976 (Sheriff John Peterson)).

A fortiori if the defendant believes his goods to be a controlled drug.

'The defendant offered to sell to Heward a quantity of Lysergide and the sale took place of some of the substance which the defendant had purchased in Leeds. At the time of this transaction both the defendant and Heward believed that the substance sold was Lysergide, a controlled drug. The substance which in fact the defendant had bought in Leeds as Lysergide, and which he sold to Heward as Lysergide, was a different drug which is known by a short name, Bromo STP. At the material time Bromo STP was not a drug which was controlled under the Act of 1971. The short point therefore is this: bearing in mind that the defendant was charged and convicted of the offence of offering to supply a controlled drug, it is the fact that what he in fact did supply, and that which was intended to be the physical subject of his offer to supply, turned out to be something which was not a controlled drug.

'In my judgment the offence was completed at the time when, to follow the findings of the justices, the defendant met Heward and offered to sell him a quantity of Lysergide. To my mind that was a clear situation in which the justices were right to find that there was an offer to supply a controlled drug, an offer made by the defendant to Heward.

'It matters not in relation to the offence of offering to supply that what is in fact supplied pursuant to that offer, the offer having been accepted, is not in fact a controlled drug' (*Haggard* v *Mason* [1976] 1 WLR 187 per Mr Justice Lawson at p 190).

For 'attempt to supply' (contrary to section 19) there must be a controlled drug: *Mieras* v *Rees* [1975] Crim LR 224, as corrected at [1980] Crim LR 47. For 'attempt to produce' there must be a possibility of success.

'Steps on the way to the commission of what would be a crime, if the acts were completed, may amount to attempts to commit that crime to which, unless interrupted, they would have led; but steps on the way to the doing of something which is thereafter done, and which is no crime, cannot be regarded as attempts to commit a crime' (*R* v *Percy Dalton (London) Limited* (1949) 33 Cr App R 102 per Lord Birkett at p 110).

'Equally, steps on the way to do something which is thereafter not completed, but which if done would not constitute a crime, cannot be indicted as attempts to commit that crime' (*R* v *Smith* [1975] AC 476 per Lord Hailsham of St Marylebone LC at p 497).

The scene changes if more than one person is involved and conspiracy is charged.

'It is necessary to consider what constitutes the crime of conspiracy according to the law of Scotland. That crime is constituted by the agreement of two or more persons to further or achieve a criminal purpose. A criminal purpose is one which if attempted or achieved by action on the part of an individual would itself constitute a crime by the law of Scotland. It is the criminality of the purpose and not the result which may or may not follow from the execution of the purpose which makes the crime a criminal conspiracy' (*Maxwell and Others* v *HM Advocate* 1980 SLT 241).

In England equally, 'agreement is the necessary ingredient in conspiracy' and 'a proximate act is that which constitutes the crime of attempt'.

'But the distinction has no relevance in determining whether the impossibility of committing the substantive offence should be a defence. Indeed upon the view of the law authoritatively explained and accepted in *Owen*'s case [1957] AC 602, logic and justice would seem to require that the question as to the effect of the impossibility of the substantive offence should be answered in the same way whether the crime charged be conspiracy or attempt' (*Director of Public Prosecutions* v *Nock and Another* [1978] 3 WLR 57 per Lord Scarman at p 69).

'The appellants made a number of attempts—all of them, of course, unsuccessful—to extract cocaine from their powder. It was not until after they had been arrested and the powder seized by the police and sent for analysis that they learnt to their surprise that there was no way in which cocaine could be produced from it.

'The trial judge in his direction to the jury, and the Court of Appeal in their judgment dismissing the two appeals, treated this impossibility as an irrelevance. In their view the agreement was what mattered: and there was plain evidence of an agreement to produce cocaine, even though unknown to the two conspirators it could not be done. Neither the trial judge nor the Court of Appeal thought it necessary to carry their analysis of the agreement further. The trial judge described it simply as an agreement to produce cocaine. The Court of Appeal thought it enough that the prosecution had proved "an agreement to do an act which was forbidden by section 4 of the Misuse of Drugs Act 1971". Both descriptions are accurate, as far as they go. But neither contains any reference to the limited nature of the agreement proved: It was an agreement upon a specific course of conduct with the object of producing cocaine, and limited to that course of conduct. Since it could not result in the production of cocaine, the two appellants by pursuing it could not commit the statutory offence of producing a controlled drug' (ibid at p 67).

'The important point to note is that the agreement that is said to have been an unlawful conspiracy was not an agreement in general terms to produce cocaine, but an agreement in specific terms to produce cocaine from a particular powder which in fact, however treated, would never yield cocaine. In order to see whether there is a criminal conspiracy it is necessary to consider the whole agreement. The specific limits of the agreement cannot be discarded, leaving a general agreement to produce cocaine, for that would be to find an agreement other than that which was made: and that is not a permissible approach to any agreement, conspiracy or other' (ibid per Lord Russell of Killowen at p 65).

'This is a case not of an agreement to commit a crime capable of being committed in the way agreed upon, but frustrated by a supervening event making its completion impossible, which was the Crown's submission, but of an agreement upon a course of conduct which could not in any circumstances result in the statutory offence alleged, ie, the offence of producing the controlled drug cocaine' (ibid per Lord Scarman at p 70).

The distinction between agreeing 'to pursue a course of action which could never in fact have produced cocaine' (Lord Scarman in *Nock, supra*) and agreeing or attempting to produce a drug with the wrong ingredients or by a wrong method is a fine one. Nevertheless, somewhere between the two scenarios, a line is crossed.

'The appellant with four others attempted to make the drug amphetamine. They had the correct chemical formula but when they mixed the chemicals concerned in a pan on a stove they failed to produce amphetamine; not only because one ingredient was wrong but also because they lacked knowledge of the proper process. The appellant was convicted of conspiracy with others to produce a controlled drug, amphetamine, contrary to section 4 of the Misuse of Drugs Act 1971. He appealed against conviction on the ground that the alleged conspiracy was one which, in relation to himself and the others concerned, was impossible of fulfilment.

'*Held*, that the appellant and the co-defendants had acquainted themselves with the proper process to produce amphetamine, and thus had entered into an agreement to do an unlawful act which was inherently possible of consummation; accordingly he had been rightly convicted' (*R v Harris* (1979) 69 Cr App R 122).

An attempt to lay on the Crown an evidential burden of proving that the agreement was capable of being carried out produced the following decision in the Court of Appeal.

'In our judgment, the position of the Crown, at any rate in cases of common law conspiracy, is as follows: (*a*) The burden of proof of course rests on the Crown; (*b*) If the Crown has in its possession evidence which might show that at the time when the agreement was made the carrying out of the agreement would have been impossible (as in *DPP v Nock*, where the evidence came from the Police Forensic Laboratory—see p 118 and p 981 of the respective reports) it is the duty of the Crown either to call the evidence or to make it available to the defence; (*c*) If the Crown has no such evidence, it is not their duty in the first instance to call evidence that the carrying out of the agreement would have been possible; the evidential burden of proving impossibility then shifts to the defence; (*d*) The probative burden remains on the Crown, and if there is some evidence of impossibility the question must be left to the jury with appropriate directions; (*e*) If there is no evidence of impossibility, the judge need not direct the jury about it. (*R v Bennett and Others* (1979) 68 Cr App R 168 per Lord Justice Browne at p 177).

For a conviction of producing a controlled drug, contrary to section 4(2)(*a*), there must be some identifiable participation in the process of production. In *R v Farr* [1982] Crim L R 745, the defendant allowed others to use his kitchen, knowing that they were producing heroin there. It was held by the Court of Appeal that the appropriate charge would have been under section 8, of permitting such an offence to take place on his premises.

Some prosecutors act as though section 4(3)(*b*) did not exist and prefer to charge the offence of possession of a controlled drug with intent to supply it to another, in contravention of section 5(3), even where the evidence points to the accused's being a 'courier' or depositary, ie, an active or passive link in the distributive chain. Some cases are apparently decided without the court's being referred to the interpretation of the word 'supplying' provided by section 37(1). In *R v Delgado* the court took the surprising course of describing the statutory definition as 'of little help to us', and continued:

'Thus we are driven back to considering the word "supply" in its context. The judge himself relied upon the dictionary definition, which is a fairly wide one. This Court has been referred to the *Shorter Oxford English Dictionary*, which gives a large number of definitions of the word "supply", but they have a common feature, viz: that in the word "supply" is inherent the furnishing or providing of something which is wanted.

'In the judgment of this Court, the word "supply" in section 5(3) of the Act of 1971 covers a similarly wide range of transactions. A feature common to all of those transactions is a transfer of physical control of a drug from one person to another. In our judgment questions of the transfer of ownership or legal possession of those drugs are irrelevant to the issue whether or not there was intent to supply.

'In the present case on his own evidence the appellant had possession of a substantial quantity of cannabis. His intention was to transfer control of it to his two friends at an agreed time and place' (*R* v *Delgado* [1984] 1 WLR 89 per Mr Justice Skinner at p 92).

This decision by the Court of Appeal not to follow its own decision in *R* v *Greenfield (infra)* seems to dispose of that decision (by a court constituted also of the Lord Chief Justice and Mr Justice Skinner in the majority, as in *Delgado*). The report in *Criminal Law Review* is not readily comprehensible as it omits the fact that the judge charged the jury that for the appellant to hand back to X drugs which he was looking after for X was not a supply.

'On the assumption that the handing back of the drugs to X, as the judge directed the jury, was not a supply, what we have to ask ourselves is whether the intention undoubtedly held, if his statements to the police are accepted, by this man, namely, the intention that these drugs should be supplied by X to another, is a sufficient offence in the words of the Act. It is not an altogether easy point. We have come to the conclusion that the intent of somebody else to supply is not enough. The words of the Act are plain, that is to say, "with intent to supply", which in our judgment predicate that it should be the intent on the part of the person who possesses to supply, and not the intent of someone other than that who is in possession of the drugs to supply. Consequently it follows that whichever way one looks at the matter, the judge was not correct in leaving the matter in the way he did to the jury. There is no doubt that had the matter been left simply on the question whether this man himself intended to supply, the jury may very well have come to the conclusion that that was made out' (*R* v *Greenfield* [1983] Crim LR 397 per Lord Lane CJ at p 5 of the transcript, as quoted by Mr Justice Skinner in *R* v *Delgado* [1984] 1 WLR 89 at p 91).

It seems that the Crown would have done better not to ignore section 4(3)(*b*) in this case, in which the accused's own words to the police were an explicit admission of being concerned in supplying. The judgment would be less difficult to reconcile with the statute if it had not clearly held the accused to be in possession ('it should be the intent on the part of the person who possesses' refers to him). On the view that the accused had only custody while the sole possessor was X, a view which seems possible if section 37(3) is held to apply to the situation, it is easier to accept that the resumption of custody by the possessor did not involve supply by the custodier. Except on that narrow view, no link in the chain of distribution should expect to escape conviction in reliance on *Greenfield*.

Section 4(3)(*c*) is 'particularly widely drawn' so as to involve people who, for example, tout for business for a supplier. Police officers on duty in a street in

London observed Mr Ronald O'Connor approaching young people and heard him say: "Do you like grass?" One of the group said: "Do you know where we can get some?" O'Connor said: "I have a friend who can fix you up. He has got a flat nearby." They then went off together and O'Connor was heard to say to one of the group: "That will cost you £15. Have you got enough?" Then the group spoke together, clearly to discover what their financial resources were. They then arrived at Mr Jason Joseph Blake's flat and Blake said to O'Connor: "Is it shit they want?", that word being understood to refer to cannabis. The police were there and it became obvious to Blake that the men were policemen, and Blake told them he was just going to get a newspaper, and pretended that he did not know O'Connor.

'This Court has considered that evidence and has come to the conclusion that the inference most certainly could be drawn if the matter was properly left to the jury. The learned judge said to them: "But before Blake can be guilty of count two there would have to be some previous arrangement or understanding between him and O'Connor." Whether that precise direction in that narrower form is absolutely necessary in every such case, this Court does not have to consider. It is sufficient to say that the evidence before the jury, in the view of this Court, perfectly justified the inference being drawn by the jury, as it was drawn, particularly when no other explanation was given as to the reason for the conduct of the two accused in this case.

'The Court has been invited to say that the offence of being concerned in the making to another of an offer requires a specific and close involvement in the particular offer that was made in Piccadilly on that day, and if we understand counsel's argument properly, he is saying that Blake, not knowing that that particular offer was made, could not be guilty of that offence. This Court rejects that submission. It is clear that section 4(3)(c) has been particularly widely drawn to involve people who may be at some distance from the actual making of the offer' (*R v Blake and Another* (1979) 68 Cr App R 1 per Lord Justice Eveleigh at p 2).

Section 6 is the cultivation section and has fallen into desuetude since the redefinition of cannabis by section 52 of the Criminal Law Act 1977. Since the effect of the amendment is to make all parts of the cannabis plant a controlled drug, which before it was not, it follows that cultivation of such a plant is production of a controlled drug and can be prosecuted under section 4.

The question of what constitutes cultivation, one of the methods of production envisaged by section 37(1), does of course remain, and enlightenment on that score is to be found in *Tudhope v Robertson and Another* in which judicial photosynthesis animates the arid page of the *Shorter Oxford English Dictionary*:

'There is a finding of a negative character which, as will be seen, had some considerable influence upon the view taken by the sheriff in finding the charge not proven. That finding is that in the course of the search the searching officers did not find any watering-can, spray, tools or other implements with which to tend the cannabis plants. Now what the sheriff did on this factual basis was to ask himself what is meant by the verb "to cultivate" in the context of this particular subsection. He said that the offence is the offence of cultivation and that Parliament had not made it an offence to grow the cannabis plant. At that point one detects already a possible misdirection by the sheriff because it is difficult to distinguish between the active content of the verb "to grow" and the verb "to cultivate". However that may be, the sheriff went on to accept a submission which had been made by the solicitor for the accused that the word "cultivate" is an active verb (and he was right about that), and that it involves the bestowal of labour and care upon plants, and their improvement by such bestowal of such labour and such care. The sheriff accordingly asked himself where he could find evidence of the bestowal of the required labour and care, and he came to the conclusion that there had been no such evidence placed before him. In particular he emphasised the absence of horticultural equipment in the bedroom which might have led him to conclude that an act of cultivation had occurred. He went on to say that no inference of cultivation could be drawn from the short period of 48 hours during which the plants had been under observation in the house and that the presence of the cannabis seeds was not of sufficient importance to allow him to draw any inference of a connection between the plants in the bedroom and the seeds in the livingroom.

'For the Crown, the attack on the sheriff's judgment was short, sharp and certain. It was that the sheriff had misdirected himself by taking far too narrow and restricted a view of the meaning of the verb "to cultivate" in relation to plants in a pot in a house. He himself appeared to be prepared to hold that the respondents were growing these plants. He ought to have found therefore that they were cultivating these plants. It was nothing to the point that there were no purpose-built pieces of horticultural equipment in the bedroom, because everyone knows that a potted plant requires very little specialised equipment for its care. The milk-jug, the spoon and the domestic fork will do perfectly well enough. The sheriff also failed to observe the significance of the position of the pot. The plants were placed in the window of the bedroom. The act of placing them there was an act of cultivation for they were placed there, no doubt, in order that the process of photosynthesis could take place and lead to the development of the plant. The cannabis seeds were significant too. From these seeds such plants could be grown and the answers given by the respondents demonstrated that the plants were not kept for their decorative function, but with a view to cropping them at the appropriate time, for, as the male respondent put it, "hash".

'In reply counsel for the respondents valiantly supported the reasoning of the learned sheriff, and he drew our attention to two statutes and one decided case. We have examined the statutes and the case and derive no assistance from any of them. The statutes in question, in particular, contain their own definition of the verb "to cultivate" which includes the mere keeping of bees and the growth of vegetables and plants. To allow a plant to grow in the window is not enough, said counsel for the respondents. It must be shown that it was deliberately placed there for a purpose and was tended.

'There is a short answer to this appeal. The sheriff was plainly wrong. He did as the Crown suggested take a too narrow and restricted view of the verb "to cultivate", in the context in which it appears, in relation to plants in a pot. There was ample evidence to demonstrate sufficient cultivation to lead to conviction of the offence libelled. That evidence lay in the positioning of the plants to secure the light necessary to growth, the condition of the plants, the presence of the seeds, and the objective which the respondents had in mind in having the plants in their house at all' (*Tudhope* v *Robertson and Another* [1980] SLT 60 per Lord Emslie, Lord Justice-General at p 62. See also *R* v *Rotherham*, Unreported, referred to in *Taylor* v *Chief Constable of Kent* (1981) 72 Cr App R 318).

Section 28 defences apply to section 4 and section 6 offences. For an unsuccessful attempt to invoke section 28 in a case of cultivation of cannabis, see *R* v *Champ* [1982] Crim LR 108.

CHAPTER 5

Section 5(1)—Possession

Section 5 is the 'possession' section, and no doubt for every offence of production, smuggling, supplying, etc, there are a hundred or more cases of unlawful possession. According to press reports, there may be half a million people at risk of being charged with 'simple' possession of cannabis or cannabis resin from time to time in Scotland, so the volume of prosecutions under section 5(2) should cause no surprise. As for section 5(3), inferentially anyone convicted under it is a supplier and the number of such convictions contrasted with the much smaller number of convictions under section 4 only illustrates the difficulty of detecting controlled drugs at the point of delivery, usually effected between consenting adults in private.

Regulation 20 of the Dangerous Drugs (No 2) Regulations 1964, provided: 'A person shall be deemed to be in possession of a drug if it is in his actual custody or is held by some other person subject to his control or for him and on his behalf.' On account, presumably, of the unsatisfactory nature of this formulation, the attempt was not repeated and possession is not defined in the 1971 Act. Whatever it turns out to mean, however, it is extended by section 37(3) as follows: 'For the purposes of this Act the things which a person has in his possession shall be taken to include any thing subject to his control which is in the custody of another.' Assuming that some degree of physical custody, the ability to put one's hand on the thing, is an ingredient of possession as normally understood, this can be seen to be a considerable extension.

Subsection 1, without creating an offence, declares the unlawfulness of a person's having a controlled drug in her or his possession (unless authorised in terms of section 7 of the Act). No further guidance being given by the Act as to the meaning of the concept of possession, that has to be sought elsewhere. It is as well to accept in advance that the search will not be easy. According to Lord Parker CJ in *Towers & Co Limited* v *Gray* [1961] 2 QB 351 at p 361, 'the term "possession" is always giving rise to trouble'. Lord Wilberforce in *Warner* v *Metropolitan Police Commissioner* [1969] 2 AC 256 at p 309 described it as 'a concept which is both central in many areas of our legal system and also lacking in definition'. He went on to quote with approval Earl Jowitt in *United States of America and Republic of France* v *Dollfus Mieg et Cie SA and Bank of England* [1952] AC 582: 'the English Law has never worked out a completely logical and exhaustive definition of possession'. The fate in store for anyone who might be tempted to try is illustrated by Ribeiro and Perry, 'Possession and Section 28 of the Misuse of Drugs Act 1971' in [1979] Crim LR 90. Of the 'eight distinct modes or situations of possession' which they argued were discernible from the decided cases, at least two came to grief: No 7, 'Possession of traces', based on the shifting sand of *R* v *Carver* [1978] 2 WLR 872, and No 8, 'Consumed Drugs', based on the palpably erroneous decision in *Hambleton* v *Callinan and Others* [1968] 2 QB 427. But they correctly emphasise the importance of context, quoting Lord Morris of Borth-y-Gest's dictum in Warner that 'The word "possession" is much to be found in the vocabulary of the law and it cannot always be given the same meaning in all its divers contexts'. Lord Wilberforce is strong on context, describing possession as 'a term which is inconclusive as to the finer shades of mental intention needed, leaving these to be fixed in relation to the legal context in which the term is used' (the report as corrected by Lord Wilberforce in correspondence with the author). He proposes that a jury should be invited to consider first custody and the 'modes or events' by which it commences, then proceed to the mental element. Professor Walker has it the other way round: 'Two elements are relevant to possession, *animus possidendi*, or the mental claim to hold the thing as against others or to retrieve it from them, and *corpus possessionis*, or the actual control of the thing' (*Principles of Scottish Private Law*, p 1456). Professor T. B. Smith also emphasises the mental element: 'Possession in Scots law is to be distinguished from custody, when a person holds a conditional or limited right without the *animus possidendi*' (*A Short Commentary on the Law of Scotland*, p 461). Professor Smith continues: 'The right of possession is established by sharing the elements of *corpus* and *animus possidendi*. The *animus* or "act of the mind" will only suffice where it is manifested in a sufficient environment of fact—*corpus*.'

The 'act of the mind' and 'act of the body' are from Stair II, I, XVII:

'Possession is the holding or detaining of any thing by ourselves, or others for our use. It is not every holding or detaining which makes possession; for depositors do detain, but because it is not for their use, they do not possess. To possession there must be an act of the body, which is detention and holding; and an act of the mind, which is the inclination or affection to make use of the thing detained.'

Professor Gerald Gordon in the first edition of *The Criminal Law of Scotland* pointedly illustrated the lack of statutory or judicial precision by stating only that 'the courts would probably accept the American view that possession to be criminal must be "conscious and willing"'. That passage and his quotation from the American Law Institute's proposed Model Penal Code, 'Possession is an act if the possessor knowingly procured or received the thing possessed or was aware of his control thereof for a sufficient period to have been able to terminate his possession', are excised in the second edition in favour of a discussion of the intervening case of *Warner* v *Metropolitan Police Commissioner* [1969] 2 AC 256.

When considering possession, knowledge has for long been seen as an essential ingredient.

'A man can hardly be said to be in possession of something without knowing it' (*R* v *Woodrow* (1846) 15 M & W 404 per Pollock CB at p 415).

'The question of "knowingly", it appears to me, is involved in the word possession. That is, a man has not in his possession that which he does not know to be about him ... it is clear therefore that possession includes a knowledge of the facts as far as the possession of the article is concerned' (ibid per Anderson B at p 417, both quoted by Professor Gerald Gordon in *The Criminal Law of Scotland*).

Other English-speaking jurisdictions reach the same conclusion, eg, India:

'Whether the possession is that of the owner or of another person, it is clear that the person who is said to possess the thing must have knowledge of the existence of the thing. In other words, possession to be punishable under the criminal law must be possession with knowledge' (*Dula Singh* v *R* (1928) ILR 9 Lah 531 per Shadi Lal CJ at p 536).

But knowledge is part of the mental element. There could be no 'mental claim', or intention to possess, without knowledge of the existence of the thing. Consequently, knowledge need not be treated as a separate element. The two essential ingredients are the intention or at least willingness to possess, and, subject to section 37(3), the actual custody of the thing. Knowledge by itself is not enough.

'There is no doubt from the findings in fact that there was a very substantial quantity of cannabis resin found in the flat and a very large number of articles used and designed for the smoking of cannabis resin were also to be seen there, especially in the living-room. There is no doubt also that from the findings in fact it is a clear inference that the appellant knew perfectly well of the presence of the drug and smoking equipment and that the smoking of cannabis resin was taking place in the flat. It was, however, not enough for the prosecutor to demonstrate, if a conviction was to be secured, that the appellant had knowledge of the articles and the drug in the flat and that smoking of cannabis resin was taking place there on a very large scale. It was in addition essential that in addition to knowing about the drug and the articles, and the smoking of cannabis resin in the flat, cannabis resin, or some of it, was in the possession and control of the appellant' (*Mingay* v *Mackinnon* 1980 JC 33 per Lord Cameron at p 35).

Although not in terms overruling *Allan and Others* v *Milne*, *Mingay's* case can be seen as stating the law more reliably, particularly as the sheriff correctly stated in *Mingay*: 'The present case is much stronger than *Allan* where the appeal against conviction failed.'

'The first three appellants had been joint tenants of the flat for over a year. The evidence did not show for how long the fourth appellant had lived there but it had certainly been for a period of at least some weeks. On the evidence before me they were the only occupiers and there was nothing to suggest that the cannabis might have been placed there by any other person. If any of the appellants had been previously ignorant of the possibility of the presence of drugs in the flat, the first police search on 13th October would have brought the question actively into their minds. From the police evidence it was clear that the appellants were on close terms with one another. In the circumstances I considered it virtually inconceivable that any of them would or could have kept cannabis on the premises without the knowledge of the others. The quantity of cannabis found, four ounces with, according to the police evidence, a market value in drug circles of about £100, was much larger than any one individual was likely to have possessed for personal consumption. The evidence did not disclose the precise sleeping arrangements in the flat but the kitchen/living-room was clearly used communally. The scales which were found standing openly on the kitchen table were produced at the trial and were of a type used for medical or similar purposes; I was satisfied that they were not there, and could not have been thought by any of the appellants to have been there, for ordinary kitchen use. In the absence of any evidence to the contrary the only reasonable inference from these circumstances was that all the appellants had knowledge of the presence of cannabis in the flat, and of its whereabouts. I was further satisfied that any of the appellants had access to the cannabis and could use it as he or she chose' (*Allan and Others v Milne* 1974 SLT (Notes) 76 (sheriff's note)).

Despite the elaborate findings as to the quantity and value of the cannabis, and the scales, the sheriff acquitted all the accused of contravening section 5(3). Without issuing opinions, the court upheld convictions on the charge under section 5(2).

If *Allan and Others v Milne* was a case in which knowledge and very little else was held to have been enough for conviction, *Lustmann and Others v Stewart*, the first reported case in Scotland on the point, is to the opposite effect.

'On Tuesday, 3rd November 1970, Inspector McMartin, accompanied by Constables Malcolm McAlpine and John Glass, carried out a search of the premises. The appellants, Lustmann and Treacy, accompanied the police during part of the search.

'Production No 2 is a rough sketch of the bottom floor of Ballivicar Farm. Production No 3 is a rough sketch of the upper floor of the farm.

'The police found the premises to be dirty, untidy, sparsely furnished and decorated in parts in a psychedelic fashion. On the ground floor the police found a mattress and a heap of dirty clothes which, when pulled back, revealed the presence of the appellant Duncan Sloan. On the upper floor room 2 was found to be laid out in such a way as to suggest its use as a shrine. The lighting was dim orange with blue spots, with paintings of what appeared to be Buddhas on the walls. A small table was in the centre of the room covered with blue velvet in the form of an altar, with candles and twigs on it. There was also a number of books on eastern religion and Tibetan folklore. There was a mattress on the floor covered with a blanket, which appeared to be used as a prayer mat, and some cushions were also on the floor. In room 3 were found a number of musical instruments. The room was garishly decorated and had some drawings on the walls which the police described as obscene. Of the other two rooms on the upper floor one seemed not to be used at all and the other, though sparsely furnished, appeared to be used as a bedroom.

'In room 2 were several ashtrays with the ends of hand-rolled cigarettes. These were placed in envelopes and labelled. Label No 2 is of stuff taken from the mantlepiece of this room, and label No 3 contains the remains of three hand-rolled cigarettes with rough pieces of cardboard inserted in the form of filters. Label No 1 contains loose tobacco taken from various ashtrays.

'The labelled envelopes were conveyed to the identification bureau of Glasgow Police for analysis. The result was spoken to by Detective Chief Inspector George Cook, who is a Licentiate of the Royal Institute of Chemistry, corroborated by Detective Inspector Angus Davidson, who is a Master of Science of Strathclyde University and a Licentiate of the Royal Institute of Chemistry. No trace of drugs was found in any of the envelopes labelled No 1 and No 2, but in the envelope labelled No 3, the cigarette ends were found to contain small fragments of cannabis.

'As a result of these findings, the three appellants were on 29th November 1970, cautioned and charged as libelled, by Constable McAlpine and Constable Glass. In reply to the first charge, the appellant Lustmann replied: "There are things which happen here which I can't control"' (*Lustmann and Others* v *Stewart* 1971 SLT (Notes) 58 (case stated by Sheriff Donald McDiarmid)).

Here knowledge was conceded in the reply to the charge of possession, yet the High Court quashed the convictions, the Lord Justice-Clerk (Lord Grant) remarking that the sheriff might have been on stronger ground to convict of the charge of permitting the premises to be used for the purpose of smoking cannabis and acquit of possession than vice versa. In the absence of opinions the *ratio decidendi* has to be deduced from the argument presented for the appellants, that they could not be held to have been in possession in respect that there was no finding in fact that the drug was actually in the custody of any of them. The counter-arguments were that the appellants were the sole occupiers of the house, that they were engaged in an experiment in communal living and that the drug was found in a room obviously used for communal purposes. This was sufficient to infer that the appellants must have known that the cigarette ends were there even if they did not know what they contained. The evidence against Lustmann was particularly strong in view of his answer to caution and charge. Similarly, in England, in *R* v *Searle* [1971] Crim LR 592 the Court of Appeal held that where drugs are found in a place which is used by more than one person and the prosecution are unable to attribute the possession of any particular drug to any particular person, it is not sufficient to show mere knowledge of the presence of the drugs.

In *R* v *Irala-Prevost* [1965] Crim LR 606 a direction that 'if two people start off on a journey together, one actually is the owner and driver of the car, and something is in the back of the car, and they are both intending that it should be taken along in the car, and the passenger who is there knows about it, then he would be in joint possession along with the person who is driving the car' was disapproved, and the conviction quashed, on the ground that 'it was incumbent on the judge to say something to the jury to make them realise that some degree of control must be established'.

The effect of knowledge without control is best illustrated by the leading case of *Black and Another* v *HM Advocate*. It concerned possession not of drugs but of explosives, in contravention of section 3(*b*) or alternatively section 4(1) of the Explosive Substances Act 1883.

'Whether or not the case is to be treated as one of concert or, as the Crown insisted, solely of individual guilt and responsibility, upon either view it is vital that "possession or control" of the explosive substance should be established and, in our opinion, it is necessary that a jury should receive adequate guidance and direction as to what may, in the particular case, be held by them to be sufficient to constitute such possession and control. Counsel for both applicants maintained that no such direction was given and further that such direction as was given by the judge was erroneous, in that it equiparated knowledge of the presence of explosives in the house with possession or control of these explosives by both accused. The passages to which counsel drew attention do not indicate that anything more than knowledge of the presence of explosives is required to establish possession or control. Indeed the last sentence of the judge's charge, dealing specifically with the charge of breach of section 4(1), is in these terms: ". . . in relation to the alternative charge, you cannot convict of the alternative charge unless you hold it proved that there was knowledge on the part of one or other of the accused, if you are disposed to convict either." This statement puts the matter negatively—it is not difficult to imply from the negative that the positive would suffice in terms of knowledge (of the presence of explosives) to establish that which would suffice for convictions. We observe also that this sentence was added after the judge inquired of counsel for Black whether he wished him "to add anything further about knowledge as opposed to possession and control?" Now the only passage in the charge which bears upon this materially or at all is one at which the learned judge referred to a statement alleged to have been made by Megeary after caution but outwith the presence or hearing of Black, to this or a similar effect, "I suppose you found the stuff in the cupboard", ie, in the room occupied as a bedroom by Black. What the judge said was: "It is for you, ladies and gentlemen, to decide what is the proper construction to be put on the evidence whether it indicates knowledge on the part of Megeary that his lodger was keeping these explosives in the house." In these circumstances we think it is the legitimate, if not the only, inference to be drawn from this passage in the charge, and we can find no other which deals with the question of possession or control, that proof of knowledge of the presence of explosives could be sufficient at least to establish such possession and control as to satisfy the requirements of proof of breach of section 4(1). The English cases cited by counsel for the applicants support the proposition that mere knowledge of the presence of explosives on occupied premises or in a vehicle is not by itself sufficient to bring home a charge of possession or control of those explosives. As it was put in the case of *Searle* [1971] Crim LR 592, "mere knowledge of the possession of a forbidden article in the hands of a confederate is not enough for joint possession to be established". We would agree with that proposition, and with the deduction from it that knowledge alone is not proof of either possession or control in the case of the individual charged alone. In our opinion, where an individual is charged with possession or control of explosives which are found in premises occupied by him and another or others, the mere fact that it is proved that at the time when he is interrogated or charged in respect of the presence of the explosives he has knowledge of their presence on the premises is not, by itself, sufficient to establish possession or control of those explosives. Proof of knowledge is certainly essential to conviction either of breach of section 3(*b*) or section 4(1) of the Act, but more must be proved to saddle an accused with responsibility as for possession or control, be it joint or individual. What more is necessary must depend upon the circumstances of the particular case, but whatever the nature or amount of the evidence required to be advanced, it must be more than, and in addition to, mere knowledge. In our opinion, therefore, it is necessary that a judge, when charging a jury in a case of alleged breaches of these sections of the Explosives Act, should give to the jury a direction which makes it clear that there must be corroborated evidence which demonstrates either that the accused has himself acquired or been in possession of and retained the possession of explosives or, if they are found in premises, that fixes the accused not only with knowledge of the presence of the substance in premises which he occupies or over which he exercises or is able to exercise control but with acceptance of the substance into his premises or at least permission for or connivance at its remaining there in the knowledge of its character. What in a particular case will suffice to satisfy the requirements of "possession or control" must be a matter of circumstance, but in our opinioin it is essential that there should be proved facts and circumstances from which a jury can infer that the accused is in a position to exercise practical control over the presence or dispose of the substance in question, and that this is not established by mere proof of knowledge of the presence of the substance and of its character' (*Black and Another* v *HM Advocate* 1974 JC 43).

There need be no hesitation in accepting the authority of this case as applicable to unlawful possession of controlled drugs, not only because the opinion itself acknowledges the identity of the problem by invoking a drugs precedent, but also because of the general nature of the principles enunciated. The use of the expression 'possession and control' derives from section 4 of the Explosive Substances Act: 'Any person who makes or knowingly has in his possession or under his control any explosive substance. . . .' It is therefore appropriate enough in such cases, but insofar as it suggests that control is additional to, rather than inherent in, possession it might be better avoided in others, specifically those under the Misuse of Drugs Act where the word possession connotes all the control necessary and, in addition, by section 37(3), control without custody.

It seems certain that the presiding sheriff had the judgment in *Black* in mind when he charged the jury in the case of *Balloch and Others*. Nevertheless, because he stopped short of explaining the necessity for 'practical control' by the accused the direction was found to be defective and the convictions quashed.

'I should try to explain what is meant by possession, particularly after what has been said to you by the solicitor for the accused, that it was ridiculous, or words to that effect, to say that any of these accused were in possession. Well, you must be able from the evidence to infer that an accused person had knowledge of the presence of these bottles with tablets and capsules in them and that an accused person had knowledge of the general character of what was in these bottles, and either that he accepted these items when they came into the room where he was, accepted their presence, or at least he permitted that they should stay there or connived at their remaining there knowing the character of what they were. You must be able to infer knowledge in an accused person that these bottles were there and what the character of their contents were and he at least permitted them to stay there or connived at their staying there' (*HM Advocate* v *Balloch and Others*, Unreported, Glasgow Sheriff Court, 20th October 1976 (Sheriff S. E. Bell's charge to the jury)).

'These are applications for leave to appeal against conviction by Donald Balloch, Peter Kerr, John Rennie and Mary Cameron or Balloch. The four applicants were convicted of a contravention of the Misuse of Drugs Act 1971, section 5(2). The only ground of appeal in each case that we have found it necessary to consider is the first, which is in the following terms: "The presiding judge misdirected the jury in respect that in charging them he confused knowledge with possession and failed to indicate (as under the circumstances he should have done) that evidence showing that the applicant may have known of the existence of the controlled drugs libelled in the charge was not in itself proof that the applicant had possession of them." Associated with that ground is the second ground of appeal which merely points out that there was no question of concert in the incident. Accordingly it was necessary that the case against each accused should be treated by itself, and proof of possession was necessary in relation to each accused, irrespective of the evidence which may have related to any of the other accused. There is a statutory definition of possession in the Misuse of Drugs Act 1971 in section 37(3). The learned judge in his charge to the jury made no reference to this. He did, however, seek at pages 5 and 6 of his charge to direct the jury on the appropriate law. I pause to point out that nowhere did he talk about possession and control except in relation to what I am about to say. At page 6, after dealing with knowledge of the presence of the bottles containing the drugs in the house, and I pause to observe that knowledge in itself is not sufficient to warrant a conviction under this subsection, he went on to direct the jury that if an accused accepted these items when they came into the room where that particular accused was, or at least permitted them to remain there or connived at their remaining there, knowing the character of what they were, then that would entitle them to convict that particular accused. No distinction was drawn between any of the accused in this regard. What he there said could possibly be accepted, despite its imperfections, as being an appropriate direction in relation to a person who was proved to be the occupier of the house and in control of the premises. It would have no application to a person who did not fall into that category' (*Balloch and Others* v *HM Advocate*, Unreported, High Court of Justiciary, 14th January 1977 (opinion of the Lord Justice-Clerk)).

Knowledge without more of the mental element, or without control, being thus insufficient proof of possession, the converse is also true. Control which is not 'conscious and willing', ie, without some degree of knowledge and intent, does not constitute possession.

'Possession does not consist merely in manual detention. Suppose I request a bystander to hold anything for me, it still remains in my possession' (*R* v *Sleep* (1861) LE & CA 44 per Mr Justice Willes at p 57).

The modern version of the truism that mere custody without the intention to possess is insufficient is to be found in a much-quoted dictum of Lord Parker.

'It is quite clear that a person cannot be said to be in possession of some article which he or she does not realise is, for example, in her handbag, in her room, or in some other place over which she has control. That I should have thought is elementary; if something were slipped into your basket and you had not the vaguest notion it was there at all, you could not possibly be said to be in possession of it' (*Lockyer* v *Gibb* [1967] 2 QB 243 per Lord Parker CJ at p 248).

Apart from *Mingay's* case (*supra*), the same solution has been arrived at in Scotland on several occasions, of which the case of *Calder* is an example.

'The appellant was convicted after trial at Edinburgh Sheriff Court of a charge that on 29th January 1974 in the house occupied by him at

7 Gladstone Terrace, Edinburgh, he did unlawfully have in his possession a controlled drug, namely cannabis, contrary to the Misuse of Drugs Act 1971, section 5(1) and (2). As the facts show, the cannabis mentioned in the charge was found during a police search of the house in two cigarette ends in a wastepaper basket in the appellant's bedroom. The facts, however, also show that the appellant shared occupancy of the house with others, that the others were permitted to use his bedroom as a sitting-room, and that although some of the others were present at the time of the search the appellant was not. Indeed there is no finding as to when the appellant was last in his bedroom before the search and there is nothing to show when he last slept in the room or in the house. In all these circumstances, it is quite impossible to hold that the possession of the cannabis in question had been brought home to the appellant' (*Calder* v *Milne*, Unreported, High Court of Justiciary, 18th February 1975 (per Crown Office Circular No 1337 of 1st April 1975).

Soon after *Lockyer* v *Gibb*, the House of Lords warmly endorsed Lord Parker:

'I entirely agree' (*Warner* v *Metropolitan Police Commissioner* [1969] AC 256 per Lord Reid at p 282).

'I agree with what Lord Parker CJ said in *Lockyer* v *Gibb*' (ibid per Lord Morris of Borth-y-Gest at p 286).

'There is no possession by a man until he knows what he has got' (ibid per Lord Guest at p 298).

'You do not (within the meaning of the Act) possess things of whose existence you are unaware' (ibid per Lord Pearce at p 307).

'There is no difficulty in the case of wholly ignorant control, put by Lord Parker CJ in *Lockyer* v *Gibb* [1967] 2 QB 243 where something is slipped into a person's custody without his knowing it is there. This is the classic case of the money in the sacks of Joseph's brethren' (ibid per Lord Wilberforce at p 311).

The House then embarked on a study of the mental element in possession so exhaustive and complex that an account of it and its repercussions is undertaken in a separate chapter.

CHAPTER 6

Warner Revisited

'If a judge on a drug case, feeling disheartened, perhaps, after a close study of *Warner's* case . . .' (Lord Pearce, one of the judges in *Warner's* case, in *Sweet* v *Parsley* [1970] AC 132 at p 157).

The case of *Warner* v *Metropolitan Police Commissioner* [1969] 2 AC 256 on appeal from *R* v *Warner* is a cornerstone of the modern English law on possession of a prohibited substance. The House of Lords had a field day (or six). The *Appeal Cases* report occupies almost sixty pages. Their Lordships refer to forty-seven precedents in their opinions, and a further twenty-nine were cited in argument. Lord Reid is said to have dissented from one ground of decision, Lords Guest and Morris of Borth-y-Gest from another. Lord Pearce suggested a legislative way out of 'a difficult position' which led in due course to section 28 of the 1971 Act. Lord Wilberforce dismissed as irrelevant discussion of *mens rea* as a 'separate requirement' and stated: 'The statute contains its own solution as to the kind of control penalised by the Act.'

The report is replete with contradictions, yet it is, so to speak, in constant use. It accordingly seems necessary to approach the case in an analytical way in order to identify with certainty the propositions of law for which it is authority. That this is not easy is hardly the fault of the reader since their Lordships are at odds as to the points at issue. Thus Lord Reid says at page 271: 'I understand that this is the first case in which this House has had to consider whether a statutory offence is an absolute offence in the sense that the belief, intention, or state of mind of the accused is immaterial and irrelevant.' He then discusses *mens rea*. Lord Wilberforce, on the other hand, says at page 308: 'I take this [the certified question] as raising the general question as to the nature and extent of knowledge or awareness, which must be shown against an accused person found in actual control of a prohibited substance', and at page 312: 'There is no need, and no room, for an inquiry whether any separate requirement of *mens rea* is to be imported into the statutory offence.'

There is no clarity either about the grounds of appeal, said to be misdirection of the jury as to possession. Lord Morris of Borth-y-Gest states: 'The jury were directed in these terms: "Now then, members of the jury, it was under control because possession means that you have control. This man quite clearly had, and does not deny he had, control of these pills, and if he had and it is a matter for you to make up your minds about because you are the judges of facts—if you think the evidence is, he does not dispute it, that he had control of that box which in fact turned out to be full of amphetamine sulphate, that creates the original offence; it is only mitigation that he did not know." ' Lord Wilberforce, however, states at page 312: 'The summing-up did in fact, in addition, put before them, as in my view it should have done, the circumstances in which the package was received by the accused and found in his custody and the unsatisfactory explanations which he offered to the police: these were just what the jury should have been asked to consider on the question of possession.' At most, therefore, the judgments amount to disapproval of a judicial charge to the jury had it consisted only of the passage quoted by Lord Morris of Borth-y-Gest.

The 'point of law of general public importance' eventually certified by the Court of Appeal was 'Whether for the purposes of section 1 of the Drugs (Prevention of Misuse) Act 1964, a defendant is deemed to be in possession of a prohibited substance when to his knowledge he is in physical possession of the substance but is unaware of its true nature.' Lord Morris of Borth-y-Gest, quoting the point of law at page 284, adds tersely: 'It will be seen that there is a certain ambiguity in this formulation.' It will also be seen at once that although *Warner* was a 'package' case, the package aspect was omitted from the point of law, thus opening the case up to a general survey of the law relating to possession. The rubric, however, allows the decision of the House to be governed by the limitation: 'Where, as here, the prohibited drugs were contained in a parcel.' The rubric, it must be said, is an unreliable guide to the decision in the case. It attributes to the majority of the judges the finding that 'the prosecution had to prove not only that the accused possessed the parcel but also that he possessed its contents'. What Lord Pearce said at page 307, in the course of a 'model' charge to a hypothetical jury, was:

'The prosecution here have proved that he possessed the parcel, but have they proved that he possessed the contents also?'

It goes without saying that it was the contents, ie, the controlled drug amphetamine sulphate, which alone the prosecution had to prove to have been in the possession of the accused. The trial judge had not made any such mistake, charging the jury that

'they have got to prove that this man had these tablets in this box in his possession'.

Inexplicably, this passage in his direction is suppressed in the House of Lords report and is to be found only in the Court of Appeal report (*R* v *Warner* [1967] 1 WLR 1209; [1967] 3 All ER 93).

The outstanding fact about *Warner* is that it has come to be regarded as an authority on *mens rea* in statutory offences. The question of *mens rea* was not raised in the court of first instance, it was not canvassed in the Court of Appeal and it was not involved in the certified point of law. How it came to be pleaded at such length before the House of Lords is, therefore, something of a mystery, but pleaded it was, though both the questions asked and the answers to them were irrelevant to the point of law which required to be decided. Not surprisingly, the decision on *mens rea* is given pride of place in the rubric, supported by reference to *dicta* by four out of the five judges. The passages indicated, however, fall short of a coherent, still less unanimous, statement of law. Those in the judgment of Lord Morris of Borth-y-Gest at pp 295 G and 296 B-D are on the subject of knowledge of possession, not *mens rea*, while the citation of Lord Wilberforce's opinion consists of a mere four words describing the statute as 'absolute in its terms'. Not only do the words come in a sentence which deals with the problem of the state of knowledge or means of knowledge involved in possession, but that sentence is both preceded and followed in its short paragraph by the *dicta* already quoted in which Lord Wilberforce declines to deal with *mens rea* as a separate issue in the case. This analysis leaves Lord Guest and Lord Pearce in a minority of two in holding *mens rea* to have been excluded by the statute, and Lord Guest blows hot and cold about it, thus:

'I am not inclined to place much weight on whether there is or is not a presumption that *mens rea* is a necessary ingredient in a statutory offence, but if there was, the presumption has to some extent been whittled down in recent years (see *Harding* v *Price* [1968] 1 KB 695, 701) and in any event the language of section 1 [of the 1964 Act] in my view is sufficient to rebut any such presumption. The very doing of the act, as has been said, imputes *mens rea*' (p 300 G).

The last sentence of the passage quoted is strikingly reminiscent of Lord Wilberforce's 'no room for an inquiry whether any separate requirement of *mens rea* is to be imported into the statutory offence'. However, Lord Guest ends resoundingly:

'I unhesitatingly answer that the offence is absolute. In fact, I would go further and say that to require *mens rea* would very largely defeat the purpose and object of the Act' (p 301 D).

The rubric is set out in three numbered paragraphs, with two *dicta*, one each by Lord Pearce and Lord Wilberforce, in addition. Paragraph 1 deals with *mens rea* without, however, employing the term. It describes the offence of possession as 'absolute'. The *dicta* on which it is based are all preliminary to the consideration which the House then gave to the question of the mental element involved in possession. That word in this paragraph must accordingly be read in an anticipatory way. Paragraph 3 applies the proviso in view of the known facts of the case, and need not be considered further. Paragraph 2 undertakes to deal with the question of knowledge and does so exclusively by reference to Lord Pearce's 'model' direction at pages 307-308, from which Lords Guest and Morris of Borth-y-Gest are recorded as dissenting. In fact, it was Lord Reid who dissented from the narrow 'escape' allowed by the model direction.

'A mistake as to the quality of the contents, however, does not negative possession. If the accused knew that the contents were drugs or were tablets, he was in possession of them though he was mistaken as to their qualities' (per Lord Pearce at p 307).

Lord Reid said of this:

'It still leaves subject to injustice persons who in innocent circumstances take into their possession what they genuinely and reasonably believe to be an ordinary medicine, if in fact the substance turns out to be a prohibited drug' (p 282).

Small wonder if Lord Reid was troubled by Lord Pearce's own illustration of the effect of his *dictum*, at page 305.

'Though I reasonably believe the tablets which I possess to be aspirin, yet if they turn out to be heroin I am in possession of heroin tablets. This would be so I think even if I believed them to be sweets. It would be otherwise if I believed them to be something of a wholly different nature.'

The puzzled comment of Professor J. C. Smith, Barrister-at-Law, in [1972] Crim LR at p 780

'If sweets are not different in kind from heroin tablets, there seems to be little room left for a defence of mistake as to nature'

is but one indicator that the last word has not yet been said on this subject.

Warner, as has been said, was a 'package' case, and it has been followed by 'package' cases where special considerations have been held to apply (eg, *R v Fernandez* [1970] Crim LR 277). But the 'package' aspect is a red herring, and the point of law certified by the Court of Appeal was more correct in ignoring it than Lord Pearce was in concentrating on the evidential specialty to the exclusion of the general principles applicable to knowledge of possession. Ignorance of the presence of a thing does not depend on its being in a package. It may be lying openly for all to see, and yet be overlooked, or fortuitously shielded from one person's sight. No question of packaging then arises, but that of knowledge does so with equal force. Nor does ignorance of the nature of a thing hinge on concealment. A person may just as likely believe a thing in the palm of his hand to be an innocent substance, as the contents of an unopened package. In neither case is there any logical justification for erecting special rules to deal with the accident of packaging, which is no more than a point in a wide spectrum of evidential possibilities. The solutions proposed by *Warner* raise as many new questions as they purport to settle. Thus:

'[I]f he suspected that there was anything wrong about the contents when he received the parcel, the proper inference is that he was accepting possession of the contents by not immediately verifying them' (p 308).

There seem to be at least three objections to this proposition. First, it is at direct variance with the sentence which precedes it:

'If, though unaware of the contents, he did not, at the first opportunity, ascertain what they were, the proper inference is that he was accepting possession of them' (p 307).

These propositions cannot co-exist in the same judgment. Either suspicion is required, to incur liability, or it is not. Second, what meaning ought to be given to the words 'anything wrong about the contents'? A person might believe that the contents were explosives, he not being entitled to have possession of them, and so be 'completely mistaken' (p 257 G). Third, revealing the contents is not, in a matter as sophisticated as the identification of a controlled drug, by any means the same thing as 'verifying' them. Uncertainty as to their nature may well continue until expert examination has taken place. In *R* v *Chatwood and Others* [1980] 1 WLR 874 the evidence of a forensic scientist was that he could not tell whether a substance was diamorphine without analysing it, and that of an experienced police officer was that, while he might have a strong suspicion that the substance was diamorphine he could not be certain.

In *HM Advocate* v *Ferreira and Others*, Unreported, Glasgow Sheriff Court, 2nd April 1976:

'There was evidence from these drug officers that real cannabis looks exactly like this, and it smells like that too, and this effect can be produced by putting fake cannabis in proximity to the real thing, so that the article thus produced looks very like it. You may remember that in this case the officers of the Drugs Squad were taken in by the appearance and smell of these articles to the extent that they thought they were real cannabis, until laboratory tests proved they were beeswax and dye, and nothing else' (Sheriff Peterson's charge to the jury).

Again, from Lord Pearce's 'model' direction in *Warner*:

'If the accused knew that the contents were drugs or were tablets, he was in possession of them though he was mistaken as to their qualities' (p 307).

Lord Reid is not recorded as having dissented from this supposed ground of decision, yet his judgment was quite different.

'The object of this legislation is to penalise possession of certain drugs. So what would be required would be the knowledge of the accused that he had prohibited drugs in his possession: it would be no defence, though it would be a mitigation, that he did not intend that they should be used improperly. And it is a commonplace that, if the accused has a suspicion but deliberately shuts his eyes, the court or jury is well entitled to hold him guilty. Further, it would be pedantic to hold that it must be shown that the accused knew precisely which drug he had in his possession. Ignorance of the law is no defence and in fact virtually everyone knows that there are prohibited drugs. So it would be quite sufficient to prove facts from which it could properly be inferred that the accused knew that he had a prohibited drug in his possession. That would not lead to an unreasonable result' (pp 279–280).

Lord Reid's use of the words 'prohibited drugs' places him in diametric opposition to the model direction's 'drugs or tablets', and still further from Lord Pearce's aspirins and sweets (p 305). To put the matter beyond doubt, Lord Reid approved of the application of the proviso because of

'the prevarications of the accused before he produced his final story and the whole circumstances',

but specifically dissociated himself from the decision in *Lockyer* v *Gibb* [1967] 2 QB 243 that

'while it is necessary to show that the defendant knew that she had the articles which turned out to be a drug it is not necessary that she should know that in fact it was a drug or a drug of a particular character (per Lord Parker CJ at p 249)

and from its adoption by Lord Pearce. His reason was that it

'leaves subject to injustice persons who in innocent circumstances take into their possession what they genuinely and reasonably believe to be an ordinary medicine' (p 282).

Lord Wilberforce speaks of a person's

'intention to possess, or knowledge that he does possess, what is in fact a prohibited substance',

and states:

'If he has this intention or knowledge, it is not additionally necessary that he should know the nature of the substance' (p 311).

He gives an example which effectively distances him from the idea that belief in possession of an aspirin would be enough.

'A man asks for a harmless remedy and is given by mistake a package containing a prohibited substance: this should not be possession under the Act at least until he knew or possibly had the opportunity of knowing what he had received' (p 311).

It seems strange that Lord Wilberforce, like Lord Reid, should be associated with the broad proposition in Lord Pearce's model direction, and that the latter should be advanced as the *ratio decidendi*.

A closer study of the report gives ground for the following synopsis:

1   The point of law did not raise the issue of *mens rea* but only the issue of knowledge of the nature of a substance in a person's control.

2   The case was decided on the basis that the direction given to the jury was defective, in respect of equating control with possession and dismissing knowledge as a factor.

3 The major proposition in *Lockyer* v *Gibb* [1967] 2 QB 243 was affirmed, to the effect that 'a person cannot be said to be in possession of some article which he or she does not realise is, for example, in her handbag, in her room or in some other place over which she has control' (per Lord Parker CJ at p 248).

4 However, that case was overruled insofar as it had laid down that 'while it is necessary to show that the defendant knew she had the articles which turned out to be a drug, it is not necessary that she should know that in fact it was a drug (per Lord Parker CJ at p 249). This was the *dictum* which the Court of Appeal applied in *R* v *Warner*, and which was consequently negatived when the House of Lords reversed the Court of Appeal's decision on the point of law.

5 The point of law was answered by reference to general principles of the law relating to possession, which are not different in 'package' cases (cf, Lord Reid: 'in his premises or in a container' at p 280; Lord Morris of Borth-y-Gest: 'article or thing or substance or package or container' at p 290; Lord Wilberforce: 'the substance, or something which contains it' at p 310).

Accordingly, *Warner's* place is with other authorities on possession, the package aspect being treated as an evidential circumstance without legal significance in principle. The report's most helpful and consistent formulations are as follows:

Lord Reid: 'What would be required would be the knowledge of the accused that he had prohibited drugs in his possession' (p 279 G).
'If the accused had a suspicion but deliberately shut his eyes, the court or jury is well entitled to hold him guilty' (p 279 G).
'It would be quite sufficient to prove facts from which it could properly be inferred that the accused knew that he had a prohibited drug in his possession' (p 279 H).

Lord Wilberforce: 'One single question should be asked—what kind of control with what mental element does the Act intend to prohibit?' (p 309 B).
'I am strongly disinclined, unless compelled to do so, to place a meaning upon this Act which would involve the conviction of a person consequent upon mere physical control, without consideration, or the opportunity for consideration, of any mental element. The offence created by the Act is a serious one and even though nominal sentences, or conditional discharges, may meet some cases, there may be others of entirely innocent control where anything less than acquittal would be unjust' (p 309 C-D).
'If room is to be found, as in my opinion it should, in legislation of this degree of severity for acquittal of persons in whose case there is not present a minimum of the mental element, a line must be drawn which juries can distinguish. The question, to which an answer is required, and in the end a jury must answer it, is whether in the circumstances the accused should be held to have possession of the substance, rather than mere control. In order to decide between these two, the jury should, in my opinion, be invited to

consider all the circumstances—to use again the words of Pollock and Wright (*Possession in the Common Law*, p 119)—the "modes or events" by which the custody commences and the legal incident in which it is held. By these I mean, relating them to typical situations, that they must consider the manner and circumstances in which the substance, or something which contains it, has been received, what knowledge or means of knowledge or guilty knowledge as to the presence of the substance, or as to the nature of what has been received, the accused had at the time of receipt or thereafter up to the moment when he is found with it; his legal relation to the substance or package (including his right of access to it). On such matters as these (not exhaustively stated) they must make the decision whether, in addition to physical control, he has, or ought to have imputed to him, the intention to possess, or knowledge that he does possess, what is in fact a prohibited substance. If he has this intention or knowledge, it is not additionally necessary that he should know the nature of the substance' (p 310 F - 311 A).

In a long and difficult report, Lord Wilberforce's last-quoted *dictum* stands out as summarising the majority views most effectively and has the special merit of dealing, as he set out to do, with the issues of *mens rea* and knowledge as a unitary problem. While giving due emphasis to the disclaimer of exhaustiveness, the proposed guidelines are sufficiently practical to be applied to most foreseeable circumstances. This appears to be the gold in the Warner river.

In the years which have elapsed, *Warner* has been invoked, no doubt, in innumerable unreported cases. Some of those which have found their way into the books may be mentioned. In the celebrated case of *Sweet v Parsley*, a House in which four of the five judges were the same as in *Warner's* case applied *Warner* to a charge under section 5(*b*) of the Dangerous Drugs Act 1965. Lord Pearce reverted to his judgment in *Warner* and explained:

'By the term "absolute", I mean an offence to which the normal assumption of *mens rea* does not apply, but in which the actual words of the offence (without any additional implication of *mens rea*) may well import some degree of knowledge, eg, the word possession as in *Warner's* case. In saying that the section relating to possession (which was there under discussion) was absolute, I was using it (as the context was intended to show) in that loose and convenient sense which had been used in the argument' (*Sweet v Parsley* [1969] 1 All ER 347 per Lord Pearce at p 358).

Lord Wilberforce applied his familiar standard, declining to consider *mens rea* as a separate issue where the statutory prohibition 'contains its own solution'.

'As in *Warner v Metropolitan Police Commissioner*, the word "possession" carried its own content of mental intention so, perhaps *a fortiori*, do the words "concerned in the management of any premises used for any such purpose . . ." and there is no occasion to look beyond them for some separate ingredient which might, in fact, be difficult to define' (ibid per Lord Wilberforce at p 360).

Lord Diplock applied *Warner* in similar terms.

'Where the prohibited conduct consists in permitting a particular thing to be done the word "permit" connotes at least knowledge or reasonable grounds for suspicion on the part of the permittor that the thing will be done and an unwillingness to use means available to him to prevent it and, to take a recent example, to have in one's "possession" a prohibited substance connotes some degree of awareness of that which was within the possessor's physical control' (ibid per Lord Diplock at p 361).

In *R v Hussain* the Court of Appeal applied *Warner* to a charge under section 304(*b*) of the Customs and Excise Act 1952.

'It is, of course, essential that he should know that the goods which are being imported are goods subject to a prohibition' (*R v Hussain* [1969] 2 QB 567 per Lord Parker LCJ at p 572).

In respect of a second count, of unlawful possession, *Warner* was also applied.

'The chairman gave the type of direction which was common before the recent decision of the House of Lords in *Reg v Warner* [1969] 2 AC 256. In other words, the direction in regard to possession was to the effect that it was only necessary for the jury to be satisfied that the accused was in control of the goods, and did not go on to invite the jury to consider whether the accused was aware of the character of the goods.

'In particular, towards the end of the summing-up the point is put very shortly. The chairman says to the jury:

'". . . are you satisfied that he consented to have that stuff put in his cabin without knowing precisely what it was, knowing that there was stuff there in those packages that were being hidden with his consent. . . ."

'He is clearly there obscuring any importance which might arise from the fact that the accused might not know the nature and character of the goods of which he was alleged to be in possession.

'Then in regard to control and physical possession the chairman, having stated quite correctly, in our view, that the test of possession is control, goes on again quite properly to say:

'"It is sufficient for the purposes of this case for me to tell you as a matter of law that if a man willingly receives and hides something for somebody else, as a matter of law he is in possession of those goods."

'We think that, as applied in this case, if the jury had been satisfied that the defendant had willingly received and hidden in a bulkhead something which another had asked him to hide, he would properly be said to have been in control and possession. The chairman enlarges on this and points out that if the truth of the matter is that the defendant was forced by superior officers in a high-handed way to allow the panel of his cabin to be removed and the goods to be put behind it, then the defendant should be acquitted, because there the proper inference would be that he was not in control. He goes on in these terms:

'"If, on the other hand, you think that what was done, although it may not have been done by his hand, that although he had not used the screwdriver it was done with his consent, the hiding of those goods in his cabin, then he had those goods in his possession. . . . If, on the second count they have proved that he consented to that cannabis being hidden in his cabin, once again they have proved he is in possession."'

'Acknowledging, as we do, the difficulty of summing up in these cases, this court is somewhat concerned that a direction on possession and control which started promisingly on the previous pages has become watered-down to little more than a direction that if the accused had consented to the second engineer and the carpenter putting these goods behind the bulkhead that would be enough to establish he was in control and, therefore, possession.

'This court feels that this was an unsatisfactory direction and, when coupled with the fact that there is really in this case no direction as regards the mental element of possession as required in *Warner's* case [1969] 2 AC 256, we have little hesitation in saying that this was an unsatisfactory verdict' (ibid).

The case of *R* v *Marriott* is variously credited with 'explaining' and 'distinguishing' *Warner*. The assistant recorder's charge to the jury was reminiscent of the judge's in *R* v *Warner*.

'The prosecution do not have to establish knowledge on the part of the accused person, otherwise, you may think, a coach and horses could be driven through the purpose of the Dangerous Drugs Act. Let us take an example. Imagine a man is charged with possessing a dangerous drug, and the prosecution's case is that there is found in his home a pound of that dangerous drug amongst other materials in a cupboard, the accused man would be able to say: "I did not know it was a dangerous drug and, therefore, I am not guilty." What the law says is this, that a person shall not be in possession of a drug unless he is licensed or authorised to be in possession of it. It is a mandatory section' (*R* v *Marriott* [1971] 1 All ER 595).

As this direction flies in the face of all the opinions in *Warner*, it was charitable of Lord Justice Edmund Davies to begin his criticism as he did.

'The learned assistant recorder doubtless had the decision of the House of Lords in *Warner* v *Metropolitan Police Commissioner* in mind. But that was a case significantly different in its facts from the present case. There the police found in the appellant's van two cases, one containing scent and the other prohibited drugs. The accused's defence was that he had gone to a café, expecting to collect one case of the sort of scent in which he dealt as a side-line which was to be left there for him by a man, and that he assumed that both the cases which he found had been left for him contained nothing but scent. The judge directed the jury that if the accused had control of the case which, in fact, turned out to be full of drugs, an offence was committed and the fact that he did not know what the contents were would be relevant only in mitigation. He was convicted and his conviction was affirmed by the Court of Appeal. The matter then went to the House of Lords who dismissed the Appeal' (ibid per Lord Justice Edmund Davies at p 597).

The court were too sanguine when they summarised their understanding of *Warner*.

'Not all members of the House of Lords expressed themselves in precisely the same way, but for the purposes of this present appeal the result of *Warner's* case may broadly speaking and (we hope) with accuracy be stated in this way: if a man is in possession, for example of a box and he knows that there are articles of *some* sort inside it and it turns out that the contents comprise, for example, cannabis resin, it does not lie in his mouth to say "I did not know the contents included resin". On the contrary, on those facts he must be regarded as in possession of it' (ibid).

The misunderstanding led to a doubtful conclusion.

'It might be urged that, if knowledge of the existence of some foreign matter is established, the decision in the case of Warner (*supra*) must lead to the conclusion that thereafter it would be no defence to say, "Although I could see just a speck of stuff sticking to the blade, I did not know the speck was cannabis." Perhaps the law does go as far as that. But must not the jury at least be directed that the Crown have to establish that the accused person had reason to know that there was *something* foreign on the knife? We think that nothing said in *Warner's* case (*supra*) negatives the necessity for some such direction' (ibid at p 597).

That is a far cry from proof of 'facts from which it could properly be inferred that the accused knew that he had a prohibited drug in his possession', since presumably any substance with which a knife may be contaminated is foreign to it in the sense in which the word is used here.

The high point of the tide of damage done by Lord Pearce's aspirins was reached in *Searle* v *Randolph*, decided in July 1972 when there was still a year to go before the 1971 Act came into operation (1st July 1973), bringing with it the innovation of section 28 defences.

'The defendant, who went to a police station at the invitation of a police officer, was searched with his consent and thirty-six cigarette ends were found on him. An unspecified number resulted from cigarettes he had smoked and a further unspecified number had been picked up by him in and around a tent in which he lived and which had been visited by other persons who smoked. One cigarette end was found to contain some three milligrams of cannabis and traces of it were found in two other ends. He was charged with having in his possession a quantity of a dangerous drug without being duly authorised, contrary to section 13 of the Dangerous Drugs Act 1965. The justices were of opinion that, while the defendant was aware that the cigarette end found to contain the measurable quantity of cannabis was in his possession, the prosecutor had failed to prove that the defendant knew or had reason to believe that it contained any foreign substance, namely, cannabis, and they dismissed the information. The prosecutor appealed by case stated to the Queen's Bench Divisional Court.

'*Held*, allowing the appeal, distinguishing *Marriott* [1971] 1 WLR 187 and applying *Warner* [1969] 2 AC 256 at p 305 per Lord Pearce, that the difference between a cigarette end composed of or filled wholly with tobacco and one filled with a substance including cannabis was the same kind of distinction between an aspirin tablet and heroin tablet. It was sufficient for the prosecutor to prove that the defendant had possession of the cigarette ends and that at least one of them contained a measurable quantity of cannabis; the prosecutor was not required to prove knowledge by the defendant that the end contained cannabis' (*Searle v Randolph* [1972] Crim LR 779).

It is notable that the application of *Warner* did not involve treating the cigarette end as a container. On the contrary, the distinction between a stub composed of tobacco alone and one composed of tobacco and cannabis mixed was held to be the same as the distinction between an aspirin tablet and a heroin tablet. It was this case which provoked Professor Smith's *cri de cœur*: 'If sweets are not different in kind from heroin tablets, there seems to be little room left for a defence of mistake as to nature.' As the requirement of knowledge of the existence of the 'thing' was held to be satisfied by knowledge of the existence of the contaminated stub among the others, this defendant was in no better case than one who knew that the stub contained foreign matter but did not know what it was. Indeed, if the latter were to open up the stub, see the foreign matter and believe it to be 'something of a wholly different nature' (Lord Pearce in *Warner* at p 305) from cannabis, such as an innocent herb, he would be acquitted despite his knowledge of the existence of the 'thing'. These reflections underline the importance of not relying on *obiter dicta* in *Warner*. At the same time, *Warner* cannot be regarded as a spent force and its true ratio is applicable today because (*a*) the 1971 Act does not alter the meaning of possession (*McKenzie v Skeen* 1983 SLT 121) and (*b*) section 28 does not alter the things which the prosecution have to prove, including the accused's knowledge (*R v Ashton-Rickhardt, infra*). Also of doubtful authority, though purporting to apply *Warner*, is *R v Fernandez*, in which it was held that

'In "package cases" the prosecution must satisfy the onus by proving that the accused was in physical control of articles which were dangerous drugs. If he did not know precisely the contents of the package but his conduct indicated that he was prepared to possess it whatever it was, or if he took something into possession when he should have been put on inquiry, then he would be guilty' (*R v Fernandez* [1970] Crim LR 277).

This formulation is, to say the least, less satisfactory than the distilled judgments in *Warner*, and might not be recognised by its putative parent.

By 1974 a better appreciation of *Warner* had been restored. In *R v Colyer* [1974] Crim LR 243 the requirement of knowledge of the presence of a prohibited substance was applied to circumstances where the quantity of the drug was minute.

The persuasive authority of *Warner* has been recognised in a number of English-speaking jurisdictions, including New Zealand (*Bright v Police* (1971) NZLR 1016), Jamaica (*R v Haye and Hamilton* (1972) 18 WIR 360), Canada (*R v Santeramo* (1977) 36 CR 1) and Scotland. In *McKenzie v Skeen*, ten milligrams of cannabis had got into an opaque jar which otherwise contained only seeds. Adopting the reasoning of *Lockyer v Gibb* and *Warner v Metropolitan Police Commissioner*, the court quashed the conviction, holding that awareness of 'the existence of the thing' was essential, and stating:

> 'Having examined the findings in fact for ourselves we are satisfied that they are incapable of demonstrating, beyond reasonable doubt, that the appellant was aware of the adventitious vegetable matter, in small flakes, amongst the innocuous seeds. The jar was opaque and although the seeds were obvious one of the two police officers searching for drugs noticed nothing but the seeds and one forensic scientist declared that the minute quantity of flakes could not be seen "except possibly by holding it up to the light and manipulating it to and fro between the fingers". He himself had only detected the flakes by tipping out the contents and carefully segregating the seeds' (*McKenzie v Skeen* 1983 SLT 121 (opinion of the Lord Justice-General) (This passage unreported)).

The Lord Justice-General dealt with the 'package' aspect in a way similar to *Warner*, but without attempting to classify or define exceptions to the general rule.

> 'In most cases possession of a container will support the inference of possession of its actual contents but it must always be a question to be decided in the particular circumstances of the particular case' (ibid (This passage unreported)).

This decision obviously represents a solution to be preferred to those in *Marriott* (*supra*), *Fernandez* (*supra*) or in *Searle v Randolph* (*supra*).

Attempts to undermine *Warner* by claiming that the passing of the 1971 Act superseded its authority were laid to rest in England by the case of *R v Ashton-Rickhardt*. The idea was that the definition of possession provided by Regulations for the 1964 Act had been repealed and 'possession' in the 1971 Act meant something different. In Edinburgh, too, the proposition was scotched.

> 'I must now deal with the argument for the Crown that possession of an article within the meaning of section 5(1) and (2) of the Misuse of Drugs Act

1971 may be established without proof that the possessor knew he had it. There is no doubt that under the corresponding provisions of the Act of 1964 knowledge on the part of the alleged possessor was an essential element to be established in proof of a charge of unlawful possession of a substance specified in the Schedule to that Act. In this respect the word "possession" was, not surprisingly, given the meaning commonly accepted in other statutory contexts, for example the Explosives Act 1883, and the English cases of *Lockyer* v *Gibb* [1967] 2 QB 243 and *R* v *Warner* [1969] 2 AC 256, which were concerned with section 1 of the Drugs (Prevention of Misuse) Act 1964, show quite clearly that for the purposes of that section a person cannot be said to be in the possession of an article which he does not realise was there at all. What was required, therefore, was proof that the alleged possessor was aware of the existence of the thing which he is said to have possessed and since the section did not demand proof of knowledge of the quality of the thing possessed, if that thing turned out to be a controlled drug proof of the offence was complete. Has the Misuse of Drugs Act 1971 made the fundamental change for which in this case the Crown contends? In my opinion the answer is emphatically in the negative' (*McKenzie* v *Skeen* High Court of Justiciary, 2nd August 1977, but not reported until 1983 SLT 121, per Lord Emslie, Lord Justice-General).

'There is the learned judge putting the question of the proof of want of knowledge directly upon the defence, although saying the burden upon the defence is less heavy than the burden of proof which rests upon the prosecution. With great respect to the judge, that direction was contrary to the decision of the House of Lords in *Warner* v *Metropolitan Police Commissioner* [1969] 2 AC 256 where it was laid down by the highest tribunal that there could not be possession of a controlled drug unless the accused person knew that the "thing" which was alleged to contain the controlled drug was in his possession, that knowledge of the presence of the thing in question was an essential prerequisite to proof of possession and that therefore the Crown had to prove, as part of its proof of possession of the controlled drug, knowledge that the thing (which was in fact a controlled drug) was there. As was pointed out, and indeed had been pointed out earlier by Lord Parker CJ—how can you have possession of something of the existence of which you do not know? Accordingly, unless for some reason the judge was justified in departing from what the House of Lords had said in *Warner* (*supra*), to which we are told he was not referred by counsel, there was a plain misdirection because, first of all, there was no reference to the need for proof of knowledge as part of proof of possession in the first part of the summing up, and secondly, in the second part of the summing up the whole question of knowledge is put as a matter of "disproof of knowledge" by the defendant, which is what the House of Lords said in *Warner* was not the position. Now Mr Gordon for the Crown has accepted that if one looks at this direction only in the light of *Warner* there was a misdirection. But he has claimed that, as is the fact, the 1971 Act was passed after the decision of the House of Lords in *Warner*, and that when one looks at the language of section 5 one should give a different meaning to the word "possession" from that which the House of Lords gave to that same word when they were concerned with section 1 of the Drugs (Prevention of Misuse) Act 1964. The earlier Act reads thus: (1) Subject to any exemptions for which provision may be made by regulations made by the Secretary of State and to the following provisions of the section, it shall not be lawful for a person to have in his possession a substance for the time being specified in the Schedule to this Act unless—(*a*) (*b*) and (*c*), which I need not read. It is true that the language of section 5(1) and (2) of the 1971 Act is not precisely the same as that of section 1 of the 1964 Act, but the word "possession" appears in both the statutory provisions. It would be strange indeed, if Parliament, being deemed to know in 1971 what the House of Lords had decided in *Warner* in 1969, should have intended a different meaning to be given to "possession" in the 1971 Act from that given by the House of Lords in *Warner* when construing that word in the 1964 Act. If that had been Parliament's intention, one would have expected to find some very clear language to that effect in the 1971 Act' (*R v Ashton-Rickhardt* (1977) 65 Cr App R 67 per Lord Justice Roskill at p 70).

(The reference to the 'thing' which was alleged to 'contain' the controlled drug is an unfortunate choice of words in view of *Warner's* notoriety as a so-called container case. It is not a reference to the parcel, but to the contents, as a previous passage in Lord Justice Roskill's opinion explains, though not without, still, an element of opacity: 'I use the word "thing" advisedly, as it was used in *Warner*, to distinguish the article from the controlled drug, which in fact it was.')

Warner accordingly marches on and, like the Bible and Shakespeare, is full of quotations.

CHAPTER 7

Section 5(2)—Unlawful Possession

Many and varied are the circumstances in which a controlled drug can be in a person's possession in contravention of the subsection. What they have in common may be summarised thus:

(a) the possession must be 'unlawful'. This is imported by the requirement of its being in contravention of subsection 1, whereby all possession of controlled drugs is declared to be unlawful unless exempted by regulations made under section 7;

(b) the possession must satisfy either the legal requirements considered to attach to that term or the partial definition of it in section 37(3);

(c) the possession must not be qualified in any of the respects provided in section 5(4)(a), 5(4)(b) or 28.

Droplets and scrapings

Hard cases make bad law and nowhere is this better illustrated than by the attempts of judges to mitigate the harshness of the code, leading to the false doctrine of usability. While the revisionism was covert, as in *Worsell (infra)*, it was allowed to pass, but when attempts to institutionalise it became too blatant, as in *R* v *Carver* [1978] 2 WLR 872 and *R* v *Webb* [1979] Crim LR 462, it had to be stopped, first in Scotland by *Keane* v *Gallacher* 1980 JC 77 and then for England and Wales by *R* v *Boyesen* [1982] AC 768. If *Worsell's* case were to recur today, he would be convicted, inasmuch as the contents of his tube were 'identifiable'. *Ex hypothesi*, if we can know what he had we can know he was guilty. There is a distinct irony in the reporting of the cases of *Worsell* and *Graham* in successive pages of the same volume of law reports. *Graham*, who genuinely believed he had nothing on him, was convicted and gaoled. *Worsell*, who knew perfectly well that his equipment was contaminated, having just had a fix, went free. (Not only so, but his was a Class A drug, Graham's Class B.)

'The sole question is, was there any evidence upon which a jury could come to the conclusion that the tube found under the dashboard contained a drug at the moment when the police discovered it?

'This Court has come to the clear conclusion that, inasmuch as this tube was in reality empty (that is, the droplets which were in it were invisible to the human eye and could only be discerned under a microscope and could not be measured or poured out), that makes it impossible to hold that there was any evidence that this tube contained a drug. Whatever it contained, obviously it could not be used and could not be sold. There was nothing in reality in the tube' (*R* v *Worsell* [1969] 2 All ER 1183; [1970] 1 WLR 111 per Lord Justice Salmon at p 112).

But it did contain a drug. According to the scientist who examined it, it contained approximately one-hundredth of one-sixth of a grain of heroin in the form of a very few small droplets. Presumably the heroin had been dissolved in water, as the examination revealed the droplets as 'a wetness inside the tube'. What cannot be gainsaid is that one-tenth of a milligram, or 100 micrograms, of herion was present.

'On August 7, 1968, the police raided a flat in Oxford where he was living with a young lady. They found some cannabis in the flat but he was not charged in respect of that. However, on the same day, the police took some scrapings from the pockets of the clothing which he was wearing. When he was asked what he would do if these scrapings were found to contain cannabis, he said: "I will plead guilty but I do not think you will find anything. If you do, that is my fault." In fact on analysis traces of cannabis were found in the scrapings from three of his pockets; I think one from his trousers and two from his jacket. In each case the quantities were very small but the scientific officer found that the quantity was capable of being weighed and measured. This case being tried before *R* v *Worsell*, no point was made by the defence that the quantities found were so minimal as in truth to amount to nothing. The case was really being run on the basis that these were very small amounts of cannabis and, that being so, it could well be that he did not know it was there and he was not truly in possession' (*R* v *Graham* [1969] 2 All ER 1181; [1970] 1 WLR 113 per Lord Justice Fenton Atkinson).

'On the evidence of the scientific officer that what was found in each of the three pockets could in fact be measured and weighed in milligrammes, we do not think that as a matter of law it could be said that there was in truth no cannabis in this young man's possession. It may be that it would have been right for the deputy recorder to leave to the jury as an issue of fact to find whether what was in his pockets was sufficient to amount to possession of cannabis but, in our view even if he had done that (and he summed up, of course, in the light of the way in which the case had been run) the end of the case would have been inevitable; there would have been a conviction. If there was any error in treating it as axiomatic that the quantities did amount to cannabis, we would apply the proviso without hesitation' (ibid at p 114).

One may wonder at the alacrity with which the court would have applied the proviso. It was the same court as had found in *Worsell* (*supra*), notwithstanding the scientific finding of heroin present, that 'in truth it was an empty tube with nothing in it'. Lord Justice Fenton Atkinson said of Mr Graham: 'He did not at first intend to appeal but was no doubt encouraged to do so by seeing or having brought to his notice the report in *The Times* newspaper of a case decided in this court, *Worsell* [1970] 1 WLR 111.' It is indeed credible that Mr Graham regarded his jacket or trouser pocket, from which the scrapings were taken, as 'in truth an empty pocket with nothing in it'.

Conflicting results have occurred in scrapings cases in Scotland by virtue of following or not following the reasoning in *Graham's* case.

'This accused, when searched at Inverness Police Headquarters, was found to have in his outside right-hand jacket pocket a quantity of debris including fragments of tobacco and a small quantity of cannabis resin subsequently measured at 0.02 grams. This is a quantity visible to the naked eye, and the analyst in evidence was able to indicate a fragment of cannabis resin among the debris taken from the accused's pocket' (*Procurator Fiscal Inverness* v *Hudson Morrison Cairns*, Unreported, 11th November 1976, Sheriff William J. Fulton).

'I think that the proper approach is that in circumstances such as arise in the present case, where a small but visible and measurable quantity of a drug found on the accused's person is involved, the Crown must prove prima facie the presence of the drug on the accused's person at the appropriate time and place. Once they have done that, the onus then switches to the defence to provide an explanation of the presence of the drug consistent with innocence' (ibid).

Almost simultaneously, Sheriff James P. Murphy came to the opposite conclusion, influenced in advance by the then unpublished argument of Mr N. L. A. Barlow on the 'relevance of minute quantities to the issue of knowledge', and acquitted in a scrapings case involving five milligrams of cannabis resin.

'What the evidence amounts to is that the respondent had, on the occasion libelled, scattered about one or more of his pockets, among the other detritus which had collected there and tucked in what corners and seams I know not, a number of small particles of cannabis resin which may not have seen the light of day for months or even years, and of whose presence he may have been for all I know sublimely unaware' (*Dean* v *McKechnie*, Unreported, Dumbarton Sheriff Court, 14th December 1976).

In a similar case at Lancaster Crown Court on 12th and 13th October 1977, Judge A. A. Edmondson acquitted on a mixture of grounds not readily summarised but apparently including the improbability that the accused would be aware of the presence of a quantity as small as 1 milligram (cf, Barlow: 'Possession of Minute Quantities of a Drug' [1977] Crim LR 26), and the artificiality of finding him guilty of possession of traces which were 'in reality nothing' (cf, *Worsell* and *R* v *Hierowski* [1978] Crim LR 563).

The burden of proving such awareness is borne by the Crown who can discharge it by various means but cannot shift it on to the accused to disprove knowledge of the facts.

'The learned chairman says: "The next thing is the question of possession. This is one of those cases where once the prosecution have proved possession the onus shifts to the accused to show that he was in lawful possession. Here there is evidence that these implements, amongst other things, were in this sack in the back of the van under his control. He has said: 'My possession was lawful because I had had that van for the purpose of re-spraying and re painting, and at the behest of the owner I was in the process of returning it to him when I was stopped. Indeed I had no idea what was in the back of it.' As I say, the onus shifts to him." That is clearly wrong because as far as the question of possession was concerned the onus remained throughout on the Crown to prove that the appellant knew' (*R v Cugullere* [1961] 2 All ER 343 per Mr Justice Salmon at p 345).

Of course, 'it would be quite sufficient to prove facts from which it could properly be inferred that the accused knew' (*Warner v Metropolitan Police Commissioner, supra,* per Lord Reid at p 279H).

The omission from section 5 of the word 'knowingly' has no effect on onus. 'All the word "knowingly" does is to say expressly what is normally implied' (*Taylor's Central Garages (Exeter) v Roper* (1951) WN 383). 'I find difficulty in seeing how it can be said that the omission of the word "knowingly" has, as a matter of construction, the effect of shifting the burden of proof from the prosecution to the defence' (ibid).

'Traces'

Practical considerations seem to have militated against too many prosecutions involving such arcane investigations as scraping out ooze from pockets, where nothing else points to guilt. Should they occur, however, defenders may with justice argue that the smaller the particle and the greater the pother of recovering it, the harder does it become for the Crown to show that the accused had possession as distinct from unconscious custody.

Not that such prosecutions are the high watermark of assiduity on the part of prosecutors.

'The facts are that on July 12, 1968, police officers went to 19A Cremorne Road [London] SW10 where the defendant occupied a basement flat. In a cupboard in the basement passage they found an old television set and inside it a polythene laundry bag which bore the defendant's name. Inside the bag was a package containing 307 grains of cannabis resin. In the defendant's flat itself according to the evidence of the police officers, there were on the mantelpiece a small clay pipe and on a table a wooden pipe and a tobacco pouch.

'The police took possession of all these articles, which were subjected to scientific analysis by Mr Cook, whose evidence was read to the jury, he having been conditionally bound over, and it was wholly unchallenged. Mr Cook identified the contents of the package as 307 grains of cannabis resin. Of the pipes and pouch he said: "I found traces of cannabis in the bulbs and stems of both these pipes and I found traces of cannabis resin amongst the tobacco within this pouch." Although no evidence was adduced as to the meaning of "traces of cannabis", the deputy chairman told the jury in his summing up: "a trace means a quantity so small that it cannot be measured scientifically in any way at all". This court is at a loss to understand why such a definition was proffered: certainly the unchallenged scientific evidence affords no basis for it' (*R* v *Frederick* [1970] 1 WLR 107 per Lord Justice Edmund Davies at p 108).

'In the course of the summing up the jury was directed in these terms: "Should you come to the conclusion that you are not satisfied that the accused was in possession of the 307 grains of cannabis, but you think he was in possession of those traces—that is to say, in his pipes and in his pouch—you will find him guilty just the same, because, members of the jury, the law is absolute. You must not have any dangerous drug in your possession, and no matter how small the quantity may be, a trace means a quantity so small that it cannot be measured scientifically in any way, at all"' (ibid at p 109).

'There was no challenge of the scientific evidence with a view to establishing that what was described as "traces" of cannabis and cannabis resin found in the pouch and both pipes in reality amounted to nothing. However, the manner in which the prosecution put their case resulted in the complication being introduced into the summing-up that the jury could find the defendant guilty if they were satisfied that he was in possession of the 307 grains *or* in possession of the traces.

'This was unfortunate and, indeed, in the view of this court quite unnecessary, for the Crown had an extremely strong case in regard to the 307 grains and could rely on the presence of the traces in the pipes and the pouch to support that case. They had no need to seek to establish, as an entirely separate ground upon which a conviction could be based, the actual presence of the drug in the pipes and pouch at the time when the police took possession of those articles.

'However that may be, the charge in the indictment was framed in words wide enough to cover the case which the Crown sought to establish, and in the way the case was run the summing up did not contain any misdirection' (ibid at p 110).

The imprecise connotation of the word 'traces' is again powerfully illustrated by the case of *Bocking* v *Roberts*. The defendant was found by police in possession of a hookah pipe the bowl of which contained 'traces' of cannabis resin. The quantity was too minute to be weighed but on chemical analysis it was found that it 'must have been' at least 20 micrograms. He was convicted, and appealed.

'In these cases, the tribunal of fact has to decide whether the quantity of traces spoken of by the expert witness is enough to justify the conclusion that the defendant was in possession of a quantity of the drug, rather than that it should amount to no more than an indication that he had on some other occasion had the drug in his possession. I do not profess to suppose that it is always or often an easy distinction to draw, and I do not think that courts trying these cases in future will be assisted by any attempt on our part to lay down any sort of mathematical formula to determine what is or what is not enough in terms of quantity to justify a conviction. I think the distinction to which I have referred must be in the mind of the tribunal of fact, that they should approach such questions, not leaving their common sense at home, bearing in mind that there is a heavy onus on the prosecution in all criminal cases to prove beyond all reasonable doubt that the offence has been committed. I think that if tribunals of fact approach this question in that way, we shall get as near to a satisfactory and consistent series of answers as by any other method.

'Having so described my views on the principle involved, I must now come back to the case in question. It is to be observed that although the quantity of cannabis in the present case could not be measured in the sense that no precise figure could be given for its weight or size, yet it was measurable in the sense that it must have been at least 20 microgrammes. The justices in this case have taken much trouble in their determination of the issues before them; they were referred to, and I think clearly comprehended, *Graham* (*supra*) and *Worsell* (*supra*), which are the two leading authorities for them to consider, and they have I think come to the conclusion that there was enough to justify the charge which was laid against the defendant; and although I am not saying that I would have reached the same conclusion if I had been a member of the bench deciding this issue, I do not find it possible to say that they have gone beyond the legal limits of determination appropriate to a tribunal of fact such as the justices' (*Bocking* v *Roberts* [1973] 3 All ER 962).

'In my opinion the traces of cannabis found in this defendant's pipe on March 30, 1972, were so microscopically small that it would be wrong in law to hold that he was at that time in possession of the drug. There was proof that he had once been in possession of it; there was not enough to prove that he was still in possession.

'If I were asked where the line should be drawn, I would be tempted to answer that it must be drawn substantially above 20 microgrammes, adding only that the difficulty of drawing the line is no reason for concluding, against common sense as I think, that the defendant was guilty of the serious offence of possessing a forbidden drug. Different tests have been proposed in some of the cases cited to us. Salmon LJ's judgment in *Worsell* (1968) 53 Cr App R 322; [1970] 1 WLR 111 suggests that no offence is committed unless there is a sufficient quantity of the drug to be used in some way. If that is the right test, the defendant should certainly have been acquitted. 20 microgrammes is not a usable quantity. *Graham* (*ante*, p 357) [1970] 1 WLR 113 speaks of a weighable and measurable quantity; the 20 microgrammes here is not a weighable quantity, nor measurable in any ordinary sense of the word. The figure, we are told by counsel, was ascertained by a chemical test; if there had not been at least 20 microgrammes present the result of the test would have been different. There was no putting of the cannabis in a weighing scale or measuring it by any instrument. Whichever test is used, that in *Worsell's* case (*supra*) or that in *Graham's* case (*supra*), it seems to me that the defendant should be acquitted.

'If his conviction is to be upheld it must follow that if a man puts cannabis in a container, whether in his pocket, his pouch or his pipe, uses the cannabis but does not destroy the container, he will continue in the eyes of the law to be in possession of cannabis so long as the container gives a positive reaction to a chemical test for the presence of that drug. I do not think that that is what the regulations mean when they speak of a man being in possession of a forbidden drug' (ibid per Mr Justice McKenna (dissenting)).

The report does not disclose that either the magistrates or the appeal judges informed themselves of the meaning of the term microgram. Mr Justice McKenna's idea that it would involve only 'a positive reaction to a chemical test' for the presence of a drug is a more convincing description than the word 'traces'. As a microgram is a one-thousandth part of a milligram (*a*) it would take 1,000,000,000 of them to make up the weight of a bag of sugar in a grocery; (*b*) it is anomalous that the case of *Worsell* should have been 'distinguished' on the ground that here there was something while there there was nothing, when the 'nothing' in *Worsell* was five times as great a mass of heroin as the 'something' in *Bocking* was of cannabis. On any view, except the ones apparently pleaded, the court should have been able to see that this case was *a fortiori* of *Worsell's*. It is pertinent to note also that if Mr Justice McKenna's use of the phrase 'positive reaction to a chemical test' was justified by any evidence in the case, and it is difficult to believe it was not, the case ought to have foundered on the fact that the chemical reaction for cannabis resin (which was charged) is the same as that for cannabis (which was not). Consequently, as the two substances are separately and differently defined (section 37(1)), it must have been impossible to tell which was, or had been, present. The presence of one cannot be extrapolated from the proved presence of the other (*Arnott v MacFarlane* 1976 SLT (Notes) 39).

Of all the reported cases on minute quantities, it is ironical that it should be *Bocking v Roberts* which contains the Lord Chief Justice's admonition to inferior judges 'that they should approach such questions not leaving their common sense at home' (ibid at p 963).

Mr Justice McKenna's did not remain a lone voice and when 20 micrograms turned up again in 1974, this time in Ipswich Crown Court before Mr Justice Stinson, the dissenting judgment was preferred to the majority one of *Bocking* v *Roberts*.

'The defendant was in possession of a pipe. It had no bowl, but could have been used either to smoke cannabis within the pipe itself or as a holder for a reefer cigarette. The police seized the pipe and it was submitted for scientific examination. The forensic scientist was unable to see whether there was anything in the pipe because of its construction. He scraped out what residue there was on the inside. He then dissolved the scrapings in a solvent which dissolved cannabis and certain other types of matter, but left other particles suspended in the liquid. The suspended matter was separated and the cannabis in the solvent isolated on a filter paper by a chromatographic process. Two reagents were applied to the filter paper. Experiments with such reagents had revealed that if there were more than 20 micrograms of cannabis present on the filter paper the reagents would change colour. One microgram is a millionth of a gram and 20 micrograms is roughly equivalent to a millionth of an ounce. At no stage in the process was any cannabis visible either to the naked eye or under a low-powered microscope. The reagents indicated the presence of at least 20 micrograms of cannabis. To say that the amount of cannabis found in this case by the methods described was measurable was stretching the meaning of the word unduly; bearing in mind the minute amount of cannabis found in this case and the elaborate methods used by the scientists to establish its presence, it could not be said that the prosecution had produced a prima facie case that the defendant knew he had it' (*R v Colyer* [1974] Crim LR 243).

Discussing 'the relevance of minute quantities to the issue of knowledge' in his important article three years later, Mr N. L. A. Barlow wrote:

'In cases where the prosecution insist upon proceeding with an allegation of possession of a minute quantity of drugs, it should be required to surmount the formidable evidentiary obstacles posed by its own evidence. It should be a common sense presumption from the prosecution case that the defendant was unlikely or unable to be aware of ... the presence of the drug the microscope has managed to find' (N. L. A. Barlow, 'Possession of Minute Quantities of a Drug' [1977] Crim LR 26).

Or even failed to find.

Minute quantities

The periodical literature on this topic would doubtless have continued had it not been cut off by *Keane* v *Gallacher* and *R* v *Boyesen*.

'The decision in *R* v *Carver* [1978] 2 WLR 872; (1978) Cr App R 352 seems to entail the importation into s 5(1) of a qualification to the term "controlled drug" namely "which is capable of being used". If that be the case, it would add an additional onus on the prosecution to prove that fact. If Parliament had intended that such a qualification should be added it would have been simple to give express effect to it. The plain unqualified words of the subsection simply refer to a controlled drug and *ex facie* anything which is capable of being identified as a controlled drug is struck at by the subsection. It is the possession of the controlled drug which is made punishable by s 5(1) and (2), not its use or potential use. There is no ambiguity in the words used and no absurdity is produced. If it is argued that anything short of a "usable" amount of the controlled drug produces an absurdity in s 5(1) it is an argument which we cannot accept. The plain wording of the subsection makes "identification in an acceptable manner" and not "capable of being used" the test' (*Keane* v *Gallacher* 1980 JC 77; 1980 SLT 144 per Lord Wheatley, Lord Justice-Clerk, at p 147).

'I find myself entirely persuaded by the reasoning of Lord Wheatley, Lord Justice-Clerk, in *Keane* v *Gallacher*' (*R* v *Boyesen* [1982] AC 768 per Lord Scarman at p 776).

'I have concluded that the "usability" test is incorrect in law. The question is not usability but possession. Quantity is, however, of importance in two respects when one has to determine whether or not an accused person has a controlled drug in his possession. First, is the quantity sufficient to enable a court to find as a matter of fact that it amounts to something? If it is visible, tangible and measurable, it is certainly something. The question is one of fact for the common sense of the tribunal. This was the decision in *Bocking* v *Roberts* [1974] QB 307, and I believe Lord Widgery CJ's approach to the question was correct in law. Secondly, quantity may be relevant to the issue of knowledge. Lord Diplock delivering the judgment of the Privy Council in *Director of Public Prosecutions* v *Brooks* [1974] AC 862, defined possession in the case of dangerous drugs as follows at p 866: "In the ordinary use of the word possession one has in one's possession whatever is, to one's own knowledge, physically in one's custody or under one's physical control." If the quantity in custody or control is minute, the question arises—was it so minute that it cannot be proved that the accused knew he had it? If knowledge cannot be proved, possession would not be established. A good illustration of the relevance of quantity to knowledge is to be found in the New Zealand case, *Police* v *Emirali* [1976] 1 NZLR 286. In the present case the question, however, does not arise. Upon the evidence which, after a correct direction on knowledge, the jury accepted the respondent knew that the traces of brown substance were there. He also knew, though this knowledge would only become relevant if he had sought to establish a defence under section 28 of the Act, that the brown substance was cannabis' (ibid at p 777).

Thus *Carver* sinks without trace, but *Worsell* and *Bocking* are saved. As to the approval given by the House of Lords to the Lord Chief Justice's approach in the latter case, the words are carefully chosen. That approach was to support the tribunal of fact, adding: 'I am not saying that I would have reached the same conclusion.'

Considering this and the cogency of Mr Justice McKenna's dissent, and the case of *Colyer*, the endorsement of *Bocking* by the House of Lords need not be seen as a green light to prosecute cannabis cases involving micrograms.

Disappearing drugs

Must a prosecution fail if the detection of the possession is too late because of consumption? On the strength of *Worsell* correctly decided, yes. Otherwise not. On the strength of *Worsell* differently pleaded, again not.

'Before parting with the case, this court would like to make it plain that if this prosecution had been run in a different way from that in which it was run at the trial, there would have been no real defence to it. His statement, plus the presence of the tube which had contained the drug would have been conclusive evidence against him' (*R* v *Worsell* [1969] 2 All ER 1183; [1970] 1 WLR 111 per Lord Justice Salmon).

That the problem is not free from difficulty is clear from Professor J. C. Smith's commentary appended to *Bird* v *Adams*. Nevertheless, both that case and the cases of *R* v *Wells* and *R* v *Chatwood and Others* resulted in convictions being upheld where no substance of any description could be produced in evidence.

'The basis of the submission was this, that although the appellant had admitted possession of what he thought to be LSD, there was no independent proof that the drug was in fact LSD, and that it might have been some innocuous substance sold to the appellant under a fraudulent description, and so it was submitted that there was no case to answer because the vital element of the prosecution case, namely, that the drug was a prohibited drug, had not been established by an admission of the appellant who himself could not know whether that which he carried was or was not the genuine drug. Now the justices rejected that suggestion, at least they were not influenced by it. They held there was a case to answer and on the case proceeding the appellant gave no evidence and he was duly convicted. Mr Reney-Davis before us today returns to the original submission in the case and says that the justices should have upheld the submission of no case because the admission of the appellant in the circumstances of this case was of no evidential value at all. Now it is clear from the authorities which have been put before us that there are many instances where an admission made by an accused person on a matter of law in respect of which he is not an expert is really no admission at all. There are bigamy cases where a man has admitted a ceremony of marriage in circumstances in which he could not possibly have known whether in truth he had been married or not because he was no expert on the marriage ceremonial appropriate in the particular place. It is quite clear that there are cases of that kind where the person making the admission lacks the necessary background knowledge to be able to make the admission at all. Again we have been referred to the *Comptroller of Customs* v *Western Lectric Co Ltd* [1966] AC 367, where a man made an admission in regard to the country of origin of certain goods when he had no idea at all where the goods had come from. Again it was held that this admission was worthless because it was an admission of a fact as to which he had no knowledge at all, and in respect of which no valid admission can be made. Mr Reney-Davis submitted that the present case is a like case with that, but in my judgment this is not so. If a man admits possession of a substance which he says is a dangerous drug, if he admits it in circumstances like the present where he also admits that he has been peddling the drug, it is of course possible that the item in question was not a specific drug at all but the admission in those circumstances is not an admission of some fact about which the admitter knows nothing. This is the kind of case in which the appellant had certainly sufficient knowledge of the circumstances of his conduct to make his admission at least prima facie evidence of its truth' (*Bird* v *Adams* (1972) per Lord Widgery CJ, quoted from the transcript by Mr Justice Forbes in *R* v *Chatwood and Others* [1980] 1 WLR 874 at p 877).

'At no time has it been suggested by Miss Wells that her belief that she had smoked cannabis with Mr Cooke and that she had taken "speed" with him was erroneous. There is even now no suggestion by her that she might have been mistaken about that admission. All that is said is it is on the prosecution to prove positively that she had been, at the relevant time or times, in possession of either cannabis or amphetamine as the case may be. But the best evidence that she has been in possession of these articles at some time might well be her admission' (*R* v *Wells* [1976] Crim LR 518 per Lord Justice Ormrod, quoted from the transcript by Mr Justice Forbes in *R* v *Chatwood and Others* [1980] 1 WLR 874 at p 878).

'The statements of the appellants in this case, either orally to the police officer, or when reduced to writing were sufficient to provide prima facie evidence of the nature of the substance which had been in their possession. One of them, Proctor, as I have indicated, gave evidence, but what I have said about his statement to the police and the fact that he was found guilty by the jury indicates quite clearly that the jury disbelieved his explanation that it was flour and believed his earlier statement to the police that he knew it was heroin.

'This court is of the view that the statements of the appellants provide, having regard to the circumstances of this case, prima facie evidence of the identity of the substance' (*R* v *Chatwood and Others* [1980] 1 WLR 874 per Mr Justice Forbes at p 879).

An admission is only enough to make good the lack of other evidence identifying the drug if there is evidence that the accused knew what it meant. The accused's belief must not rest on hearsay. Otherwise the evidence of someone contradicting or retracting the identification would equally have to be received. If *Mieras* v *Rees* [1975] Crim LR 224 failed for lack of identification of the drug, it was not because the defendant retracted his admission but because his admission was unacceptable in the first place.

For an example of a case masquerading as an instance of absent drugs, see *Hambleton* v *Callinan*. Here it was hypothesised that consumption of a drug changes its character, depriving the prosecutor of the chance to identify it even if he recovers the accused's urine at the critical time. However, a close perusal of the report reveals that the hypothesis was mistaken in this instance. Traces of the drug survived in the urine and were 'identified in an acceptable manner', the findings in fact including the following: '(*f*) that the urine samples together with 71 Durophet tablets were handed over to an officer of the Forensic Science Laboratory at Bristol on October 23, 1967; (*g*) that the Durophet tablets were on analysis found to be in the amphetamine group; (*h*) that Callinan's urine sample was found to contain amphetamine powder and barbiturate together with traces of alcohol; (*i*) that Farrier's and Graham's samples contained amphetamine powder and barbiturate'. Of course, on the basis of these findings, the justices felt able to opine that 'once a capsule or tablet entered the blood stream, it substantially changed its form' (p 429). By the time this reached the High Court it had itself been substantially changed and the justices were said by Lord Parker CJ to have felt that 'once you had consumed something and its whole character had altered and no further use could be made of it, as in this case, a man could not be said to be in possession of the prohibited substance'.

'I am quite satisfied that the justices were right. Mr Tucker has said that there may be cases where a man, as it were consumes something, puts it in his mouth or swallows it, such as a diamond or a gold ring, in order to conceal it, when nevertheless he may well be in possession of it. I entirely agree but when, as here, something is literally consumed and changed in character, it seems to me impossible to say that a man is in possession of it within the meaning of this Act' (*Hambleton* v *Callinan and Others* [1968] 2 QB 427 per Lord Parker CJ at p 431).

The judgment is possible only by virtue of the switch from 'change of form' in the case stated to 'change of character' in the appeal. Otherwise the Lord

Chief Justice's reasoning is not convincing. The Durophet tablets, on being consumed, changed their form but the amphetamine powder did not change its character. It was a finding in fact that the urine contained amphetamine. If not in the defendant's possession, then in whose? The distinction between a diamond and a drug loses force if both can be excreted unaltered. Reliance on the proposition that 'no further use could be made of it' is inconsistent with the reasoning in the cases leading from *Graham* via *Keane v Gallacher* to *Boyesen*.

In *R v Beet* (1978) 66 Cr App R 188, on similar facts, no bones were made about possession of drugs which were found in the appellant's urine and nowhere else. The report states, *tout court*, 'The sample, on analysis, disclosed the presence of amphetamine and methylamphetamine.' The Appeal Court were just as terse: 'The crux of this matter is a matter entirely of direct scientific determination as to the presence of one of the prohibited drugs.'

Lord Justice Salmon's tip in *Worsell* for avoiding failure of prosecutions by thoughtless draftsmanship is foreshadowed in *Hambleton* by Lord Parker's parting shot: 'I confess that I myself can see no reason why in another case the time when the possession is said to have taken place should not be a time prior to the consumption, because as it seems to me the traces of, in this case, amphetamine powder in the urine is at any rate prima facie evidence—which is all the prosecution need—that the man concerned must have had it in his possession, if only in his hand prior to raising his hand to his mouth and consuming it. Accordingly, it seems to me that the possible difficulty that the decision in this case raises for the police does not arise in practice because the date of his possession can always be laid prior to the consumption' (p 432).

The circularity of this view is exposed by the fact that unless the drug is found to be present, at least to the extent of 'traces', when the urine or other excretion is examined, proof of past possession will also fail.

Lord Chief Justice Parker's and Lord Justice Salmon's hints in *Hambleton* and *Worsell*, respectively, were taken eventually and in Middlesex Crown Court on 19th May 1977 Mr James Pragliola came to trial before Judge Solomons, QC, on a charge of possession based on an inference of possession at some previous date of a quantity of cannabis resin of which 'minute traces' were found in a pipe. Evidently the minute traces, which are not stated to have been quantified, were considered to be 'in reality nothing' (*Worsell*). The circumstances were that on 25th November 1974 the defendant had been convicted of possession, when after a police search of his flat, cannabis resin, a set of scales and a distinctive pipe were removed. The pipe was returned to him on 13th February 1975. In 1977 he was charged with possession between 13th February 1975 and 2nd October 1976, 1st October being the date on which police took possession of the pipe for the second time. The pipe was found to contain minute traces of cannabis resin whereas in 1974 it had appeared not to have been used. The question was whether as a matter of policy the charge could be put in this way, considering the period of time involved. It was submitted that any extension backwards in time in cases of possession is oppressive unless 'in truth and in fact the possession of cannabis in this extension back relates to that moment when the police took possession and is of restricted duration and the offence charged is in effect of recent possession of a drug'. After considering *R* v *Worsell* [1970] 1 WLR 111, in which Lord Justice Salmon had suggested a slight extension of time to cover the admission of W that he had had a fix at some time prior to the moment when the police stopped him, the learned judge indicated that he regarded recent possession as being a matter of the 'last few minutes and last few hours'. The submissions of defence counsel were upheld and the jury directed to return verdicts of not guilty (*R* v *Pragliola* [1977] Crim LR 612).

Professor Smith surmises that the judge's reason for being 'strict' is that the defendant might, for example, have lent the pipe out during the period in the charge and not have been in possession of it when it contained cannabis.

Granted that *R* v *Worsell, Mieras* v *Rees, Hambleton* v *Callinan* and *R* v *Pragliola* all foundered for various reasons, it is nevertheless true that such prosecutions can succeed. All that is required, should there be 'nothing but the smell left a-hanging on the wall', is for judge or jury to be convinced by the accused's admission that he was in possession of a controlled drug. As for the apparent disparity of status between the accused and an expert witness, the former is a 'quasi-expert'.

> 'All the evidence as to the nature of the substance is an expression of opinion. Scientists perhaps express more reliable opinions than people who have not got the advantages of scientific techniques of identifying substances. But in the last analysis, everybody is expressing an opinion' (*R* v *Wells* [1976] Crim LR 518 per Lord Justice Ormrod, quoted from the transcript by Mr Justice Forbes in *R* v *Chatwood and Others* [1980] 1 WLR 874 at p 879).

In *Lang* v *Evans* [1977] Crim LR 286 the Crown Court held that magistrates were entitled to conclude that a defendant who admitted 'giving Billy cannabis and cannabis leaves' would know the true identity of the plant. However, in view of the technical definition of cannabis, comprising only parts of the plant at that time, the conviction was quashed. Had the defendant been a scientist it would have been different.

In a case in which no mention is made of the defendant's technical knowledge, the Court Martial Appeal Court held that an unsupported admission is enough to establish the identity of a drug in his possession, 'observing that there was no evidence at all that the substances were other than as described in the applicant's statement and the question whether the substances were not the drugs described in his statement was purely hypothetical' (*R* v *Powell*, Unreported, Court Martial Appeal Court, 15th July 1975, referred to at [1977] Crim LR p 62).

What if a prosecutor has neither an identifiable drug nor an admission, need he despair? Apparently not. In *R* v *Best and Others*, police officers armed with a search warrant went to an address in Huddersfield where there were about a dozen people, including the five appellants. They found there was a pungent aroma there, which the officers believed to be cannabis. Some debris was found in ashtrays, including two 'roach' ends. In one, or possibly both, of the roaches traces of the constituents of either cannabis or cannabis resin were found.

'These five appellants were found guilty of one offence which alleged the unlawful possession of a controlled drug, namely "Cannabis or cannabis resin". The indictment had not started in that form, because initially the article possessed was described simply as cannabis resin. It was so described, so we understand, because the Crown hoped initially to have an accomplice give evidence, whose evidence it was thought would disclose that the object in question in this case was cannabis resin. However at the start of the trial, when it became clear to counsel for the prosecution that he would not have this particular witness, he had to change his tactics. He had another witness, and this other witness was prepared to say that the substance in question was either cannabis or cannabis resin. In order to put his case in a way which would be supported by the evidence, counsel for the prosecution then applied to amend the count in order to make it a count of possession of "cannabis or cannabis resin"' (*R* v *Best and Others* (1980) 70 Cr App R 21 per Lord Widgery CJ at p 22).

'In our judgment cannabis and cannabis resin seen together in that context can be charged as they were charged in this case without offending the rules against duplicity. What was alleged here was a single act, an act of possessing a particular substance which the evidence has shown to be cannabis or cannabis resin. Being in possession of that substance and none other, it was perfectly fair to proceed as was done here. In effect what the pleader is saying is "you are in possession of a substance found in an ashtray. That substance is either cannabis or cannabis resin, or part one and part another, we do not know". It matters not, because each comes under the same class and under the same rule in the Act. Indeed they are linked together' (ibid at p 23).

Omissions from the report leave some detective work to be done on it before the implications of this strange judgment can be appreciated. The indictment contained no count other than one of simple possession against each of five people. What prompted the prosecutor to take up such a thin case is not revealed. How the five accused were picked out from the twelve persons present also remains a mystery. That nobody had anything incriminating on his or her person is assumed from the fact that the case revolved round debris found in ashtrays. Whether any objection was made to the prosecution's application to amend is not stated, though the Lord Chief Justice emphasises that no objection was taken to the relevancy of the amended count, adding significantly: 'If the complaint in this case had been that it had not been disclosed with sufficient clarity just what the substance alleged to be a dangerous drug was, then all sorts of consequences might follow' (p 23). Consequently, the judgment must be read in the light of the way in which the case was pleaded. Even so, it is a matter of some surprise to find that convictions can be upheld for unlawful possession of a controlled drug where it was not known to the Crown, and never emerged, which of two controlled drugs it was. It is suggested that the linking of the two in the listing of the controlled drugs in Schedule 2 may have influenced the decision which, however, is on the ground that 'each comes under the same class'. Were it not for the linking whereby 'cannabis and cannabis resin' appear on the same line, in that form, in the Schedule, a distinction shared with no other drug in any of the classes, it seems doubtful if the fact of their being in the same class would have been treated as sufficient ground for dispensing with positive identification. The unique layout adopted in the case of 'cannabis and cannabis resin' is no doubt an acknowledgement that they are related, but the Act takes the trouble to provide separate, and mutually exclusive, definitions for the two substances respectively (section 37(1)). If the prosecutor had applied to amend cannabis resin to cannabis, the reasoning of *Arnott v MacFarlane* 1976 SLT (Notes) 39 would have been against him. If objection had been pressed to the lack of specification in the amended count, then 'all sorts of consequences' might have been expected. As it was, the case is authority for 'the combination of cannabis and cannabis resin in the way it was done here' (p 23) and, by inference, for convicting of unlawful possession of a drug which has disappeared by consumption leaving only traces, not of the drug but its 'constituents'. These constituents make frequent appearances in forensic science laboratory reports as 'active principles' and, for obvious reasons, in the case of cannabis and cannabis resin which have a common origin, are common to both. The pungent aroma presumably betokened the recent nature of the indulgence and consequently of the unlawful possession. The case is testimony to the contortions imposed on a prosecutor who has open to him no charge of 'misusing', whether by smoking or otherwise, a controlled drug with the single exception of opium (see section 9).

Modes and events

The threshold which a jury has to cross before proceeding to find possession proved, according to Lord Wilberforce in *Warner*, is a consideration of the 'modes or events' by which the custody commences. The closest possible scrutiny should be made of these phenomena. Somewhere within them is the seed from which full-blown possession grows or, alternatively, the flaw which elides it. It may matter greatly whether the alleged possessor is alone or with others, authorised or unauthorised, at home or abroad, in premises or in the open air, an occupier or a visitor. The issue may turn on such variables as packaging, concealment, duration of handling or even the time of day the postman calls and whether the addressee opens his letters or his parcels first. Reported instances will be in some measure special to their facts, but coherence should emerge eventually.

Two conflicting decisions illustrate the narrowness of the line between some modes of possession and innocence. Bearing in mind that, except for opium, it is not an offence under the statute to smoke or otherwise use a controlled drug, even where the possession of it is unlawful, the question arises, can misuse take place without possession?

'Where, as here, a person passes round a cigarette among several people in circumstances where some or all of them contemplate only taking a puff and passing it on, that does not constitute supplying the material in the cigarette as it exists. It is only a supply if at the beginning the defendant has the material in his possession and at the end it has come into the possession of another in the sense that the other can do with it as he wishes. The control over a cigarette exercised by an individual within a circle of smokers as described is not such a degree of control as to make it a "supply" by the defendant within the meaning of section 5(3)' (*R v King* [1978] Crim LR 228).

If no supply by A to B then, presumably, no possession by B. This decision by His Honour Judge John Finlay, QC, at Maidstone Crown Court did not commend itself to His Honour Judge John Baker in a similar case at Surbiton Crown Court.

'Moore had persuaded two girls who had never smoked cannabis before to leave a public house with him and go for a smoke. Outside the public house as Moore was rolling a reefer which he admittedly intended to share with the two girls, he was arrested' (*R v Moore* [1979] Crim LR 789).

'"Supply" should not be given too narrow a definition. In this case there was an offer of consumption and therefore an offer to supply' (ibid at p 790).

Since there was an offer to supply, leaving aside the factor of consumption, it follows that the recipients would have been deemed to be in possession if that supply, limited as it was to be in duration and control, had taken place. The commentary on *Moore* (and *King*) at [1979] Crim LR 790 calls for 'resolution by the Court of Appeal'.

The status of the accused may cast light on the 'mode or event' by which his custody commenced, with a consequential effect on whether his possession is judged to be unlawful.

'The way in which it is put on behalf of the Crown is that, it is impossible for a person to act in his capacity as a doctor if he is not at the time treating a patient, other than himself. Consequently a doctor who has no patient, as was so in the case of Dr Dunbar, is not acting in his capacity as a doctor. That is a proposition which we find ourselves unable to accept. There seem to us to be many occasions on which it can properly be said that a man is acting in his capacity as a doctor which have nothing to do with the existence of any patients. If the Crown were correct, it would produce the extraordinary result that no doctor, who had quite properly in his drug cupboard a Schedule 2 drug, and who quite properly decided that he required such a drug—for instance codeine—to alleviate either pain or sickness in himself, could administer to himself such a drug without committing a criminal offence. Similarly the sort of situation propounded by Miss Ellis, where a doctor, again perfectly properly carrying morphine in his bag in a car, suffers an accident, as a result of which he is in acute pain. If he were in those circumstances to remove an ampoule of morphine from his bag and inject himself to relieve the pain with morphine, he once again would be committing a criminal offence.

'We find that as a proposition unattractive. Taking the words as they stand, it seems to us that the doctor bona fide treating himself in those circumstances, is acting in his capacity as a practitioner, although it is he himself who is receiving the benefit of the drug. So much for that aspect. I emphasise the words bona fide, because there may well be cases, and the instant circumstance illustrates one of them, where the actions of the doctor are not bona fide, and where they might, on one view of the case, take him outside his acting in his capacity as a doctor. For instance the suggestion made here, namely it was said to the police that he intended to use these drugs to commit suicide, could scarcely be said, if that was his intention, that he would be acting either bona fide or in his capacity as a medical practitioner if with that view in mind he had possession of the drugs. What, in our judgment, it comes down to is this, that it is a matter for the jury to decide whether he was in fact acting in that capacity or not. If in the present case the jury had come to the conclusion that they felt sure, whilst the drugs were in his possession, he intended to use them to commit suicide, then upon a proper direction one imagines the jury would have come to the conclusion that he was not acting in the proper capacity' (*R* v *Dunbar* (1982) 74 Cr App R 88 per Lord Lane LCJ at p 92).

Similarly, in the case of a detective, authorised receipt may be converted into unlawful possession.

'In the top right-hand drawer of the appellant's desk Superintendent Thomson and Detective Sergeant Park found Label 3, a Bank of Scotland plastic bag containing resinous material. This material was then in one single piece. There was no label then attached to the bag and there was no other wrapping round it. Superintendent Thomson reminded the appellant that he was under caution and then asked him if he could account for the substance in the bag which appeared to be cannabis. The appellant replied: "It's just a spare bit of cannabis I have, that's all." There was no legitimate reason for the appellant having the substance contained in Label 3 in his desk' (*Cameron* v *MacDougall*, Unreported, Dumfries Sheriff Court, 4th June 1981 (case stated by Sheriff Kenneth Barr)).

Occupancy of premises

Occupancy of premises, whether shared or exclusive, is for obvious reasons one of the commonest bases for an accusation of possession. Such cases are entitled to succeed only against an accused person of whom it can be said, as in *Black and Another* v *Her Majesty's Advocate*, that he has 'himself acquired or been in possession of and retained the possession of' the drugs or against whom there is evidence 'that fixes the accused not only with knowledge of the presence of the substance in premises which he occupies or over which he exercises or is able to exercise control but with acceptance of the substance into his premises or at least permission for or connivance at its remaining there in the knowledge of its character'. Any ambiguity in putting this across to a jury may vitiate a conviction.

'Ms Smith was convicted of possessing Indian hemp found in a room at a house where she was. She told the police the room was hers. In evidence she denied all knowledge of the drug, said she did not live at the house and called evidence to the effect that the room was used in common by all the persons living in the house. She appealed on the ground that the judge omitted to give a direction on the meaning of possession and to remind the jury of the corroborative evidence that the room was in common use. In the course of his summing-up the judge said: "If you conclude that she did live in that room and had an interest in it so that she controlled all the things that were in it of any significance. . . ."

'It was held that the jury should have been directed that they had to decide whether the accused knew of the drug and if so whether she had possession or control of it within the meaning of regulation 20 of the Dangerous Drugs Regulations. What the judge said might have been construed by the jury as meaning that if the accused lived or had an interest in the room she must necessarily control everything in it' (*R* v *Smith* [1966] Crim LR 558).

Apart from the cases of *Black*, *Mingay*, *Lustmann*, *Balloch* and others illustrating this theme, already referred to *supra*, the principle is to be found laid down in many English cases such as *R* v *Cavendish* and *Lockyer* v *Gibb* (so far as not overruled by *Warner*).

'It is quite clear, without referring to authority, that for a man to be found to have possession, actual or constructive, of goods, something more must be proved than that the goods have been found on his premises. It must be shown either, if he was absent, that on his return he has become aware of them or that the goods had come, albeit in his absence, at his invitation or "by arrangement"' (*R* v *Cavendish* [1961] 2 All ER 856 per Lord Parker CJ at p 858).

Perhaps the nearest thing to guilt being inferred from the finding of drugs in premises without 'something more' is represented by the case of Ms Stephanie Storey. Police officers went to Ms Storey's flat with a search warrant. They were let into the flat by Ms Storey, and on the bed in the flat they found three plastic bags containing a total of 71,500 grains of cannabis resin. These represented substantial parcels in bulk. The police asked Ms Storey what it was and she said that it was 'hash', but she added at once that it did not belong to her. The police officers asked her whose it was and why it was there, and she pointed silently to the door of the lavatory. On the police officers opening the door of the lavatory they found inside the applicant Anwar. He was told that the girl had indicated that the cannabis belonged to him, and he made no comment. When he was searched, a further small quantity of cannabis resin was found on his person, and when questioned he was not prepared to give an explanation for his possession. They were taken to the police station and later the same day Ms Storey dictated a voluntary statement. She said that she had been a call-girl for about a year and had got to know an Indian who called himself Ali. That was the man Anwar. She said: 'On Friday he telephoned me and said he would like to call at my flat on Monday (today) for business. When he arrived he was carrying a carrier bag and he asked if it was all right for a friend to call to do a business transaction. I asked him why and he emptied out the bag and I saw that it was brown substance which he told me was hashish and he was going to sell it to someone, but could not do it at his home because of his wife and family and he thought I wouldn't mind if he came to my flat. I was amazed, because I thought he was coming for "other business". I was arguing with him when you arrived'.

'The question which arises in this case is whether the fact that she gave shortly afterwards an explanation which, if true, would provide a completely innocent explanation is enough to produce a situation in which the learned judge's duty was to say that there was no case to answer. The court has given careful consideration to this important point. We think it right to recognise that a statement made by the accused to the police, although it always forms evidence in the case against her, is not in itself evidence of the truth of the facts stated. A statement made voluntarily by an accused person to the police is evidence in the trial because of its vital relevance as showing the reaction of the accused when first taxed with the incriminating facts. If, of course, the accused admits the offence, then as a matter of shorthand one says that the admission is proof of guilt and, indeed, in the end it is. But if the accused makes a statement which does not amount to an admission, the statement is not strictly evidence of the truth of what was said but is evidence of the reaction of the accused which forms part of the general picture to be considered by the jury at the trial.

'Accordingly, in our judgment, in this case the fact that the cannabis was on the applicant's bed in her flat was in itself some evidence of possession to go to the jury. Her unsworn explanation, although, if true, it would have been a complete answer to the charge, did not cancel out or nullify the evidence which was provided by the presence of the cannabis. It was ultimately for the jury to decide whether that explanation was or might be true' (*R* v *Storey and Another* (1968) 52 Cr App R 334 per Lord Justice Widgery at p 337).

Drugs in vehicles

It may be that no considerations of principle apply to possession in vehicles which are not equally applicable to premises. However, when all 'modes and events' are being scrutinised, as has been suggested, the locus is not to be overlooked. Many important cases such as *Worsell*, and even *Warner*, started off in vehicles. The judgment in *Irala-Prevost* makes special reference to a car passenger throughout a long journey. During a long journey there must be occasions when the driver steps out for fuel, refreshments, to deal with Customs and the like. Suppose that the passenger remains aboard and an attack is made by an intending thief. Will any action taken by the passenger to repel the attempt put him at risk of the conviction which Irala-Prevost escaped by reason of having knowledge but no control? *Wright* (*infra*) illustrates the danger to an innocent occupant of associating as closely with guilty persons as car travel involves.

In *R* v *Ashton-Rickhardt* (1977) 65 Cr App R 67 the accused was alone and asleep in his car, a reefer in the pocket of the driver's door. 'Had the direction to the jury been a proper one it is difficult to think that they could have arrived at any verdict other than "guilty"' (Lord Justice Roskill at p 73). Where the case went wrong is described *supra* (p 52).

In *R* v *Peevey* (1973) 57 Cr App R 554 the question was whether, in addition to six Dexedrine tablets in his wallet in his pocket, the appellant was in possession of ninety-two more of the same tablets under the driver's seat. The jury did not distinguish between the two amounts in their verdict of guilty. The Court of Appeal treated it as a verdict 'in respect of the offence charged' which, however, 'did not mean that the verdict related to all the matters specified in the particulars insofar as a specific number of tablets had been mentioned' (Lord Justice Lawton at p 558).

Director of Public Prosecutions (for Jamaica) v *Brooks* is a case where a driver's disclaimer that he knew what his load was failed as a defence.

'Upon the evidence, including his own statement to the police, the nineteen sacks of ganja were clearly in the physical custody of the respondent and under his physical control. The only remaining issue was whether the inference should be drawn that the respondent knew that his load consisted of ganja. Upon all the evidence and in particular the fact that he and the other occupants of the van attempted to run away as soon as they saw the uniformed police approaching, the magistrate was, in their Lordships' view, fully entitled to draw the inference that the defendant knew what he was carrying in the van' (*Director of Public Prosecutions* v *Brooks* (1974) 59 Cr App R 185, on appeal to the Privy Council from the Court of Appeal of Jamaica, explaining the case of *Livingston* (1952) 6 JLR 95 and the meaning of 'possession' in section 7(*c*) of the Dangerous Drugs Law of Jamaica (1953 rev c 90), per Lord Diplock at p 188).

In an early case, *R* v *Carpenter* [1960] Crim LR 633, the Court of Appeal held that there was insufficient evidence of possession of Indian hemp where the appellant was in possession of a car with a small quantity locked in the boot.

Drugs by post

Where a person has ordered controlled drugs to be sent to him by post, he will be held to be in possession of them when the postman delivers the package which contains them even though they are intercepted and removed before he can exercise practical control over them.

In *R* v *Peaston* police officers went to the appellant's premises and, on entering the house, they found on the hall table a number of unopened letters, some or all of which were addressed to him. The unopened letters were handed to the appellant by the police officer who had a warrant to search the premises. The police officer went upstairs into the appellant's bedroom, where he was lying in bed, and invited him to open the unopened letters. The appellant opened the letters and from one of them fell a film capsule which contained 7.7 grams of amphetamine. The appellant then handed the envelope back to the police officer and, in due course, he was arrested and proceedings were begun. His ground of appeal was that he was not in possession of the drug at the material time.

'If the appellant, having given directions to the supplier, which he did in this case, and having consistently with those directions received the amphetamines through the letterbox of the house where he was living, it seems to us that it is beyond argument who became the possessor of those drugs when they were put through the letterbox of the house in which he was living. It may be he was asleep; it may be he was out, but those considerations do not arise so as to prevent the appellant from being in possession in the circumstances of this case' (*R* v *Peaston* (1979) 69 Cr App R 203 per Lord Widgery CJ at p 205).

The same result may ensue although the accused has not ordered the drugs.

'Even in an offence of strict responsibility there must be "an actus reus which consists of, or is the result of, voluntary conduct on the part of the accused" (Gordon, *Criminal Law*, 2nd edition, p 287). I was satisfied that there was such voluntary conduct on the part of the appellant in this case. The postal package containing the controlled drugs was sent to the appellant, not by a stranger to her, but by a man whom she knew, and with whom she was on affectionate terms. Only a few days before she received the postal package, the appellant wrote to the sender, Ian Meldrum, a letter which revealed that she was familiar with the vocabulary of people who are involved with controlled drugs, and that she knew that Meldrum had access to controlled drugs. When the appellant read the letter from the postal package she became aware of the nature of the contents of the postal package. It is true that the appellant did not examine the contents of the postal package. It seemed to me that, in the circumstances, the appellant had no reason to doubt that the contents were as described in Meldrum's letter. The appellant's action in crushing and concealing the letter which accompanied the postal package was inconsistent with repudiation of the postal package and its contents. The appellant made no statement to the police disavowing voluntary possession of the contents of the postal package either at the time when they confronted her first, or in answer to the charges against her. The appellant did not give evidence in the case. In the whole circumstances I held it established that the appellant was voluntarily in possession of controlled drugs before the police removed them from her' (*Haswell* v *McLeay*, Unreported, Lerwick Sheriff Court, 13th October 1978 (Sheriff Alistair A. MacDonald's note)).

(Dealing with an objection that the appellant's letter did not relate to the controlled drugs which were the subject-matter of the case, the learned sheriff added: 'It was clear from the evidence that the appellant's letter did not refer to the drugs in the present case and that, in fact, the two letters in the case must have crossed in the post. I took the view, however, that the Crown had the right to introduce in evidence the appellant's letter to Meldrum in order to establish that the sender of the postal package was known to the appellant, that the appellant knew that the sender was a person who dealt in controlled drugs, that the appellant was familiar with the vocabulary of people involved with controlled drugs and thus understood the terms of the letter which accompanied the controlled drugs in the postal package.') The appeal was abandoned. The decision that the accused fell on the wrong side of the line and, in the words of Lord Wilberforce in *Warner*, 'ought to have imputed to her' the knowledge necessary to transmute her custody into possession, illustrates the danger of associating with, at least, drug suppliers or even, as in *Wright* (*infra*), users. Presumably Wright, had he been intercepted by the police at the moment of receiving the tin from B, or at latest at the moment of being told to throw it out of the window, would have been in danger of being convicted. It is not clear how he could be credited with having 'no reason to suspect' the contents when he knew B used cannabis. Ms Haswell, on the other side of the line, had reason to be suspicious of correspondence from a particular source. Guilt by association being thus unthinkable, sailing near the wind may at least incur the inconvenience of being accused. That happened to Mr Patel. He was convicted of aiding and abetting the possession of cannabis by B. Police officers saw them and a third man at a bus stop. B had a bag and when he saw the officers he crossed the pavement and dropped the bag over a wall. The bag contained a packet of cannabis. The appellant, Mr Patel, said:

'"They got me out of bed to help them but I did not know what was in the bag." In evidence all three said that B never had the bag. In directing the jury the judge said *inter alia* that the prosecution had to prove that the appellant knew that the bag contained drugs or alternatively that he knew the bag contained something and was content to aid in its possession whatever it might be. It was held, allowing the appeal, that the second half of the direction was too wide. The prosecution had to prove that the appellant knew that B was in possession of a dangerous drug' (*R* v *Patel* [1970] Crim LR 274).

Fleeting contact

Are there any circumstances in which a person, not being exempt or entitled to a section 5 defence, can knowingly handle a controlled drug and elide guilt of possession? Answer, yes, by virtue of the doctrine of fleeting contact.

'As appears from the stated case, the facts found disclose an unusual and exceptional situation. The police raided the house occupied by Miss Burn. The appellant was found asleep, naked, on a couch in the living-room of that house. His clothes lay on a chair beside the couch. A thorough search of the appellant's clothes and the chair disclosed nothing. The cushion of the chair which had been removed during the search was left on end to indicate that the chair had been searched. Some time later after the appellant had dressed, sixteen tablets of Lysergide were found lying on the seat cover of the chair and it is not suggested that they were in any way concealed. It is found as a fact that in the interval between the time of the police search and the discovery of the tablets "no one had had anything to do with the chair except the appellant". It is accordingly a legitimate inference that he placed them there.

'Upon these findings the question is whether the sheriff was entitled to find that the appellant was in possession of the tablets within the meaning of section 1(1) of the Drugs (Prevention of Misuse) Act 1964. As we read the findings, all that can reasonably be inferred from them is that the appellant must have moved the tablets by hand from some unknown part of Miss Burn's living-room to the seat cover of the chair. He must therefore have had them in his hands for at most a second or two. In our opinion this proved fleeting contact between the appellant and the tablets is not in the context of the other findings in this case enough to justify a finding that he had them in his possession within the meaning of the subsection' (*Mackay* v *Hogg*, Unreported, High Court of Justiciary, 11th May 1973, per Lord Emslie, Lord Justice-General).

By the time a similar set of circumstances arose for consideration in England, the 1971 Act had come into force. A similar result was reached by the Court of Appeal.

'Wright was convicted of possessing cannabis. He was in a motor-car with others including B. A police car was following and Wright was seen to throw something from the car. This turned out to be a small tin containing cannabis. Wright in evidence said he had no cannabis and was not aware that his companions in the car had any. He did not know the car behind was a police car. B gave him the tin. He did not know what it was. Then B told him to throw it out of the window and he did so. He knew B used cannabis and on being told to throw the tin away it occurred to him that it might contain drugs.

'If a person were handed a container and at the moment he received it did not know or suspect, and had no reason to suspect, that it contained drugs and if, before he had time to examine the contents, he was told to throw it away and immediately did so, he could not be said to have been in possession of the drugs so as to be guilty of an offence against section 5 of the Misuse of Drugs Act 1971' (*R* v *Wright* [1976] Crim LR 248).

The words carry an echo of Lord Morris of Borth-y-Gest's tentative proposal in *Warner*: 'If there is some momentary custody of a thing without any knowledge or means of knowledge of what the thing is or contains—then, ordinarily, I would suppose that there would not be possession.'

This proposition is consistent with rules applied in cases involving other species of goods, where handling them does not necessarily amount to possession.

'The defendant had had his appeal against a conviction for receiving some metal ingots dismissed by Quarter Sessions, who found that he had helped to load and unload them into another's car but otherwise did not handle them or help to sell them. The Divisional Court held, allowing his appeal, that merely handling goods did not necessarily amount to taking them into possession' (*Hobson* v *Impett* (1957) 41 Cr App R 138).

'Property which had been stolen a week earlier was found with the fingerprints of the accused upon it. He said that the property had been shown to him by an acquaintance but that he had not bought it or taken it into his possession. The Ontario Court of Appeal held that the accused had not been proved to have had legal possession of the property' (*R* v *O'Keefe* (1958) 15 DLR (2d) 579 (Canadian case reported in 1959 CLY 731)).

Conclusion

Whatever the mode, whatever the event, in the last analysis the decision turns on whether an accused person 'ought to have imputed to him the intention to possess or knowledge that he does possess' the substance in question.

CHAPTER 8

Possession with Intent to Supply and Section 5 Defences

Prior to the 1971 Act, possession was possession and courts reflected their views about the intentions of possessors in the way in which they sentenced them. Section 5(3) introduced the notion of a separate offence of possession with intent to supply, in contravention of section 4(1). Where the possession is unlawful, ie, where the facts would justify conviction under section 5(2), the intent is in the nature of an aggravation of that offence. However, section 5(3) applies equally where the possession is lawful and to that extent creates a completely new offence.

In the absence of admissions, the intent to supply can often only be inferred from the quantity of the drugs found, though this yardstick is by no means conclusive. Logically speaking, no amount is too small to be passed on, and large amounts may conceivably be for personal use. Allowing that quantity alone is a fallible guide, there are circumstances which make the inference inescapable, eg, where an accused has virtually set up shop and her drugs have, like a merchant's stock, 'diversity and value' as well.

'The basis for the convictions returned on charges 1 and 2 was expressed by the sheriff thus, and he is speaking of the drugs found in the appellant's possession, and listed and analysed in production 4 which was admitted: "Their value, quantity and diversity convinced me that her possession was with the intention of supplying others and I therefore convicted her of contraventions of section 5(3) of the Misuse of Drugs Act 1971." Now that was the sole basis upon which the sheriff proceeded to convict on the first two charges in their first alternative form, and in presenting this appeal, which is directed to conviction on charges 1 and 2 only, Mr Mitchell has argued that in the circumstances of this case there was not enough to support the inference which the sheriff drew from the quantity of the drugs, their variety or their value. In this case it has to be borne in mind that it was found as a fact that the appellant was a registered heroin addict and in all the circumstances she would have had to be found in possession of larger quantities of drugs of greater value before the sheriff could have taken the leap which he did from possession to possession with intent. We have to reject that submission. In this case the starting-point was the finding of the appellant in possession of a substantial quantity of assorted drugs—four different drugs of substantial value. The appellant offered no explanation for her possession, negating the idea that it was possession with intent. Her evidence was that she knew nothing about them and that evidence the sheriff rejected. In these circumstances the sheriff was perfectly entitled, in our judgment, to draw the inference which he did from the matters to which he paid attention' (*Morrison v Smith* 1983 SCCR 171 per Lord Emslie, Lord Justice-General, at p 174).

Some case reports reveal that charges under section 5(3) have failed but, being concerned with other grounds, lack any discussion of the element of intent to supply. Such a one is *Allan and Others* v *Milne* 1974 SLT (Notes) 76. The findings in fact included: '(10) the police dog led the officers to the area of the sink in the kitchen/living-room of the flat; (11) beneath this sink the wall was panelled with plywood or hardboard; (12) between this panelling and the wall the officers found several packets of varying sizes containing a brown substance wrapped in silver paper and a chillum which is a type of pipe used for drug smoking; (13) the brown substance, which weighed altogether about four ounces, and the chillum (as later certified on soul and conscience by Dr J. P. Sword and Dr M. S. Henderson of Inveresk Research International) contained compounds of cannabis from which the resin had not been extracted; this is a controlled drug in terms of the Misuse of Drugs Act 1971; (14) on the table of the kitchen/living-room the officers found a set of scales designed to measure weights in the range of 250 grammes to 10 grammes; scales of this delicacy are suitable for measuring drugs but are not commonly used for ordinary domestic purposes.' In addition, the case stated by the sheriff included the following passage: 'The quantity of cannabis found, four ounces with, according to the police evidence, a market value in drug circles of about £100, was much larger than any one individual was likely to have possessed for personal consumption.' The charge of contravening section 5(3) was found not proven in favour of guilty verdicts against all four accused under section 5(2). In this instance the type of evidence from which intent to supply is frequently inferred, viz (1) quantity, (2) multiple packaging, and (3) the presence of scales and weights, was present, but the inference was rather that all four accused were using the supply.

Reference has been made in Chapter 4 to the cases of *R* v *Greenfield* [1983] Crim LR 397, *R* v *Delgado* [1984] 1 WLR 89 and *R* v *Buckley* (1979) 69 Cr App R 371. *Greenfield* raises the question of whether a depositary can give up the deposited drugs without 'supplying' them to the depositor. Does such a surrender of custody fall within the definition of supplying, either in its ordinary meaning or its extended meaning to include distributing? If not, as was held in *Greenfield*, we have isolated a species of possession which it is questionable if the Act envisaged, possession which is not 'for personal use' (a common gloss on section 5(2)) and which is nevertheless not with intent to supply to another. The problem arises in more acute form where the custodier does not hand back the drugs to the depositor, or do anything else actively in relation to them. Suppose that he only keeps watch over them and the original possessor resumes custody without his intervention. His, the depositary's, possession being granted, is it with intent to supply them to the depositor? The better solution might be to regard the custody as falling short of possession, in lacking the *animus possidendi* and full control. Some support for an argument directed to that end is provided by section 37(3): 'The things which a person has in his possession shall be taken to include any thing subject to his control which is in the custody of another.' One alternative would be to plug the gap by legislating for the offences of having unlawful custody of a controlled drug, with intent to yield custody to the possessor. The judgment in *Delgado* describes such a surrender as a 'transaction' and what is given up as 'physical control'. But the possessor already has control, which is why he can demand the custody of the goods to be restored to him. Prosecutors habitually charge under section 5(3), involving them in proof of both possession and intent to supply, in circumstances where a charge of being concerned in the supply, under section 4(3)(*b*), would elide the attendant difficulties.

In *R* v *Buckley* the act of dividing a supply acquired jointly was held to be distributing and hence supplying. But suppose a joint supply is held *pro indiviso*, and each of the possessors helps himself. Does any holder of the pool supply any of the others when that happens? Apparently not, if *Allan and Others* v *Milne* was correctly decided on that point, though unfortunately it is not disclosed by the report what arguments were directed towards convicting under section 5(3), and the Crown did not appeal against the acquittals. It may be that only intent to supply beyond the quartet was in issue.

Certainly, as was held in *Greenfield*, the 'intent to supply' must be that of the possessor. Where one joint possessor has the intent to supply, a second who does not have such an intent is not guilty even if he or she knows of the other's intent.

'Lord Justice Robert Goff, giving the reserved judgment of the court, said that when police searched the defendant's flat for drugs, they found a box which contained £130 in cash, three notebooks, a 27 gram block of cannabis resin and 13 packets of cannabis resin weighing about 3.6 grams. They also found scales which had traces of cannabis resin on them. In the course of police interviews the defendant said that the box and some of the cash were hers, but she denied that the drugs, documents or the scales belonged to her, and she denied being involved in the supply of cannabis resin.

'At her trial, the prosecution case was that the defendant and a co-defendant, Steven Robert Saunders, were in joint possession of the cannabis resin with intent to supply it to another, contrary to section 5(3) of the 1971 Act. Having directed the jury that they had to be satisfied that the defendant was in possession of the cannabis, the trial judge went on to say that the defendant intended to supply it to another, and was guilty of the offence charged if, either she intended to supply it to another, or she knew full well that the co-defendant was going to supply it to others, although she herself was not going to be involved in the supply and distribution.

'It was submitted for the defendant that the judge has erred in so directing the jury on the matter of the relevant intent. In *R v Greenfield* it was decided that the intent of somebody else to supply was not enough. Was it enough that the defendant who was in joint possession with her had the intention to supply? The answer was, not necessarily so, unless the person in joint possession of the drugs were engaged in a joint venture of supplying it to others. It was not enough, therefore, to direct the jury that it would be sufficient that the defendant knew full well that the co-defendant intended to supply the cannabis; for the mere fact of such knowledge without herself being involved in any joint venture with him, was not enough to establish the necessary intent on the defendant's part' (*R v Downes*, Unreported, *The Times*, 13th June 1984. See also [1984] Crim LR 552).

The High Court of Justiciary gave *Greenfield* short shrift, though not by name, and by implication cast doubts on *Downes*, while approving of *Delgado*.

'We agree with the opinion of the Court of Appeal in *R v Delgado* [1984] 1 WLR 89 at p 92: "A feature common to all of those transactions is a transfer of physical control of a drug from one person to another. In our judgment questions of the transfer of ownership or legal possession of these drugs are irrelevant to the issue whether or not there was intent to supply."

'The sheriff referred to a suggestion made by the solicitor for the appellant that it was open to the jury to decide that the accused and Colin Stewart had joint possession of the drug and that it was Colin Stewart alone who intended to supply it to another person. He said: "Well, ladies and gentlemen, intent to supply doesn't necessarily infer that the intent is to sell it. As long as the intent is that it should be passed on to somebody else, then that is enough. It is a matter for you whether, if Mary Donnelly was jointly in possession of this drug, she was in possession of it with the intention that it should be passed on to somebody else." Then follows the passage which counsel submitted was the misdirection—"even if it were that Colin Stewart was going to be the person who in fact arranged the transactions and arranged the passing on, it would be open to you to find Mary Donnelly guilty of intent to supply, if she knew that the drugs that were in her possession were to be passed on to somebody else."

'Counsel for the appellant submitted that mere knowledge of Colin Stewart's intention was not sufficient to make the appellant party to that intention. He founded upon an English Court of Appeal decision of *R v Downes*, reported in *The Times*, 13th June 1984, and [1984] Crim LR 552, in which it was said: "It was not enough, therefore, to direct the jury that it would be sufficient that the defendant knew full well that the co-defendant intended to supply the cannabis; for the mere fact of such knowledge, without herself being involved in any joint venture with him, was not enough to establish the necessary intent on the defendant's part."

'A material distinction between that case and this one is that Downes and her co-defendant were jointly charged with intent to supply on the basis of joint possession of the drugs. The trial judge appears to have directed the jury that they could convict the defendant of intent to supply, even if she had no intention herself to supply to another. That would seem to be self-contradictory.

'Be that as it may, it was plainly open to the jury on the undisputed facts in this case, to which we have referred, to convict the appellant of intent to supply to another. They may have rejected her evidence that the drugs belonged to Colin Stewart. Even if they accepted that evidence and proceeded upon the fact, or even the possibility, of joint possession, none of the packets of drugs could have been supplied to anyone else without the appellant relinquishing the physical control of the drugs which she had at the material time. In our opinion, where a large quantity of controlled drugs, separately packaged in quantities normally sold in the streets, are found in the possession of a person, it is open to a jury to infer that that person intended to supply them to another. If the appellant in this case did no more than allow Colin Stewart to uplift drugs in her physical possession, she was thereby supplying them to another, namely, Colin Stewart.

'That is the kind of direction which we consider should be given on facts similar to those in this case, whether or not the Crown charges on the basis of joint possession. It was not clearly spelled out by the sheriff in this case, but he did say that the jury could find the appellant guilty of intent to supply if she knew that the drugs that were in *her* (the emphasis is ours) possession were to be passed on to somebody else. That is tantamount to saying that, if she intended to relinquish her control of the drugs in her possession to another person, the intent to supply was proved' (*Donnelly (Mary)* v *HM Advocate* 1984 SCCR 419 per Lord Dunpark at p 421).

The disapproved charge in *Downes* (*supra*) had not raised the question of Ms Downes's relinquishing her control of the drugs in her possession to her co-defendant, but he could not have supplied them to others without her doing so. It appears, therefore, that *Downes* and *Donnelly* represent divergent views of the liability of a joint possessor for the actings of his or her partner.

The word 'intent' in the section must be given full value.

'An "intention" to my mind connotes a state of affairs which the party "intending" . . . does more than merely contemplate; it connotes a state of affairs which, on the contrary, he decides, so far as in him lies, to bring about and which, in point of possibility, he has a reasonable prospect of being able to bring about, by his own act of volition' (*Cunliffe* v *Goodman* [1950] 2 KB 237 per Lord Justice Asquith at p 253, quoted with approval by Lord Ross in his charge to the jury in *Sayers and Others* v *HM Advocate* 1981 SCCR 312 at p 318).

Section 5 defences
The remainder of section 5 consists of statutory defences provided by

subsections 4 and 5, and a declaration by subsection 6 that they are without prejudice to any other defence which may be open to an accused person. By a side wind we learn from subsection 5 that the Act does envisage the possibility of an attempt to commit an offence under section 5(2). This might have been doubted because of the nature of the offence as a passive state rather than a course of action. However, the attempt is defined as 'attempting to get' possession of a controlled drug.

Suppose police officers raid a flat. On their entering the living-room one occupant reaches out to a piece of furniture, picks up a controlled drug and hands it to them with the words: 'This is all there is.' On the hypothesis that the possession was someone else's, the occupant will not be guilty under section 5(2) or (3) because although she knew, or at least suspected, that it was a controlled drug, she took possession of it only so as to hand it over to the police, and then did so. This would hold good even if the bona fide intention of handing it over to the authorities was frustrated.

Subsection 4(*a*) constitutes the necessary protection for parents, schoolteachers, employers, landlords or others who may see fit to impound substances with a view to destroying or surrendering them.

Section 28 defences are also available against section 5 offences.

CHAPTER 9

Section 8

Section 8 replaces, *inter alia*, section 5 of the 1965 Act, introducing a subtle change. In the earlier statute the offence in relation to the smoking of cannabis, etc, was of permitting premises to be used 'for the purpose'. Hence the dictum in *Sweet* v *Parsley*: 'It is a somewhat strange use of language to say that an ordinary room in a house is used for the purpose of smoking cannabis when all that happens is that some visitor lights a cannabis cigarette there' ([1970] AC 132 per Lord Reid at p 151). The new wording, more strictly, prohibits the permitting by an occupier or manager of certain activities on his premises, whether or not that amounts to a use of the premises for the purpose of those activities. In other words, one casual instance incurs liability. The proscribed activities most commonly encountered are the smoking of cannabis and the smoking of cannabis resin. The others are:

Producing a controlled drug
Attempting to produce a controlled drug
Supplying a controlled drug
Attempting to supply a controlled drug
Offering to supply a controlled drug
Preparing opium for smoking
Smoking prepared opium.

It will be observed that although the first five listed activities are stated to be in contravention of section 4(1), the two attempts are not contraventions of section 4(1) but of section 19. There are in fact no such offences in section 4 as attempting to produce and attempting to supply. *Per contra* there are three offences in section 4, being concerned in the production, being concerned in the supplying and being concerned in the making of an offer to supply a controlled drug, which are not proscribed. This observation underlines the fact that the activities struck at by this section are not necessarily offences. Those which are not are smoking cannabis, smoking cannabis resin and preparing opium for smoking. The proscribed activities include smoking prepared opium, which is an offence under section 9, but not otherwise using prepared opium, which is also a section 9 offence. Consumption of cannabis or cannabis resin other than by smoking is not a proscribed activity. A tea-party at which a cannabis cake is consumed is thus exempt.

To the list must now be added cultivating a plant of the genus *Cannabis*, not because of any amendment of the section, but by virtue of the redefinition of cannabis by section 52 of the Criminal Law Act 1977.

'In section 37(1) (interpretation) of the Misuse of Drugs Act 1971, for the definition of "cannabis" there shall be substituted—

" 'cannabis' (except in the expression 'cannabis resin') means any plant of the genus *Cannabis* or any part of any such plant (by whatever name designated) except that it does not include cannabis resin or any of the following products after separation from the rest of the plant, namely—
(*a*) mature stalk of any such plant,
(*b*) fibre produced from mature stalk of any such plant, and
(*c*) seed of any such plant." '

The main interest of section 8 lies in the room for debate which is inherent in the notions of being the occupier, or being concerned in the management, of premises, and in the concept of permitting.

It will, of course, be appreciated by prosecutors and defenders alike that being an occupier and being concerned in the management of premises are special capacities within the meaning of sections 67 and 312(x) of the Criminal Procedure (Scotland) Act 1975 and, if not admitted, must be challenged by preliminary objection.

Occupier is not the same as occupant, and not everyone found on premises, even apparently in charge of them, qualifies to be described as an occupier.

'In order to show that these two defendants, who are charged as principals, were the occupiers of the premises, it must be the case that they were in legal possession of the premises and had control over them' (*R* v *Mogford* [1970] 1 WLR 988 per Mr Justice Nield at p 990).

'It cannot be said that they were in legal possession of the premises. The premises mean the house. They were not in legal possession of the house having in mind the fact that they were two daughters of parents who were temporarily away on holiday.

'Upon the second aspect of the test, namely control, it was no doubt open to these daughters to invite guests and, indeed, to exclude persons from their parents' house in the absence of those parents, but in my judgment that does not amount to the nature and measure of control which is envisaged in the present statute. As it seems to me, if the Act of Parliament had intended to say that it is an offence for anyone in or living in premises to permit others to smoke cannabis there it could have said so' (ibid at p 992).

In Scotland, legal title is beside the point. A squatter was held to be the occupier of his flat.

'The police officers who carried out the investigation knew that the appellant and another man lived in the flat in question. They warned both of the consequences of allowing the premises to be used for the purposes of smoking cannabis resin. The appellant then said that he was the occupier of the flat and that the other man lived there as his guest. He produced a rent book bearing his name. It is found as a fact in the case that the appellant had not paid rent since 29th August 1972. The reason for this was that the building of which the flat formed part had been condemned as unfit for human habitation. Despite that the appellant continued to live in the flat. These facts form the basis of the present appeal, the contention being that on 8th June 1973 the appellant was what is commonly called a "squatter". He lived in the premises but had no legal right or title to do so. Therefore, it is claimed, he was not an "occupier" within the meaning of the subsection of s 5 of the Act at the date when the offence was alleged to have been committed.

'This argument was wholly based on the decision in an assize court case, *R v Mogford* [1970] 1 WLR 988, in which a charge was laid under s 5 of the Act. The defendants were two sisters, aged 20 and 15. They were living in their parents' home while the parents were on holiday. It was held that the girls were not "occupiers" of the premises within the meaning of the section and on that point the Crown case was held to fail. If that was all there was to the decision of Nield J who heard the case, we might have had little difficulty, with respect, in following the reasoning of the learned judge, in that the alleged "occupation" was short, temporary and transient in nature and, in a sense, accidental. But the ground of decision in the case appears to go much further than that.

'At p 990, Nield J stated: "For the purposes of the present argument I am satisfied that in order to show that these two defendants, who are charged as principals, were the occupiers of the premises, it must be the case that they were in legal possession of the premises and had control over them, and I call attention particularly to the two words so often reiterated inevitably in the statute 'the occupier' and that must be observed to be in distinction, as it were, to an occupier or in occupation." Towards the end of his opinion the learned judge held that the defendants were not "in legal possession of the premises having in mind the fact that they were two daughters of parents who were temporarily away on holiday". As a corollary to his reasoning he added that if the Act of Parliament had intended to say that it was an offence for anyone in or living in premises to permit others to smoke cannabis, it could have said so. He remarked that his decision might hamper the police in seeking to deal with the mischief of drug taking.

'Counsel for the appellant argued that the effect of that decision was to restrict the meaning of the words "the occupier" to one who had a legal right and title to occupy premises and so his client must be acquitted. We agree that this does appear to be the view expressed by Nield J. With all respect, we are unable to accept that construction of the section.

'No violence is done to the wording of the section if the words "the occupier" are construed as bearing their ordinary meaning and connotation. In our opinion "the occupier", within the meaning of the section, is a person who has possession of the premises in question in a substantial sense involving some degree of permanency and who, as matter of fact, exercises control of the premises and dictates their use' (*Christison* v *Hogg* 1974 SLT (Notes) 33 per Lord Emslie, Lord Justice-General).

Considered in a subsequent case in the Court of Appeal, *Mogford* was found to have been correctly decided for the wrong reason.

'On the facts is is difficult to see how, on any view, it could be said that these two girls were "the occupiers" of those premises. But while therefore the decision was correct, with great respect to the learned judge, this court does not agree that the reasoning by which the judge reached that decision is correct. In the first instance it is not entirely clear what the learned judge meant by "legal possession"; whether he meant legal possession as a tenant or someone who had an estate in land in the premises in question. At one stage in his argument Mr Haworth argued that that was what "the occupier" meant. That would give a very narrow and legalistic meaning to the phrase "the occupier". A person can have exclusive possession of premises without being a tenant or having an estate in land' (*R* v *Tao* (1976) 63 Cr App R 163 per Lord Justice Roskill at p 166).

A student is the occupier of his hostel room in college.

'What are the facts relating to this young man's user—to use a neutral phrase— of room 17? It was accepted in argument that one might take the facts as they were summed up to the jury by the judge at p 20 of the transcript: ". . . room number 17 of King's College Hostel in Market Hill. That," said the judge, "is a room allotted to him in the College [hostel], and he pays for his use of that room, it's furnished for him, there's a bed, there's a washbasin, there's a chest of drawers, a desk, a table, wardrobe for his clothes, and that's where he lives. And so, for the purposes of this case, it is his home or his house or his flat or whatever you like to call it, or however you like to think of it." The judge gave the direction he did after he had rejected a submission from Mr Haworth that there was no evidence to go to the jury that the appellant was "the occupier".

'In giving his ruling, the judge said: ". . . this accused is an undergraduate. All that his occupation is, if it be occupation, of this room, is that of undergraduate or indeed, of anybody else. There can be little doubt but that is exactly what it is, but there isn't any evidence of it. And one must decide the case within the confines of the evidence as it is. Nevertheless, in my judgment, there is evidence that he is the occupier of room 17, in what's called King's College Hostel. It is a room of which he was the sole user. It is a room fitted out so that he can live a complete existence there. It's got the means of sleeping, of washing, of eating, and writing, and everything else. And he's got the key to it. He may exclude people from it if he wishes, and quite obviously he would have the power in a case like this to exclude anyone who wanted to smoke cannabis or, indeed, to smoke anything else for that matter, if he was the sort of chap who didn't like smoking taking place in his room."

'On those facts it seems to us that the correct legal analysis of the appellant's right of occupation of that room in the King's College Hostel was this: he had an exclusive contractual licence from the college to use that room. He was entitled to retain the use of that room to live in, to sleep in, to eat in and to work in: he paid the college for the use of that room. It was, in our view, clearly a licence which gave him not merely a right to use but a sufficient exclusivity of possession, so that he can fairly be said to be "the occupier" of that room for the purpose of section 8.'

In the last analysis, the decision will turn on the facts.

'It is in every case a question of fact and degree whether someone can fairly be said to be the occupier' (ibid at p 167).

'Every case will depend on its own facts. We see no reason to restrict the interpretation of the words "the occupier" to describe one who has a legal right or title to inhabit the premises' (*Christison* v *Hogg* (supra)).

Equally with the word 'occupier', the phrase 'concerned in the management' has received close judicial scrutiny, the upshot of which is to separate premises notionally from what goes on in them. Collecting rents and seeing to repairs are not instances of management within the meaning of the section. Thus an absent proprietor of a public house is outwith the ambit of the section while a humble barman falls within it.

In addition to the switch from 'permitting premises to be used for the purpose of' to permitting certain activities to take place in premises, the replacement of section 5 of the Dangerous Drugs Act 1965 by section 8 of the 1971 Act introduced the word 'knowingly' to govern the act of permitting. But the innovation has not altered the standard of proof.

'Even without such adverbs the words descriptive of the prohibited act may themselves connote the presence of a particular mental element. Thus where the prohibited conduct consists in permitting a particular thing to be done, the word "permit" connotes at least knowledge or reasonable grounds for suspicion on the part of the permitter that the thing will be done and an unwillingness to use means available to him to prevent it' (*Sweet* v *Parsley* [1970] AC 132 per Lord Diplock at p 165).

Of the two elements, knowledge and unwillingness to use available means to prevent, one would not suffice even under the 1965 Act.

'Lord Diplock had said that "'permit' connotes *at least* knowledge or reasonable grounds for suspicion . . .", and it is important to note that he throughout insists on "unwillingness" by the defendant to use means available to him to prevent the prohibited act. Both elements are, to his way of thinking, clearly indispensable to the concept of "permitting"' (*R* v *Souter* (1971) 55 Cr App R 403 per Lord Justice Edmund Davies at p 409).

The section 8 offence of knowingly permitting is such that *Souter* (and *Parsley*) adequately state the law.

'The recorder gave the direction of which counsel complains: "Let us look therefore at what 'knowingly permitted' means: actual knowledge or knowledge of circumstances which fixed him, as it were, with a suspicion or knowledge of circumstances so that it could be said that he had shut his eyes to the obvious, or had allowed something to go on, not caring whether an offence was committed or not. Of course, if a person knows, as was admitted in this case, that smoking was taking place and is unwilling to take means available to him to prevent the prohibited act, is unwilling to take steps which are open to him to prevent the prohibited act, then, members of the jury, he is at the very least shutting his eyes to what is happening, is he not? The best indication of such unwillingness is proof of failure to take reasonable steps readily available to prevent the prohibited activity.

'"In this case you will have to ask yourselves if the defendant, as he admits, knew that smoking of cannabis resin was taking place, what steps, if any, did he take that were open to him to prohibit that illegal activity. Another way of putting it is this: that knowing that the smoking of cannabis resin was taking place or shutting his eyes to the fact that it was, he took no steps or no adequate steps to prevent the prohibited act. You can tell someone to go, force them to go, threaten them with the police, take away the pipes; one could do all manner of things in a reasonable attempt to prohibit the activity that you knew was going on. You have got to ask yourselves in this particular case what steps, if any, were taken once knowledge came to the mind of this defendant that acts prohibited by the statute of 1971 were occurring."

'The first sentence of the first paragraph is an exact quotation from the judgment of Lord Parker CJ in *Gray's Haulage Co Ltd* v *Arnold* [1966] 1 WLR 534, 537F, which was accepted by Edmund Davies LJ, giving the judgment of this court in *Souter* (1971) 55 Cr App R 403, 408; [1971] 1 WLR 1187, 1191, as the proper test to be applied to a case of permitting premises to be used for the purpose of smoking cannabis contrary to section 5 (*a*) of the Dangerous Drugs Act 1965. The last sentence of the first paragraph is a quotation from pp 408 and 1191 of the same judgment in *Souter's* case (*supra*). The only thing therefore which can be said in this court to be wrong about it, is that it ignores the addition of the word "knowingly" in the Act of 1971. A direction which was correct for the offence committed by an occupier of premises who "permits" them to be used for this purpose is incorrect for the offence committed by one who "knowingly permits".

'So counsel submits that for knowingly permitting suspicion is not enough, even if coupled with shutting of the occupier's eyes to the obvious, and that nothing short of actual knowledge is enough to establish the offence—or any of the offences—created by section 8. He goes on to submit that the direction gave the jury the impression that "permitted" was to be equated with "failed to take reasonable steps to prohibit".

'This last contention misreads the direction. The recorder was telling the jury that failure to take reasonable steps to prevent the activity was evidence from which the jury could infer a necessary ingredient of permitting, namely unwillingness to take available means to prevent it. In telling them that he was quoting what Lord Diplock had said in *Sweet* v *Parsley* (1969) 53 Cr App R 221, 247, 249; [1970] AC 132, 162 and 165, as criticised and explained by Edmund Davies LJ in *Souter's* case (*supra*).

'So we come back to the question: Does "knowingly" add anything to the offence created by section 5 of the Act of 1965 which invalidates the directions approved by this court in *Souter's* case (*supra*)? We think not' (*R* v *Thomas and Another* (1976) 63 Cr App R 65 per Lord Justice Stephenson at p 68).

Sweet v *Parsley* did not expressly overrule *Yeandel and Another* v *Fisher* [1966] 1 QB 440, in which the licensee of a public house who knew nothing about the smoking of cannabis and dealing in cannabis which were going on there was convicted along with his wife who did know, both being 'concerned in the management'. But what the House of Lords thought of it is plain not only from this decision but from Lord Reid's terse allusion to its having been invoked to justify the conviction of Ms Sweet.

'This was held to be an absolute offence following the earlier decision in *Yeandel* v *Fisher* [1966] 1 QB 440. How has it come about that the Divisional Court has felt bound to reach such an obviously unjust result?' (*Sweet* v *Parsley* [1970] AC 132 per Lord Reid at p 148).

An occupier can permit anyone other than himself to engage in the proscribed activities. The person permitted to do so may be a joint owner-occupier or tenant.

'One co-tenant who knowingly permits another co-tenant to smoke cannabis or cannabis resin on those premises is just as guilty of an offence as a single tenant of premises who invites his friends into those premises and then knowingly permits them to smoke cannabis there' (*R* v *Ashdown and Others* (1974) 59 Cr App R 193 per Lord Justice Roskill at p 194).

'Permit' and 'suffer' are synonyms and a jury may be directed to consider only one of them in a case under section 8 (*R* v *Thomas and Another*, loc cit).
Section 28 defences do not apply to section 8 offences.

CHAPTER 10

Section 9

This section has the effect of singling out opium from all other controlled drugs and, among other things, making it an offence to smoke it. Apart from section 9, the Act contains no prohibition of consumption *per se*.

Opium appears in the list of Class A drugs in Schedule 2 in this form: opium, whether raw, prepared, or medicinal. Medicinal opium and raw opium are defined in Part IV of the same Schedule. Prepared opium is defined in section 37(1) as including dross and other residues remaining after opium has been smoked. Preparing opium for smoking is not an offence, though knowingly permitting that activity on premises is a section 8 offence.

The prohibition of smoking or otherwise using is confined to prepared opium and although all subsequent provisions in the section, and in section 37(1), refer only to the smoking of opium, it is reasonable to infer that such references are to prepared opium. From this it follows that raw and medicinal opium part company with prepared opium and join the other controlled drugs in respect of offences under the Act.

The section 9(b) and 9(c) offences are unique in making it an offence to frequent a place used for the purpose of smoking (prepared) opium, ie, whether that is the frequenter's purpose or not, and an offence to have certain pipes or utensils in one's possession. In the latter instance, however, the utensils must have been used, or at least be intended for use, in connection with opium. A pipe or utensil which would do for smoking prepared opium but which is intended for smoking cannabis or cannabis resin is exempt. Similarly utensils which have been used for the smoking of cannabis or cannabis resin, or in connection with preparing those substances, such as knife blades used for cutting and/or holding cannabis resin over a flame, may be possessed with impunity unless they yield a quantity of the substance which can form the subject of a charge of possession.

It is not a section 9 offence to be concerned in the management of a place used for the purpose of smoking opium. It is, however, a section 8 offence to be concerned in the management of a place, at least if the place is premises, and knowingly to permit the smoking of prepared opium to take place there. The punishment for that offence under section 8(c) is the same as the punishment for an offence of frequenting under section 9(b) and the smoking offence under section 9(a). The importance attached to these special opium offences is signified by the fact that the maximum punishment for them on indictment is twice as high as the maximum punishment for unlawful possession of opium under section 5(2).

It will be observed that the formula 'used for the purpose of' smoking opium has been retained in section 9 though abandoned when section 8 replaced section 5 of the 1965 Act. This places a greater burden of proof on the prosecution, because a casual instance of smoking opium in a place would not render a frequenter of it liable under section 9(*b*). Consequently *Sweet* v *Parsley* retains its interest on this point so far as section 9(*b*) is concerned.

Section 28 defences apply to section 9 offences.

Section 9A

By section 34 of the Drug Trafficking Offences Act 1986, this new section of the 1971 Act prohibits supplying or offering to supply 'any article which may be used or adapted to be used (whether by itself or in combination with another article or other articles) in the administration by any person of a controlled drug to himself or another', where the supplier believes that 'the article (or the article as adapted) is to be so used in circumstances where the administration is unlawful'. This is an offence by virtue of subsection 1 punishable, on summary conviction only, by imprisonment for 6 months or a level 5 fine or both.

Subsection 3 makes it an offence, similarly punishable, to supply or offer to supply any article which may be used to prepare a controlled drug for administration by any person to himself or another, where the supplier believes that the article is to be so used in circumstances where the administration is unlawful.

As has been stated earlier in this work, neither administration nor self-administration having hitherto been unlawful, except in the case of opium, it is necessary for these new offences that that should be changed. This is done by subsection 4 which provides that 'any administration of a controlled drug is unlawful', still however without making it an offence. Exceptions are provided in the subsection where administration is not unlawful supply under section 4 (1) and where self-administration does not derive from unlawful possession.

Subsection 2 excepts hypodermic syringes and any parts thereof, for obvious reasons. Cocaine spoons are at risk, unless sold as ornaments, and so are all manner of smoking utensils and appliances including cigarette papers. Presumably the bigger the cigarette paper the more a supplier may be expected to believe that it is to be used for rolling a cannabis cigarette. But tobacco is also used in cannabis cigarettes, so tobacconists must now beware of selling tobacco, and even factory-made cigarettes, to cannabis users.

CHAPTER 11

Sections 7, 10 to 18 and 22; and Schedules 3 and 6

It will have been observed that section 3 contains an exemption in favour of controlled drugs specified in regulations. Similarly, section 4, 5 and 6 offences may be elided, as the opening words of each section proclaim, by invoking regulations made under section 7. It is not for the prosecution to prove the accused's lack of authorisation. In a case under the Drugs (Prevention of Misuse) Act 1964, the onus is defined and allocated.

'It is tolerably plain that there must be many statutory prohibitions which would become incapable of enforcement if the prosecution had to embark upon inquiries necessary to exclude the possibility of a defendant falling within a class of persons excepted by the section when the defendant himself knows perfectly well whether he falls within that class and has or should have readily available to him the means by which he could establish whether or not he is within the excepted class. That consideration has proved a powerful one in enabling courts in the past to construe enactments such as the section now before us and we think that it is of the utmost persuasive importance in relation to this section and we take the view that the burden did lie on this defendant to show that he fell within the excepted class of a person who has possession of this scheduled drug as a result of the prescription of a qualified medical practitioner' (*R* v *Evans* [1967] 1 QB 322 per Mr Justice Melford Stevenson at p 330).

Section 7 empowers, and in some instances ordains, the Secretary of State to make regulations. Subsection 2 makes provision for licences to be issued for doing things which would otherwise be unlawful, including having controlled drugs in one's possession. Subsection 3 protects doctors, dentists, vets and pharmacists acting in their respective capacities. But where the Secretary of State is of the opinion that it is in the public interest for the production, supply or possession of a particular controlled drug to be either wholly unlawful or unlawful except for purposes of research, he may designate that drug by Order, whereupon the protection flies off.

Section 7 regulations in force are The Misuse of Drugs Regulations 1973 (SI 1973 No 797), hereinafter referred to as the principal regulations, as amended.

The amendments to the principal regulations are in SI 1974 No 402; SI 1975 No 499 (revoked in part); SI 1975 No 1623 (revoked); SI 1977 No 1380; SI 1979 No 326; SI 1983 No 788; and SI 1984 No 1143.

The designation order in force is The Misuse of Drugs (Designation) Order 1977 (SI 1977 No 1379), as varied by The Misuse of Drugs (Designation) (Variation) Order 1984 (SI 1984 No 1144). It designates:

Bufotenine
Cannabinol
Cannabinol derivatives
Cannabis (Class B)
Cannabis resin (Class B)
Coca leaf
Concentrate of poppy-straw
Eticyclidine
Lysergamide
Lysergide and other *N*-alkyl derivatives of lysergamide
Mescaline
Psilocin
Raw opium
Rolicyclidine
Tenocyclidine
4-Bromo-2,5-dimethoxy-*α*-methylphenethylamine
N,*N*-Diethyltryptamine
N,*N*-Dimethyltryptamine
2,5-Dimethoxy-*α*,4-dimethylphenethylamine

and their stereoisomers, esters, ethers and salts and any preparation or other product containing these drugs.

These drugs, considered by the Secretary of State to have no legitimate medicinal use, are wholly unlawful and their production, supply and possession are prohibited by the Order except under licence.

The designation order may be varied or revoked by a subsequent order, and may be annulled by resolution of either House of Parliament, but no such order may be made in the first place except after consultation with, or on the recommendation of, the Advisory Council on the Misuse of Drugs.

Section 10 empowers the Secretary of State to make regulations, governing a wide field of activities, ostensibly 'for preventing the misuse of controlled drugs', though most of the regulations envisaged, in paragraphs (*a*) to (*f*) of subsection 2 go no further than preventing unauthorised dissemination of controlled drugs. Paragraphs (*g*) (*h*) and (*i*) are aimed at doctors and pharmacists and include the requirement of notification of addicts, and restriction upon the supply of certain controlled drugs to addicts.

The regulations made in pursuance of section 10 are The Misuse of Drugs (Safe Custody) Regulations 1973 (SI 1973 No 798) and The Misuse of Drugs (Notification of and Supply to Addicts) Regulations 1973. The safe custody regulations have been amended by regulations in 1974 (SI 1974 No 1449), in 1975 (SI 1975 No 294) and in 1984 (SI 1984 No 1146), and the notification of addicts regulations by regulations in 1983 (SI 1983 No 1909).

The principal regulations reveal that the controls exercised by the Act are not identical in respect of each and every controlled drug. Sections 4 and 5 do not apply to poppy-straw, and a number of substances are, subject to certain requirements of keeping records, excepted from sections 3 and 5. These substances are listed in Schedule 1 to the regulations and consist of preparations comprising controlled drugs in certain specified compounds and concentrations, eg, '2. Any preparation of cocaine containing not more than 0.1 per cent of cocaine calculated as cocaine base, being a preparation compounded with one or more other active or inert ingredients in such a way that the cocaine cannot be recovered by readily applicable means or in a yield which would constitute a risk to health'. The following provision is in similar terms in relation to preparations of medicinal opium or morphine containing not more than 0.2 per cent of morphine.

Practitioners will normally be guided by forensic scientists, but should have these and all other exceptions made by regulations in mind in cases where the identification of any substance as a controlled drug is in question, and also where the status of a person intromitting with controlled drugs may be relevant.

Regulation 5 of the principal regulations legalises the production, supply, offer to supply and possession of any controlled drug by a person who has a Secretary of State's licence authorising the relevant activity.

Regulation 6 authorises possession without licence by constables, carriers, postmen, customs officers and scientists in the course of duty. The word 'forensic' in paragraph (*e*) should presumably be read to mean 'scientific': 'a person engaged in the work of any laboratory to which the drug has been sent for forensic examination'. Paragraph (*f*) extends the authority to 'a person engaged in conveying the drug to a person authorised by these Regulations to have it in his possession'. This provision could prove useful to defence solicitors who were able to arrange to borrow Crown productions for independent laboratory examination (on the authority, if required, of *William Turner Davies, Petitioner,* 1973 SLT (Notes) 36).

Regulation 7 authorises the administration of drugs by doctors and dentists, by other persons on their directions, and without medical direction, in accordance with categories of drugs. Regulations 8, 9 and 10 authorise the production, supply and possession of drugs in the same categories and by specified categories of persons.

Regulation 11 saves the use by certified midwives of pethidine, a controlled drug of Class A. By regulation 21(3), midwives have to keep records of the pethidine which they obtain and administer.

Regulation 12 legalises the cultivation of plants of the genus *Cannabis* if done under licence, and regulation 13 exempts from section 8 of the Act approved premises where cannabis or cannabis resin is smoked for purposes of research.

As regards cultivation, judicial solicitude has offered advice to unsuspecting licensees.

'The only thing which has disturbed me is a point to which Forbes J drew attention, namely, that you may well find that there are reputable horticulturists who have licences to cultivate the cannabis plant, licences granted under regulations made under section 7, which would protect them under section 6. Following the amendment of the 1977 Act they may, in theory at any rate, now be open to a charge under section 4 or possibly under section 8 as occupiers of premises on which cannabis is being cultivated and therefore the cannabis drug is being produced contrary to section 4. They would need special authorisation to protect them in respect of that activity, which is the same activity but could be impugned under a different section.

'Mr Cripps says that we do not have to worry about that because the police will be sensible about their prosecutions. That may be but it is not a very happy approach to the situation. If any person has a licence to cultivate the cannabis plant, he should ensure that it is a licence which authorises not only cultivation, which would otherwise be prohibited by section 6, but also the production of a drug, which would also be prohibited under section 4' (*Taylor v Chief Constable of Kent* (1981) 72 Cr App R 318 per Lord Justice Donaldson at p 322).

Regulations 14 to 23 set out requirements as to the documentation of authorised activities in relation to controlled drugs, including prescriptions, labelling and the keeping of records.

The safe custody regulations make elaborate and detailed structural requirements for safes, cabinets and rooms used for keeping controlled drugs in retail pharmacies, nursing homes and similar institutions. Alternatively, a retail pharmacist may obtain a police certificate that his safe, cabinet or room provides an adequate degree of security. When controlled drugs are out of their locked safe, cabinet or room, the person having possession of them is required by regulation 5 to ensure that they are kept in a locked receptacle. A motor-car, though locked, does not comply. In *Kameswara Rao v Wyles* the appellant, a registered medical practitioner, who was a person legally authorised to be in possession of drugs, left a leather case, which was unlocked, and which contained a variety of drugs to which the Dangerous Drugs Act 1920 and the regulations made under it applied, in a motor-car the doors of which he had locked and which he had left in a car park. Held, on appeal, that a motor-car could not be regarded as a receptacle.

'I am not speculating on what might be the result if different facts had been found, such as that this case itself had been locked, or if the motor-car had contained a locker in which these drugs were kept locked up' (*Kameswara Rao v Wyles* [1949] 2 All ER 685).

Exemptions are provided in favour of the drugs specified in Schedule 1 to the principal regulations and certain other preparations.

The notification of addicts regulations specify the fourteen controlled drugs, all of Class A, to which they apply, viz:

Cocaine	Hydromorphone	Oxycodone
Dextromoramide	Levorphanol	Pethidine
Diamorphine	Methadone	Phenazocine
Dipipanone	Morphine	Piritramide
Hydrocodone	Opium	

They define an addict: 'A person shall be regarded as being addicted to a drug if, and only, if, he has as a result of repeated administration become so dependent upon the drug that he has an overpowering desire for the administration of it to be continued.'

Regulation 2 requires a doctor who attends an addict to report certain particulars in writing to the Chief Medical Officer at the Home Office.

Regulation 3 prohibits the administration or supply to an addict, except under licence, of (*a*) cocaine; (*b*) diamorphine, or (added by amendment in 1983) dipipanone; or their salts.

Contravention of any of these section 10 regulations is an offence, with the exception of any contravention of a regulation made under subsection 2(*h*) or (*i*), in which cases the sanction is a direction by the Secretary of State under section 13. By section 37(1), contravention includes failure to comply.

Section 11 empowers the Secretary of State to direct the taking of precautions for the safe custody of controlled drugs on premises supplementary to regulations made under section 10, contravention being an offence.

Section 12 empowers the Secretary of State to give directions prohibiting named practitioners or pharmacists from possessing, prescribing, supplying, etc, controlled drugs where they have been convicted of drugs offences, including smuggling. Any such direction must be published in the London, Edinburgh and (not or) Belfast Gazettes and takes effect when a copy of it is served on the person to whom it applies. Contravention is an offence.

Section 13 makes similar provision in respect of practitioners who have contravened section 10(2)(*h*) or (*i*), and also in respect of practitioners who in the Secretary of State's opinion have been prescribing, administering or supplying controlled drugs in an irresponsible manner. Contravention of a direction made in either case is an offence.

Before the Secretary of State can give a section 13 direction, he must go through the procedure provided, in detail, in section 14, including reference to a tribunal and, if the tribunal recommends making a direction, to an advisory body. Both the composition of and the procedure to be followed by tribunals and advisory bodies are found in Schedule 3.

In cases of urgency, section 15 allows the Secretary of State to put a temporary stop to irresponsible prescribing, administering or supplying of controlled drugs by a practitioner, by giving a section 13(2) direction without going through the section 14 procedure. He must, however, first refer the matter to a professional panel. Again, the constitution and procedure for the panel are in Schedule 3. The direction lasts for six weeks, and may be kept in force longer if the case is referred to a tribunal under section 14.

Section 16 introduces Schedule 3 and provides for publication of section 14 and 15 orders, directions and notices in the London, Edinburgh and Belfast Gazettes.

Section 17 empowers the Secretary of State to require doctors or pharmacists in any given area to furnish him with particulars of the prescription, administration or supply of any drugs, by reference to quantities supplied and the number and frequency of such occasions of supply, etc. It is important to stress that this provision is part of the Secretary of State's armoury against the dangerous or otherwise harmful drugs of the long title to the Act, not simply against misuse of controlled drugs. Clearly the information obtained in the manner described might form the basis of a decision to amend the lists of controlled drugs by Order in Council. The powers given by the section cannot, however, be used as a fishing diligence to determine whether a section 13 direction should be given in respect of a particular practitioner, as the section comes into operation only if it appears to the Secretary of state that there exists in any area of Great Britain a social problem caused by the extensive misuse of dangerous or otherwise harmful drugs in that area. Non-compliance and giving false information are offences.

Section 18 makes it an offence to contravene any of the foregoing regulations, except those made under section 10(2)(*h*) or (*i*), to contravene a condition or other term of a licence, to give false information for the purpose of obtaining a licence or renewal and to give false information in response to a requirement.

Section 22 empowers the Secretary of State by regulation to exclude from prescribed cases any offence under the Act and any of the smuggling offences. He may also make regulations for applying the provisions of sections 14 to 16 and Schedule 3, anent tribunals, advisory bodies and professional panels, to directions under section 12 or to regulations generally.

Sections 29, 30 and 31 make provision for the service of notices or directions, and for the making of regulations.

The sections under which notices are served are 11, 14, 15(6) and 17; the sections under which directions are given are 12, 13, 15 and 16.

The sections authorising the making of regulations by the Secretary of State are 7, 10 and 22.

CHAPTER 12

Section 19—Attempts

Section 19 provides the only basis for prosecuting attempts to commit offences under the Act. It provides for it to be an offence to attempt to commit an offence under any other provision of the Act and, in addition, to attempt to commit the section 19 offence of incitement. Incitement to commit an offence under any provision of the Act other than section 19 is an offence. These offences of attempt and incitement are described in section 25 as being 'under section 19', not under the section appropriate to the substantive offence. Notwithstanding this, prosecutors frequently prefer charges of attempt without reference to section 19, eg, attempting to produce a controlled drug contrary to section 4. There is no such offence under section 4, although it is a proscribed activity under section 8, as is also attempting to supply a controlled drug. All attempts to commit offences should be prosecuted under section 19 on pain of failure.

'Charge 3 can be disposed of on the simple ground that attempting to cultivate plants of the genus cannabis is an offence under section 19 of the Misuse of Drugs Act 1971. Accordingly, attempting to cultivate the plants is not an offence under section 6(2). No motion to amend was made and so findings of not guilty will be made on this charge' (*Mingay* v *Mackinnon* 1980 JC 33. (This passage in the sheriff's judgment unreported.)).

The punishment for an offence under section 19 follows the punishment for the substantive offence to which the attempt, incitement or attempted incitement was directed. Similarly, section 19 offences may be prosecuted summarily or on indictment and are punishable accordingly.

A charge of attempting to commit the offence of having unlawful possession of a controlled drug in contravention of section 5(2) is undoubtedly competent under section 19. Specific reference is made to it in section 5(5) where it is described as attempting to get possession of such a drug.

Where, before the Act, attempts to procure cannabis and heroin were prosecuted at common law, a mere inquiry for the drugs was held not to be an attempt to procure them.

'According to police officers they followed two men who had sold a substance to known drug addicts in Piccadilly, London, and had gone to a nearby street when the defendant came out of a club and s..id to them: "What you got tonight, boys, hash or heroin? I got money upstairs", and then, observing the officers, added: "Not now, push off—law!" and the two men ran off. The defendant was searched and no drugs were found. The magistrate was referred to *Davy* v *Lee* [1968] 1 QB 366, and was of opinion that the words spoken by the defendant, coupled with the evidence of the actions of the two men observed by the officers, amounted to the offence charged and he convicted the defendant, who appealed.

'Lord Parker CJ said that, although the evidence established an intention to obtain drugs, mere intention was insufficient, and some further step was necessary for the defendant's actions to move to the stage of an attempt. Since the words used by him could be given no wider meaning than that of an invitation to treat or make an offer, they were not sufficient. Moreover, the evidence could not have supported a finding of guilt on both of the charges' (*Kyprianou* v *Reynolds* 1969 SJ 563).

For a charge under section 19 of attempting to supply a controlled drug, unlike a charge under section 4(3)(*a*) of offering to supply a controlled drug, there must be a controlled drug: *Mieras* v *Rees* [1975] Crim LR 224.

CHAPTER 13

Sections 23 and 24—Search and Arrest

These sections contain the powers of search, detention, seizure and arrest given to the police.

In respect of producers or suppliers of controlled drugs (ie, under licence), the powers are extended to persons, other than police officers, authorised by the Secretary of State, but limited to entering premises and demanding to be allowed to inspect documents and stocks of drugs. No warrant is required to go that far under subsection 1, but if documents or drugs are to be seized a warrant must be obtained under subsection 3, of section 23.

The power to detain a person under subsection 2 and search him or her extends to taking the suspect to a police station for the purpose: *Farrow* v *Tunnicliffe* [1976] Crim LR 126. But arrest without warrant is unlawful unless one of the preconditions in section 24(1) is satisfied, and where the detention is unlawful the search is so too.

'The respondent was approached by police officers at Elgin railway station, who told her that she was being apprehended under the Misuse of Drugs Act 1971 on suspicion of being in possession of a controlled drug or drugs. It was made clear to the respondent that she was under arrest and was to be taken to Elgin police office and searched for drugs. She was told that she would not be kept there any longer than necessary. She was further told that when the police had received information of a suspected drug offence they were bound to take suspects to a police station to be searched for drugs; they told her she would be released as soon as possible. According to the sheriff, the police officers gave clear and unequivocal evidence that the respondent was arrested at the railway station under the Misuse of Drugs Act 1971.

'If this is so, then the arrest in my opinion was unlawful. It was not an arrest under s 24, but was a purported action under s 23(2)(*a*). But that section does not give authority to arrest, only to "detain" for a limited purpose. There is a vital distinction between "arrest" and "detention" (*Swankie* v *Milne* 1973 SLT (Notes) 28, Lord Cameron at p 29). It is true that under s 23(2)(*a*) of the 1971 Act the police are entitled to detain the person suspected for the purpose of searching him, and for this purpose may be entitled to take him to a place where the search may take place. This place might conveniently be the nearest police station. But a penal statute must be construed strictly. In my opinion, in deference to the rights of the citizen, it must be made perfectly clear to the person against whom action is being taken under s 23(2)(*a*) that that is what

103

is being done and that he is not being arrested. If, as apparently happened in this case, the respondent was arrested and told that she was to be taken to the police station under arrest, then in my opinion that was an unlawful arrest. It will not do, in my opinion, to say that she was bound to know the law and so was bound to realise that, although the police officers used the word "arrest", they really meant "detain", and were proceeding under s 23(2)(*a*). The police also should know the law and if they were proceeding under s 23 they should have done so explicitly' (*Wither* v *Reid* 1979 SLT 192 per Lord Robertson at p 197 (Lord Wheatley, Lord Justice-Clerk, dissenting)).

A warrant may be granted under section 23(3) to search premises for drugs or documents relating to drugs offences, if the justice of the peace, magistrate or sheriff is satisfied by information on oath that there is reasonable ground for suspecting their presence. The warrant lasts for a month and extends to searching persons found in the premises. The authority is limited to seizure of drugs and documents, but under subsection 2(*c*) anything which appears to a searching constable to be evidence of an offence under the Act may also be seized.

Subsection 4 creates the offences of obstructing searches, etc, concealing documents or stocks of drugs where that is relevant under subsection 1 and failing to produce documents for inspection. In the latter case, reasonable excuse is a defence, proof being on the accused. Section 28 defences do not apply.

Evidence concerning a search carried out under the authority of a search warrant which has been shown to the accused at the time of the search but which is not produced at the trial is admissible: *Nocher* v *Smith* 1978 SLT (Notes) 32.

Evidence obtained in the course of a search made without a valid warrant may be admissible: *Walsh* v *MacPhail* 1978 SLT (Notes) 29.

Or it may be held to be inadmissible. Where the name of the officer enforcing the warrant and the address of the premises were left blank, evidence was held to have been illegally obtained.

'The failure to insert the name of the officer to whom the warrant was granted raises a much more serious matter. The explanation offered by the procurator fiscal seems to me entirely irrelevant. It matters not to which force the officer who executed the warrant belonged because no officer was in fact named in the warrant. This failure was a clear breach of section 23(3) which requires that the warrant must authorise any constable acting for the police area. If no name be entered, then in my opinion no constable is authorised to enter and search. To countenance a situation where any police officer might seek entry under section 23(3) armed only with a blank warrant, would in my opinion be quite contrary to the intention and spirit of the Act and would amount to taking an unfair advantage of the occupier. It follows that it would also be unfair to an accused. For these reasons I am unable to excuse this irregularity which indeed, I regard as quite fatal to the warrant.

'The failure to insert a specific description of the premises to be searched seems to me also to be a clear breach of the requirements of section 23(3) which requires the premises to be named in the warrant. The printed words "the said premises at" followed by the blank space, makes it perfectly clear that the address of the premises to be searched must be there inserted. No explanation as to how this vital omission came about was offered by the Crown except that it had been overlooked in the urgency of the operation. I cannot accept this explanation nor do I consider that the linking of the printed words "said premises at" with the printed word "aforesaid" will suffice to cure the defect.

'The procurator fiscal sought to argue that all the omissions and defects were in fact due to the urgency of the need to search and the haste involved. Urgency may well excuse a search without any warrant in very special circumstances but once a warrant had been obtained I can see no reason why proper care should not have been taken to complete the warrant in proper form. The officers from the Scottish Crime Squad who undertook the search would, I have no doubt, have been well acquainted with the formalities attending a search. I would respectfully agree with the observation of the Lord Justice-General (Cooper) in *McGovern* v *HM Advocate* 1950 JC 33 at 37: "Unless the principles under which police investigations are carried out are adhered to with reasonable strictness, the anchor of the entire system for the protection of the public will very soon begin to drag"' (*HM Advocate* v *Cumming* 1983 SCCR 15 (Sh. Ct)).

The powers are guarded.

'A police officer testified that at about 2 am he saw an Austin Mini car parked in a public car park. He suspected that the car might have been stolen and requested information from the police computer by radio. He was informed that the car was suspected of being involved in drug trafficking. It was submitted that the search was illegal as the officer did not suspect the defendant was in possession of the drug but that the vehicle was. The Crown argued that section 23 gave the officer such a power. *Held*, that section 23 gives the police power to search a person or any vehicle when he has reasonable grounds to suspect that the person is in possession of a controlled drug. In this case it was the vehicle that was suspect, not the defendant, and consequently the search was illegal' (*R* v *Littleford* [1978] Crim LR 48).

The obstruction of officers in the exercise of their powers under section 23 must be 'intentional' but need not be physical (*R* v *Ford* 81 Cr App R 19; *Carmichael* v *Brannan* 1985 SCCR 234).

Section 24 authorises arrest without warrant where at least one of the conditions listed in the section is satisfied. Either an offence under the Act must have been committed or the arresting constable must have reasonable cause to suspect the person to be arrested of having committed one. Then he must have reasonable cause to suspect that the person will otherwise abscond, or is not giving a true name or address.

CHAPTER 14

Sections 21, 25, 27 and 33; and Schedule 4—
Prosecution and Punishment of Offences

Section 21 renders officers of a body corporate liable to be convicted, along with the company or other body of which they are officers, of offences committed by the body corporate. Guilt on the part of such officers is proved by (*a*) their consent to the commission of the offence; (*b*) their connivance at the offence; or (*c*) any neglect on their part, presumably either to prevent the commission of an offence by the body corporate or to secure compliance with requirements such as the safe custody regulations. As the liability is confined to offences under the Act, smuggling is not included, but section 171(4) of the Customs and Excise Management Act 1979 is to the same effect as regards the smuggling offences.

Section 25 and Schedule 4 set out, the latter in tabulated form, the way in which offences under the Act are punishable. A column is provided in the Schedule ostensibly to show whether the offence is punishable on summary conviction, on indictment or in either way, but with a single exception all offences are triable summarily or on indictment. The exception is failure to comply with a section 17 notice.

Subsection 3 provides that attempts which are offences under section 19 shall be punishable in the same way as the substantive offences to which they were directed.

Subsections 4, 5 and 6 increase to twelve months the time within which proceedings may be taken summarily, notwithstanding the limitations in the Magistrates' Courts Act 1980, the Criminal Procedure (Scotland) Act 1975 and the Magistrates' Courts Act (Northern Ireland) 1964.

Section 26 has been repealed by the Customs and Excise Management Act 1979, section 177(3) and Schedule 1. That Schedule takes the place of this section.

Section 27 empowers the court by or before which a person is convicted under the Act to order the forfeiture of anything shown to the satisfaction of the court to relate to the offence in question. The forfeiture is usually for destruction, but the court may order a different disposal. The controlled drug in question is the invariable target of a motion for forfeiture, and even where an accused is acquitted he can hardly resume, or take, possession of any such production. Next come scales and other implements such as smoking utensils and it will be a matter of fact in every case whether they have been shown to relate to the offence. Money may or may not relate to the offence, though it is difficult to see how it can ever relate to certain offences such as possession under section 5(2) unless there were evidence that a drug had been bought and not paid for, which would be exceptional.

'The justices concluded that the defendant had offered to supply lysergide to Heward and therefore convicted him of the offence of offering to supply. They sentenced him to a fine. They imposed a sentence of imprisonment which they suspended for two years in the exercise of their powers under section 20 of the Criminal Courts Act 1973. They made an order for the destruction of seven drops of Bromo STP, which were the subject of the transaction between the defendant and Heward (the matter to which the information related) and they finally ordered the forfeiture of a sum of money which was apparently in the defendant's possession. In making that order of forfeiture the justices purported to act under section 27 of the Misuse of Drugs Act 1971, which provides that the court by or before which a person is convicted of an offence under the Act may order anything shown to the satisfaction of the court to relate to that offence to be forfeited or dealt with in such other manner as the court may order.

'In my judgment the justices had no power to make an order such as they purported to make in this case' (*Haggard* v *Mason* [1976] 1 WLR 187 per Mr Justice Lawson at p 190).

The same result was achieved in appeals in section 5(3) cases. *Ex hypothesi* if controlled drugs are in the accused's possession with intent to supply them to another, money simultaneously in his possession is not the product of, or even 'connected with', that offence. In *R* v *Morgan* [1977] Crim LR 488 an order for forfeiture was quashed where the court held that the money 'was no doubt part of his working capital for trade in drugs'. *R* v *Ribeyre* [1982] Crim LR 538 is to the same effect.

The disposal of things forfeited will vary according to their nature. Drugs are almost always ordered to be destroyed. Any different disposal ordered must not be whimsical, but may be ingenious.

'My powers under section 27(1) are virtually unrestricted. I can order the destruction of the property, or I can order that it should be dealt with in such a manner as the court may order. Obviously I must adopt a judicial and not a whimsical approach as regards the words "In such other manner as the court may order".

'In my judgment the sum of £3,978 will be forfeited, and of that sum the sum of £3,478 I order to be paid to Customs and Excise, and the balance I order to be paid to the sheriff of the City of London. I make no bones about it, I am not by that order intending to enrich the sheriff of the City of London or reducing the rates in the City, because what I am now going to do is to proceed to make an order of reward for Mr Galloway, whom I thought a very brave officer. He executed his duty admirably and he is a great credit to the service under which he serves.

'I observe that I invited argument on the powers of the court but I think that Mr Galloway should have more than a pat on the back. I, therefore, order that a reward should be paid to Mr Galloway, in the sum that I have ordered should be paid to the sheriff of the City of London, and that reward be paid by the sheriff of the City of London' (*R* v *Beard* [1974] 1 WLR 1549 per Mr Justice Caulfield at p 1551).

An owner or other interested party must be given an opportunity to show cause why forfeiture of anything should not be ordered. This includes, but is not confined to, the accused (subsection 2).

The court's powers are significantly different, and greater, if section 223 of the Criminal Procedure (Scotland) Act 1975 is invoked.

'Mr McLean argued that the forfeiture of the money found was incompetent. It could not be justified, he argued, under reference to a number of cases in England, under section 27(1) of the Misuse of Drugs Act 1971 and it could not be justified either under section 223(1) of the Criminal Procedure (Scotland) Act 1975. In reply the learned advocate-depute conceded that if the order depended upon the justification given by section 27(1) it could not be supported, and with that concession we entirely agree. Section 27(1) could not protect this order if that is all that we have to look at in determining the competency of the forfeiture. Coming, however, to section 223 of the Act of 1975, a different question arises, because we have to examine what was done to see whether it can be supported by the power given to the court in that section. Now the section says this: "Where a person is convicted of an offence and the court which passes sentence is satisfied that any property which was in his possession or under his control at the time of his apprehension—(*a*) has been used for the purpose of committing, or facilitating the commission of, any offence; or (*b*) was intended by him to be used for that purpose, that property shall be liable to forfeiture."

'Now in this case the learned advocate-depute has argued that the order of forfeiture was competent under both head (*a*) and head (*b*) or either of them in section 223(1). In our opinion the order was competent, under section 223(1)(*b*). In the circumstances of this case the judge was entitled to be satisfied that the money found concealed in the flat in association with the paraphernalia of trafficking, and, indeed, the cannabis resin, was intended to be used by the appellant for the purpose of committing an offence and, for that matter, an offence under the Misuse of Drugs Act 1971. The intention was there to be seen and it arises as a reasonable inference from the material which was before the trial judge' (*Donnelly (Edward)* v *HM Advocate* 1984 SCCR 93 per Lord Emslie, Lord Justice-General, at p 95).

All offences created by the Act are extradition crimes within the meaning of the Extradition Acts 1870 and 1932. Section 33 of the 1971 Act adds the common law crime of conspiring to commit any such statutory offence to the list of extradition crimes.

Since the beginning of 1986, further penal consequences of a monetary character have attached to certain drugs-related offences. In Scotland the provisions are contained in the Law Reform (Miscellaneous Provisions) (Scotland) Act 1985 and were brought into force (by section 60 (3) (*d*)) on 30th December 1985. The offences are those created by sections 4 (2), 4 (3) and 5 (3) of the 1971 Act and by sections 50 (2), 50 (3), 68 (2), 170 (1) and 170 (2) of the Customs and Excise Management Act 1979. The principal innovatory provision is that where a person is convicted on indictment of one of the offences and sentenced to imprisonment (or detention) 'the Court shall, unless it is satisfied that for any reason it would be inappropriate to do so, also impose a fine.'

The Legislature's thinking in introducing such provisions is revealed by subsection 2:

'In determining the amount of a fine . . . the Court shall have regard to any profits likely to have been made by the offender from the crime (*sic*) in respect of which he has been convicted.'

Despite the mandatory character of the provision, the fact that no commercial element is essential to the commission of any of the offences listed is presumably recognised by the escape clause. Granted that forfeiture of controlled drugs in possession is inevitable on conviction, it must be supposed that most section 5 (3) offences, and others of production, importation, etc will result in losses and not profits to the offender, and that the full effect of the provisions will be felt only in cases of commercial supply under section 4 (3) of the 1971 Act. The words 'profits likely to have been made' must await judicial interpretation, as to whether they can have a future or only a past connotation. In practice, the onus of satisfying a Court that a fine is inappropriate will fall on the defence.

The Drug Trafficking Offences Act 1986, which received the Royal Assent on 8th July 1986, and is to come into force on an appointed day or days, provides for confiscation orders in England and Wales. The drugs trafficking offences are defined in section 38 (1) and are those in the Scottish legislation plus offences under section 20 of the 1971 Act, conspiracy under the Criminal Law Act 1977, attempts under the Criminal Attempts Act 1981, incitement under section 19 of the 1971 Act, 'aiding, abetting, counselling or procuring' any such offence and, finally, a new offence under this Act. This is found in section 24 and defined as assisting another to retain the benefit of drug trafficking. Drug trafficking is defined in section 38 (1) in such a way as to overlap with the drug trafficking offences. But they are not coterminous: there are these innovations, (a) that drug trafficking includes 'transporting or storing' a controlled drug where its possession presumably by this offender and not only by the consignor, consignee or depositor, is unlawful; and (b) drug trafficking also includes making arrangements to facilitate the retention or control of the proceeds of drug trafficking, presumably by any means, but 'laundering' funds is particularly struck at.

For 'profit' in the Scottish legislation, read 'benefit' in this Act, section 1 (2). Benefit means any payment or reward, not necessarily a profit, and if there has been any benefit as so defined the Court orders confiscation of it. Duplication with fines, payment orders, forfeiture orders, criminal bankruptcy orders and deprivation orders is avoided, but the opposite applies to imprisonment or any other disposal. It is to be left out of account.

Section 2 provides for the proceeds, and hence the benefit, of drug trafficking to be assessed in accordance with formulae which permit the assumptions, except where rebutted in (not 'by') the defendant's case, that all his acquisitions for six years back from the institution of proceedings against him, plus his current assets, are proceeds of trafficking.

Sections 3 and 5 contain detailed provisions supplementary to the assessment provisions while section 4 provides that the amount to be recovered under a confiscation order is the amount assessed or the value of the defendant's realisable property if less. Realisable property includes gifts which, in accordance with section 5, may be clawed back from donees.

Sections 6 to 23 provide elaborate mechanisms for enforcement of confiscation orders in England and Wales and for enforcement, after registration, of certain ancillary orders in Scotland.

Investigations into drug trafficking are to be facilitated by search powers under section 28 and production orders under section 27.

CHAPTER 15

Section 28

Section 28 is innovatory. It applies to all the production and supplying offences in section 4, to both possession offences in section 5 and to the special opium offences in section 9. The section also in terms is made applicable to section 6, a provision whose effect was increased when the redefinition of cannabis by section 52 of the Criminal Law Act 1977 made the cannabis plant as such a controlled drug.

The genesis of section 28 is said to be Lord Pearce's suggestion in *Warner* v *Metropolitan Police Commissioner*: 'It would, I think, be an improvement of a difficult position if Parliament were to enact that when a person has ownership or physical possession of drugs he shall be guilty unless he proves on a balance of probabilities that he was unaware of their nature or had reasonable excuse for their possession' ([1969] 2 AC 256 at p 307). Whether Parliament has hit that target is a matter of debate.

If, to take the terms of subsection 2, it is necessary for the prosecution to prove some fact in order to bring home guilt to an accused, presumably that fact is, or is part of, the *actus reus* of the offence in question. But knowledge is part of the *actus reus* of all section 4 and 5 offences and consequently the subsection does not operate to transfer the burden of proof to the defence in any degree.

'I must now deal with the argument for the Crown that possession of an article within the meaning of section 5(1) and (2) of the Misuse of Drugs Act 1971 may be established without proof that the possessor knew he had it. There is no doubt that under the corresponding provisions of the Act of 1964 knowledge on the part of the alleged possessor was an essential element to be established in proof of a charge of unlawful possession of a substance specified in the Schedule to that Act. In this respect the word "possession" was, not surprisingly, given the meaning commonly accepted in other statutory contexts, for example the Explosives Act 1883, and the English cases of *Lockyer* v *Gibb* [1967] 2 QB 243 and *R* v *Warner* [1969] 2 AC 256 which were concerned with section 1 of the Drugs (Prevention of Misuse) Act 1964 show quite clearly that for the purposes of that section a person cannot be said to be in the possession of an article which he does not realise was there at all. What was required, therefore, was proof that the alleged possessor was aware of the existence of the thing which he is said to have possessed and since the section did not demand proof of knowledge of the quality of the thing possessed, if that thing turned out to be a controlled drug proof of the offence was complete. Has the Misuse of Drugs Act 1971 made the fundamental change for which in this case the Crown contends? In my opinion the answer is emphatically in the negative. Apart from the fact that section 5(2) of that Act is introduced by the words "Subject to section 28 of this Act" it is not suggested that it is possible to distinguish the offence created by that subsection and the offence created under section 1 of the Act of 1964. Section 28(2) is in these terms: "Subject to subsection (3) below, in any proceedings for an offence to which this section applies it shall be a defence for the accused to prove that he neither knew of nor suspected nor had reason to suspect the existence of some fact alleged by the prosecution which it is necessary for the prosecution to prove if he is to be convicted of the offence charged."

'It will be observed at once that this subsection is extraordinary in that it appears to restrict the prescribed defence to proof of ignorance "of the existence of some fact . . . which it is necessary for the prosecution to prove . . .". Why it was thought necessary so to provide is astonishing since no conviction could possibly be returned on the evidence as a whole unless the Crown proved all that required to be proved. Be that as it may the defence is clearly not available with respect to any fact which it is not necessary for the prosecution to prove and the submission for the Crown, insofar as it rests upon the language of section 28(2), simply cannot get off the ground unless it can be demonstrated that in the formulation of the substantive offence, section 5(2) by itself changes the meaning of "possession". The subsection does nothing of the kind' (*McKenzie* v *Skeen* 1983 SLT 121 per Lord Emslie, Lord Justice-General).

In a word, section 28 does not reduce the matters the prosecution had to prove before the Act, and still has to prove, nor alter the burden of proof in respect of them. It merely provides fresh defences not hitherto available (*R* v *Colyer* [1974] Crim LR 243). That terse statement in a Crown Court, while receiving no nominate credit, was confirmed in the Court of Appeal.

'It is sought to say that the effect of section 28(1) and (2) and perhaps (3) of the 1971 Act is to alter the meaning to be given to "possession" so that the Crown no longer has to prove beyond reasonable doubt that the accused person knew that he had "the thing", as it has been called, in his possession. Mr Gordon did not shrink from saying that section 28 removed from the shoulders of the Crown on to those of the accused the "burden of disproof" of knowledge that he had the "thing" in his possession.

'We look, therefore, at section 28 to see what its ambit is. Section 28(1) provides: "This section applies to offences under any of the following provisions of this Act, that is to say section 4(2) and (3), section 5(2) and (3), section 6(2) and section 9." We are, of course, here concerned with section 5(2). Section 28(2) goes on: "Subject to subsection (3) below, in any proceedings for an offence to which this section applies it shall be a defence for the accused to prove that he neither knew of nor suspected nor had reason to suspect the existence of some fact alleged by the prosecution which it is necessary for the prosecution to prove if he is to be convicted of the offence charged.'

'The argument is that the effect of that subsection, and of subsection (3)—which I need not read—is to put the whole burden of disproving knowledge upon the accused. With all respect to the argument, we think it is wrong as a matter of the construction of the section. When one construes these sections in the 1971 Act together with section 5(1) and (2) and one realises that section 5(2) and indeed (3) are each made subject to section 28 of the Act, it is apparent that whatever the precise scope of the various subsections of section 28 may be, their manifest purpose is to afford a defence to an accused person where no defence had previously existed. Historically, it may well be that the reason for this was because of what was said by the House of Lords and, in particular by Lord Pearce, in *Warner* (*supra*) (and later repeated by him in *Sweet* v *Parsley* (1969) 53 Cr App R 221; [1970] AC 132, 157). But, of course, what the House of Lords said in *Warner* (*supra*), and indeed in *Sweet* v *Parsley* (*supra*) cannot help construe the language of a statute passed some time after those two decisions. We must look at the language of the 1971 Act and construe the language there as it appears.

'It would be very odd indeed, if one effect of section 28, which as we said a moment ago is plainly designed to afford a defence where no defence had previously existed, was at the same time to remove from the shoulders of the Crown the burden of proof of one of the essential elements of the offence as stated by the House of Lords in *Warner* (*supra*). It seems to us plain that there is nothing in section 28 which in any way alters the burden which rests upon the Crown so that when the Crown seeks to prove unlawful possession of a controlled drug, proof of that possession involves proof of knowledge by the accused that he had control of the "thing" in question' (*R* v *Ashton-Rickhardt* (1977) 65 Cr App R 67 per Lord Justice Roskill at p 71).

What then does section 28(2) amount to? The answer given by Ribeiro and Perry is nothing ('Possession and section 28 of the Misuse of Drugs Act 1971' in [1979] Crim LR p 90). While that may be the case so far as section 5 offences are concerned, the section 6 offence is to be distinguished. Section 6 prohibits not the cultivation of any controlled drug, so that the cultivation of one in the belief that it was another would be no defence, but only the cultivation of a plant of the genus *Cannabis*. Consequently it is of the essence of the offence, and part of the *actus reus*, that the accused should know that she is cultivating that plant, which the prosecution must prove. In *R* v *Champ* the appellant claimed misdirection of the jury by the trial judge in ruling that it was not necessary for the prosecution to prove that the appellant knew that she was cultivating cannabis.

'The appellant sought to show that she did not know that she was cultivating a cannabis plant. Subsection (2) of section 28 makes it clear that she had to prove that defence. There was no burden on the prosecution to prove that she knew that she was cultivating a plant of the genus cannabis. On the contrary, she had to prove that she did not know that she was doing so' (*R* v *Champ* (1981) 73 Cr App R 367 per Lord Justice Lawton at p 369).

The interpretation of section 28(2) is manifestly wrong. If there was no burden on the prosecution to prove the accused's knowledge of what she was doing, subsection 2 does not come into play as it applies only to 'some fact alleged by the prosecution which it is necessary for the prosecution to prove'. As the Lord Justice-General stated in *McKenzie* v *Skeen* (*supra*), 'the defence is clearly not available with respect to any fact which it is not necessary for the prosecution to prove'.

Section 28(3) provides, apart from a defence in paragraph (*b*)(ii) available only to a person entitled to be in possession of some controlled drug or another, a defence that the accused neither believed nor suspected nor had reason to suspect that the substance or product involved in a charge was a controlled drug. Paragraph (*a*) emphatically excludes the operation of the defence where the only mistake consists in believing the substance or product to be a controlled drug other than the one in question.

Insofar as all the activities which become offences under sections 4 and 5 can also be legitimated by regulations, a distinction is to be drawn between them and section 9 offences. The activities struck at by section 9 are inherently illegal and no justification for them is provided by law. But again the *actus reus* of the offences involves knowledge of their essential ingredients. Since the essential element of a section 9 offence is intromitting with opium, the prosecution must prove an *actus reus* which involves knowledge of the nature of the drug. Subsection 3 therefore seems to be otiose as far as section 9 offences are concerned. Of course, opium no less than any other controlled drug is included in the section 4 and section 5 offences to which section 28(3) applies, and in which the *actus reus* is not limited to the controlled drug libelled.

Of the three elements in section 28(3), belief, suspicion and reason to suspect, the first two are to be judged subjectively, the last with 'objective rationality', so that the accused's being drunk at the time is irrelevant.

'It is contended that the three requirements are to be read as one, all of which require consideration of the effect of alcohol on the appellant's actual personal ability to believe, suspect, or have reason to suspect. In other words, the subjective approach applies throughout and the introduction of the test of the reasonable sober man is not appropriate. For the prosecution it is submitted that the words "nor had reason to suspect" introduce the concept of that which is reasonable and this affects the belief and suspicion also. That being so, it is said that it was correct to introduce the objective test of the reasonable sober man.

'We were referred to various authorities. In support of the prosecution case the most recent authority is *R* v *Woods* (1981) 74 Cr App R 312. That laid down that a defendant's self-intoxication was not a relevant consideration which a jury were entitled to take into account on a charge of rape in deciding whether there were reasonable grounds for his belief that the woman in question was consenting to sexual intercourse. We would not require authority for that proposition. It is clearly the law that when reasonable grounds for belief are canvassed, self-intoxication will not avail.

'For the appellant it is contended "had reason to suspect" is not the same thing as "reasonable grounds for belief". Reliance is placed on the decision of the Divisional Court in *Jaggard* v *Dickinson* [1981] QB 527. That is authority not binding upon this court, but nevertheless persuasive for the proposition that where there is an exculpatory statutory defence of honest belief, self-induced intoxication is a factor which must be considered in the context of a subjective consideration of the individual state of mind. The objective test of a reasonable sober man is irrelevant. Accepting and applying this decision as we do, it would lead to the conclusion that, insofar as the belief and suspicion are concerned, there would have been a misdirection in the instant case. But it leaves untouched the problem created by the introduction of the third limb, which is an integral part of the exculpatory defence. The remaining question is whether a reason is something entirely personal and individual, calling for an entirely subjective consideration, or involves the wider concept of an objective rationality. We are of the opinion that it is the latter. It follows therefore that, in our judgment, it was a correct direction that the self-induced intoxication did not avail. Moreover, it was an unnecessary gloss to introduce the concept of the reasonable sober man. Nevertheless, this gloss did not vitiate the fundamental direction that the self-intoxication was no defence. The drunkenness relied upon could not assist in considering whether or not the accused had no reason to suspect. The effect of this conclusion is that self-induced intoxication is not a relevant consideration in the exercise of this statutory defence' (*R* v *Young* [1984] 1 WLR 654 per Mr Justice Kilner Brown at p 657).

CHAPTER 16

Sections 36 and 37—Definitions

Section 37 is the interpretation section, but definitions for the purposes of the Act and Regulations are scattered here and there in other parts, eg, section 36, Schedule 2 and regulation 2 of the Notification Regulations.

Section 36 defines 'corresponding law' for the purpose of section 20 offences. 'Corresponding law' also appears in section 23(3)(*b*), dealing with the granting of warrants to search for documents, which are not confined to those relating to offences under the Act but include those relating to offences against the provisions of a corresponding law.

The words and phrases defined in section 37(1) are a miscellany which includes three controlled drugs and two words descriptive of offences. The drugs are cannabis, cannabis resin and opium. The separate definitions of cannabis and cannabis resin underline the fact that they are two drugs, not one, despite their coupling in paragraph 1(*a*) of Part II of Schedule 2, and the unconvincing attempt in *R* v *Best and Others* (1980) 70 Cr App R 21 to fudge the distinction. The fact that drugs have a common origin has not elsewhere in the Schedule prevented their having individual placings, so the manner of listing these two remains a mystery. The redefinition of cannabis by section 52 of the Criminal Law Act 1977 has, if anything, prised them further apart, in that cannabis now means the whole plant whereas formerly it was confined to the flowering or fruiting tops containing the resin. The essential difference is that cannabis is vegetable material (though it may contain resin) while cannabis resin is resinous material (though it may be impossible even in extreme refinement to exclude microscopically small particles of plant material). The common slang terms 'grass' and 'hash' are a convenient guide. See also *Muir* v *Smith* [1978] Crim LR 293 in which Mr Justice Wein held that cannabis and cannabis resin were 'two entirely different substances as defined by section 37'.

The degree of separation required, or resultant crudity tolerated, by the definition was concerned in *R* v *Thomas*. The defendant was in possession of a brown substance which had been produced by compacting the shakings or scrapings of a plant of the genus *Cannabis*. On microscopic examination the substance was seen to contain intact glandular trichomes from which the resin had not been removed. A submission that insufficient separation had occurred for the substance to comply with the statutory definition was rejected and the defendant convicted. It was held by the Court of Appeal that the presence of the trichomes did not prevent the substance from being cannabis resin. It was crude cannabis resin (*R* v *Thomas* [1981] Crim LR 497). In fact what Ms

Thomas had was a mixture of cannabis resin and cannabis, the surviving plant material contained in the mass of resin. Even when purified to a much greater degree than in her case, cannabis resin yields microscopically observable particles of plant material, ie, cannabis. Strictly speaking, therefore, since the redefinition of the latter, a person in possession of cannabis resin could almost always be successfully charged also with possession of cannabis.

The third drug definition contains a unique provision. Prepared opium means not only the substance indicated but also 'dross and any other residues remaining after opium has been smoked'. It is apparent that this definition has two different uses for prosecutors. In the first place, it will allow prosecution of section 9 offences to proceed on the basis of opium-related activities being provable though none of the drug is found. More significantly, however, it would provide the evidential basis for a section 5 charge which might otherwise founder for failure to prove the presence of the drug. It is direct statutory authority for convicting of possession of an absent drug.

The inclusion of the words 'dross' and 'other residues' also raises a doubt as to whether some prosecutions, such as those in *Searle* v *Randolph* and *Muir* v *Smith*, are justified, when all that is found of cannabis or cannabis resin is the debris of smoking in cigarette ends, pipes or ashtrays. If Parliament has intended the 'dross and any other residues remaining' after cannabis had been smoked to come within the definition of cannabis, or cannabis resin, it seems on the evidence of this section that it could have said so. The point, apparently, remains to be argued in a suitable case. It was not invoked by Mr Justice McKenna when he said in his dissenting judgment in *Bocking* v *Roberts* [1973] 3 All ER 962 that a mere positive reaction to a chemical test for the presence of a drug is not 'what the regulations mean when they speak of a man being in possession of a forbidden drug'.

The definitions of cannabis and cannabis resin being mutually exclusive, no extrapolation can be made from one to the other.

'As the definition section in the Act shows, cannabis and cannabis resin are two quite distinct and different drugs within the same class. In these circumstances the first point taken by the appellant was that since the charge was of possession of cannabis, a finding of possession of cannabis resin did not establish the contravention. With that proposition the learned advocate-depute for the Crown very properly agreed and the only remaining point in the case is whether the sheriff was entitled to proceed upon the finding of cannabis resin to hold that cannabis resin must have been derived from the smoking of cannabis, and that that smoking denoted possession of cannabis on 2 April 1975 or thereabouts. In our opinion the sheriff was not entitled on the material before him to draw either inference' (*Arnott* v *MacFarlane* 1976 SLT (Notes) 39).

The offences defined are producing and supplying. Producing includes manufacture, cultivation and any other method. What other methods there may be is a question of fact. Separation is one, at least if it is a chemical process.

> 'Mr Du Cann submitted that an agreement to separate a mixture so as to isolate a constituent substance cannot in law be an agreement to produce that substance. The interpretation section of the Act (section 37(1)) provides that the word "produce" shall have the meaning assigned to it, namely, "produce, where the reference is to producing a controlled drug, means producing it by manufacture, cultivation or any other method . . .". What the defendants intended to do, and tried to do, was to get cocaine from what they believed to be a mixture of two substances by the use of sulphuric acid. The separation was to be by a chemical process, not a mechanical one. We have no doubt at all that such a method of separation amounted to producing cocaine' (*Director of Public Prosecutions* v *Nock and Another* [1978] 3 WLR 57 per Lord Justice Lawton at p 61).

(The decision of the Court of Appeal was reversed by the House of Lords on other grounds.)

Supplying is defined as including distributing.

Section 37(2) defines misuse, though the term does not see the light of day after section 1 and there are no relevant penal provisions except in section 9, where the verbs used are smoke and use, not misuse.

Section 37(3) extends possession to things in the custody of another subject to the control of the first person. No doubt this formula does not preclude the same conclusion where the person having *de facto* custody is also in possession.

CHAPTER 17

Sections 38 to 40; and Schedules 5 and 6—Miscellaneous

Section 38 makes special provision for Northern Ireland, where the Ministry of Home Affairs takes over from the Home Secretary, under exceptions listed in subsection 1.

Section 39(1) and Schedule 5 contain savings and transitional provisions with particular reference to regulations made, licences granted and directions given under the Act's predecessors, which remain unaffected by the repeal of the Acts in question. Subsection 2 and Schedule 6 contain the repeals of the Drugs (Prevention of Misuse) Act 1964, and the Dangerous Drugs Act 1965 and 1967, which swept the board for the 1971 Act. By subsection 3 the Secretary of State is empowered to repeal or amend, by statutory instrument, any local Act where a provision 'is inconsistent with, or has become unnecessary or requires modification in consequence of, any provision of this Act'.

Section 40 contains the short title, extent and commencement. Commencement was delayed by more than two years from the passing of the Act on 27th May 1971 to 1st July 1973.

CHAPTER 18

Schedule 2

Schedule 2 is in four parts. Part I contains a description of Class A drugs in six paragraphs. Part II describes Class B drugs in four paragraphs. Part III describes Class C drugs similarly. Part IV provides definitions of six Class A drugs.

Class A drugs and Class B drugs are described as substances and products, Class C drugs only as substances. In each class, Paragraph 1 consists of an alphabetical listing. Paragraphs 2, 3 and 4 of Class A add, with minor exceptions, the stereoisomers, esters, ethers and salts of the listed drugs. In Classes B and C, paragraphs 2 and 3 bring in the stereoisomers and salts of their respective drugs.

Paragraph 5 of Part I and paragraph 4 of Parts II and III specify any preparation or other product containing any of the preceding entries. In this connection it must be noted that where a Class B drug is contained in a preparation designed for administration by injection it becomes *ipso facto* a Class A drug, and in consequence it leaves paragraph 4 of Part II and joins Part I in paragraph 6. The exceptions made by regulation 4 of and Schedule 1 to the principal regulations, in favour of extremely dilute preparations, should also be borne in mind.

The listings of the controlled drugs in Classes A, B and C are not homogeneous but a mixture of systematic chemical names, approved names for chemical compounds and words descriptive of naturally occurring substances. The more obscure substances are listed under their systematic chemical names. Where an approved name is current it has been used. Proprietary names are not used. These substances are synthetic. Naturally occurring substances in the lists include some which can be synthesised.

Few controlled drugs present problems of definition which are not resolved by expert testimony. Lord Diplock's classic exposition in *Goodchild* disposed at a stroke of an attempt to convict of possession of a Class A drug, a cannabinol derivative, a person in possession of the Class B drug cannabis, and explained generally the relationship between the naturally occurring substances and other substances in Schedule 2.

'The appellant, Goodchild, was found to be in possession of about ¼ lb of leaf and stalk of the cannabis plant. He was in due course charged on indictment with unlawful possession of controlled drugs contrary to section 5(2) of the Misuse of Drugs Act 1971. In three counts, which were laid in the alternative, the drugs were described as:

(1) a Class B controlled drug, namely, cannabis;
(2) a Class B controlled drug, namely, cannabis resin, and
(3) a Class A controlled drug, namely, a cannabinol derivative.

To understand what lies behind the application of these three different descriptions to the leaves and stalk of the cannabis plant it is necessary to understand a little of the botany and pharmacognosy of the plant *Cannabis sativa*, the botanical name for Indian hemp. It can be grown in a wide range of climates from tropical to temperate, including the United Kingdom, although its cultivation here is now prohibited by section 6 of the Misuse of Drugs Act 1971. It is one of the oldest of cultivated plants in Asia where its fibrous stalk is used for making rope and cloth, its seed for birdseed, fish-bait and cattle food, and oil from the seed is used for soap and paint making. The plant contains hallucinogenic ingredients, of which the chemical names are cannabinol and other substances of closely related molecular structure known to chemists as cannabinol derivatives. Of these one of the most potent and important is the tetrahydro derivative of cannabinol known familiarly as THC.

'*Cannabis sativa* is an annual. It grows to a height of 4 feet to 16 feet and flowers and fruits in October to November. The floral structure is formed at the top of the stems and is associated with a mass of small leaves known as vegetative tops. The lower parts of the plant also have a luxuriant growth of leaves which differ, and are to be distinguished, from the vegetative tops. The hallucinogenic ingredients are found in the resin of the plant. These are secreted in the hairs of trichomes on the leaves and on the flowering and fruiting tops. They are present in increasingly greater concentration as one moves from bottom to top of the plant. There is very little in the stem itself or in the ripe seeds. The concentration in the flowers is about two and a half times, and in the vegetative tops is about twice, the concentration in the lower leaves. The resin can be extracted from the plant by brushing it off the leaves and flowers. The hallucinogenic ingredients, cannabinol, THC, can then be extracted from the resin.

'The narcotic effect of the cannabis plant when subjected to no other treatment except drying thus varies with the portion of the plant that is used. The resin when separated from the plant contains a higher concentration of narcotic than the plant itself; while the highest narcotic content is to be found in cannabinol and cannabinol derivatives after they have been extracted from the resin.

'The Misuse of Drugs Act 1971 specifies in Schedule 2 what are the controlled drugs dealt with by the Act and allots them to three classes, A, B, and C. By section 5, it is an offence for a person to have a controlled drug in his possession. (This is subject to some exceptions that do not affect the instant case.) By section 25 and Schedule 4 the maximum penalty on prosecution on indictment for having possession of a controlled drug is progressive, according to the class of drug involved. It is a maximum of seven years' imprisonment for a Class A drug, five years for a Class B drug, and two years for a Class C drug.

'Schedule 2 contains a list of more than 120 different drugs. Most of these are in Class A, but cannabis and cannabis resin are listed in Class B. The majority of drugs in all three classes are synthetic substances only, that is to say they are man-made. All these are described in Schedule 2 by their scientific name which, to a skilled chemist, would indicate their molecular composition. There are, however, a few drugs which also occur naturally in plants, in fungi or in toads. Apart from cannabis the most important of these are opium and its narcotic constituents, which include such well-known alkaloids as morphine, thebaine and codeine. "Opium" is specified as a Class A drug under that name (which is not a scientific one). It consists of the coagulated juice of the opium poppy. All parts, except the seeds, of the opium poppy, are also included separately in the list of Class A drugs under the description "poppy straw"; while morphine, thebaine and other alkaloids contained in opium appear as separate items in Class A, and codeine as an item in Class B. Cocaine occurs naturally in coca leaf which is the leaf of a plant of the genus *Erythroxylon*: "coca leaf" and "cocaine" appear as separate items in Class A.

'These, together with cannabis are instances of where a naturally occurring substance which contains drugs specified by their scientific names in Schedule 2, is itself included as a separate item in the Schedule. There are other drugs listed under their scientific names which also occur in nature, but the natural source from which they can be obtained is not itself specified as a controlled drug in the Schedule. The following are examples.

'Lysergamide and lysergide occur in nature in the stalks, leaves and stem of the flowering plant known as Morning Glory; mescaline is found in the flowering heads of the Peyote Cactus; psilocin and psilocybin are to be found in a toadstool sometimes called the Mexican magic mushroom; and bufotenine occurs in the common toadstool and in three other varieties of toadstool; in the stalks and leaves of a semi-tropical plant, and even as a secretion of the common toad and natterjack toad' (*Director of Public Prosecutions* v *Goodchild* on appeal from *R* v *Goodchild* (No 2) [1978] 1 WLR 578 per Lord Diplock at p 579).

The case having been decided in the courts below before the redefinition of cannabis, the judge continued:

'Cannabis and cannabis resin are defined respectively in section 37 as follows: "''Cannabis' (except in the expression 'cannabis resin') means the flowering or fruiting tops of any plant of the genus *Cannabis* from which the resin has not been extracted, by whatever name they may be designated. 'Cannabis resin' means the separated resin, whether crude or purified, obtained from any plant of the genus *Cannabis*."

'They are included as items in the list of Class B drugs, but "Cannabinol, *except where contained in cannabis or cannabis resin*", is an item in Class A; so is "Cannabinol derivatives", an expression which is defined in Part IV of Schedule 2 as meaning "the following substances, *except where contained in cannabis or cannabis resin*, namely tetrahydro derivatives of cannabinol and 3-alkyl homologues of cannabinol or of its tetrahydro derivatives". The italics here are my own.

'Following upon the lists of controlled drugs specified by name in each of the three classes are additional paragraphs designed to incorporate in the class closely related chemical analogues of the listed drugs, such as stereoisomers, esters, ethers and salts. In addition there is a paragraph which incorporates within the relevant class "any preparation or other product containing a substance or product for the time being specified in [the list of drugs] above".

'At the first trial of the appellant in the Crown Court in June 1976, the expert scientific evidence was given in the form of written statements. It was common ground that it was not proved that any part of the leaf and stalk of the cannabis plant that had been found in his possession consisted of flowering or fruiting tops, but that it was proved, though by qualitative analysis only, that some THC was present in the specimen that had been subjected to analysis. Upon this evidence the judge ruled that the material found in the appellant's possession was cannabis. The judge also ruled that the appellant had in his possession a cannabinol derivative, THC, since this had been identified as a constituent of that material; but that the appellant was not in possession of any cannabis resin.

'In consequence of those rulings, the appellant pleaded guilty to the count of unlawful possession of the controlled Class B drug, "cannabis". He pleaded not guilty to the count of being in unlawful possession of the Class A drug "a cannabinol derivative". This count was left upon the file; and the appellant was sentenced to a fine of £100 or six months' imprisonment in default of payment on the count of unlawful possession of "cannabis".

'His appeal to the Court of Appeal against his conviction on this count was allowed on December 10, 1976, on the ground that the statutory definition of cannabis is restricted to the flowering or fruiting tops of the plant, and that leaf and stalk alone, in the absence of any such flowering or fruiting tops, does not fall within the definition. This was, in my view, obviously right. No argument to the contrary has been advanced before your Lordships' House.

'The appellant underwent a second trial upon the count remaining on the file which charged him with unlawful possession of "a cannabinol derivative". This was held in the Crown Court on March 3, 1977, and was presided over by a different judge. He too ruled that possession of leaf and stalk of the cannabis plant which proved on analysis to contain traces of THC amounted to possession of "a cannabinol derivative" within the meaning of section 5 of and Schedule 2 to the Act. Faced by this ruling the appellant once more changed his plea to guilty and was sentenced to a fine of £25. Once more too he appealed to the Court of Appeal who upheld the judge's ruling and certified that a point of law of general public importance was involved in the decision, namely:

'"Whether on the true construction of the Misuse of Drugs Act 1971 a person in possession of some leaves and stalk only from a plant or plants of the genus *Cannabis* may thereby be in possession of a cannabinol derivative naturally contained in those leaves, in contravention of section 5(1) of that Act."

'My Lords, the Misuse of Drugs Act 1971 is a criminal statute. It makes it an offence to be in possession of any of a long list of drugs and makes the gravity of the offence depend upon the class of listed drug into which the particular substance in his possession falls. Most, though not all, of the listed drugs in the three Classes A, B and C are described by their precise chemical name and are synthetic substances which do not occur in the natural state. In the case of these drugs there is no room for doubt or ambiguity. A substance either is the described synthetic drug (or a preparation or other product containing the described synthetic drug) or it is not. But there are some listed drugs which, although they can be synthesised, also occur in the natural state in plants, fungi or animals, and these include some of the most used narcotic drugs. It would not in my view be a natural use of language to say, for instance, that a person was in possession of morphine when what he really had was opium poppy straw from which whatever morphine content there might be in it had not yet been separated; nor do I think it would be apt use of language to describe the poppy straw as a "preparation or other product" containing morphine, since this expression is inappropriate to something that is found in nature as distinct from something that is man-made. Regarded simply from the point of view of language the matter is in my view put beyond doubt as respects the specific narcotic ingredients found in opium poppies by the inclusion in the list as separate items "opium" and "poppy straw" as well as morphine, thebaine, codeine and several other specified alkaloids which are or may be constituents of opium and of poppy straw. A similar indication of the meaning of references in the Schedule to specific drugs by their scientific names is to be found in the inclusion as separate items of "cocaine" itself and "coca leaf" which contains cocaine and from which cocaine can be extracted. I should conclude, therefore, that prima facie a reference in Schedule 2 to a specific drug by its scientific name does not include a reference to any naturally occurring substance of which the specific drug is a constituent but from which it has not yet been separated.

'So prima facie one would not suppose that possession of naturally occurring leaf and stalk of the plant *Cannabis sativa* of which a cannabinol derivative THC, was an unseparated constituent could be charged under the Act as possession of a "cannabinol derivative".

'The argument to the contrary depends upon the presence of the words of exception which I have italicised in the description of cannabinol in the list of Class A drugs and in the definition of cannabinol derivatives in Part IV of Schedule 2. These, it is suggested, give rise to an inference that but for the exception, cannabinol and cannabinol derivatives notwithstanding that they were contained in the natural substances cannabis or cannabis resin would have fallen within the definition; and that, accordingly, possession of cannabinol and cannabinol derivatives in however small a quantity if contained in any naturally occurring material other than one falling within the statutory definition of cannabis or cannabis resin would constitute the offence of possession of a Class A drug under the Act.

'My Lords, such inference as to the ambit of enacting words as can be derived from the presence of a proviso or an exception is notoriously a weak one, since the proviso or exception may have been inserted *per majorem cautelam.* In any event it must give way whenever the consequences of applying it would be irrational or unjust. In the instant case the consequence, at the time that the appellant was prosecuted, would have been that he would be liable to be convicted of the more serious offence of unlawful possession of a Class A drug, whereas if what he had had in his possession had included part of the flowering or fruiting tops of the cannabis plant and so contained a greater concentration of cannabinol derivatives, he could only have been convicted of the lesser offence of possession of a Class B drug, to wit cannabis itself.

'I would construe the Act in such a way as to avoid this irrational and unjust result. A man should not be gaoled upon an ambiguity. I would allow the appeal and quash the conviction of the appellant for the offence of unlawful possession of a cannabinol derivative.

'The question directly involved in this appeal will not arise again in future, as the definition of "cannabis" has now been amended by section 52 of the Criminal Justice Act 1977, so as to include the whole of the plant except the mature stalk and fibre produced from it and the seeds. However, similar questions may arise in relation to those other listed drugs described by their scientific names, but which also occur naturally in plants or fungi or animals. As I have already indicated, as a necessary step in the reasoning which has led me to the conclusion in the instant appeal that no offence was committed by the appellant, the offence of unlawful possession of any controlled drug described in Schedule 2 by its scientific name is not established by proof of possession of naturally occurring material of which the described drug is one of the constituents unseparated from the others. This is so whether or not the naturally occurring material is also included as another item in the list of controlled drugs' (ibid at p 581).

Mr Justice Lawton performed a similar service for cocaine, though the issues were less sharp in that both the naturally occurring substance, coca leaf, and the drug derived from it, cocaine, are in the same class, Class A. The decision relieves draftsmen of specifying, and prosecutors of proving, which stereoisomer, or other derivative, of a drug is present. So long as it can be described by the name in paragraph 1, it matters not if it can also be described in terms of paragraphs 2, 3, 4, or 5 of Part I.

'"Cocaine" can be a natural substance or a substance resulting from a chemical transformation; but both substances are cocaine. In our judgment the word "cocaine" as used in paragraph 1 is a generic word which includes within its ambit both the direct extracts of the coca leaf, the natural form, and whatever results from a chemical transformation. Paragraphs 2 to 5 of Part I of the Schedule, in our judgment, deal with the various kinds of substance which can result from chemical transformations. It is significant that in each of these paragraphs what is referred to is a chemical form "of a substance specified". What sections 2 and 5(3) are dealing with are "substances or products". This case is concerned with the substance "cocaine" which may have a number of forms but they are still cocaine' (*R* v *Greensmith* [1983] 1 WLR 1124 per Mr Justice Lawton at p 1127).

The same result was achieved for the Class B drug amphetamine in *R* v *Watts* in which the complicated issue was born of the fact that amphetamine has two steroisomers of which one but not the other has an alphabetical listing in paragraph 1. If it were the case that only the unlisted stereoisomer was present in the sample, *quid juris?* The provisions of paragraph 2, introducing the stereoisomers, justified conviction. The inclusion of one of the stereoisomers by name in paragraph 1 was otiose.

'We have come to the conclusion that greater effect will be given to the intention of Parliament, as disclosed by the content and context of the statute, by holding that amphetamine embraces both forms of it. The addition of dexamphetamine was unnecessary, and its inclusion is certainly not sufficiently strong to justify the application of the maxim already cited, which would have the startling effect that one of two stereoisomeric forms of amphetamine would be excluded from the category of drugs, quite apart from the fact that it would raise considerable practical difficulties in analysing the all too frequently small amount of the drugs that is available. Taking the question of construction in the round we have therefore come to the conclusion that the full generic meaning of the word "amphetamine", where it appears in paragraph 1 of Part 2 of Schedule 2 to the Act of 1971, should be given to it' (*R* v *Watts* [1984] 1 WLR 757 per Lord Justice Purchas at p 762).

The converse of the *Goodchild* dictum that possession of a drug was not proved by possession of a naturally occurring substance, such as poppy-straw, which contained it but from which it had not yet been extracted, is that possession of a naturally occurring substance is not proved by possession of a synthetic substance with the same chemical properties. The section 37(1) definition of cannabis is clearly descriptive of 'something that is found in nature' as distinct from something that is man-made' (Lord Diplock in *Goodchild*). Cannabis resin is obtained from the plant by mechanical separation, not chemical transformation. Hence the plant origin is an essential element of its identification and the relevant expert is a botanist, not a chemist. Where the latter, or any scientist, gives evidence of identification, he must be able to exclude synthetic production.

'The sheriff found as a fact that the respondent at the material time was in possession of various articles, all "contaminated with a brown syrupy material" and that that material on chemical analysis was "found to contain a purified form of cannabis resin", being "cannabis oil" which "had been reduced from cannabis resin". It was argued for the appellant that standing these findings in fact, the sheriff was bound to convict.

'The sheriff, however, made a further finding in fact in these terms: "There was no evidence from either of the two analysts (who gave evidence for the prosecution) that the material found in the possession of the respondent could be obtained only from a plant of the genus *Cannabis*." "Cannabis resin" is defined in section 37 of the Act as follows: "Cannabis resin means the separated resin, whether crude or purified, obtained from any plant of the genus *Cannabis*." The sheriff stated his reasons for his decision to acquit the respondent in the following terms: "Evidence that the drug could be produced synthetically was not investigated or enlarged upon by re-examination of either of the two analysts. Without further evidence I inferred that synthetic production meant that there were other methods of producing the chemical compound than as a derivative from the plant of the genus *Cannabis*. Neither was asked and neither gave evidence that the substance analysed could be obtained only from a plant of the genus *Cannabis*. When the respondent's solicitor had submitted his argument the procurator fiscal depute was given an opportunity to reply, but made no further submissions."

'In that situation we remitted to the sheriff to enquire "if any evidence was led in relation to the synthetic production of cannabis resin and if so which witnesses gave such evidence, and what was the effect of that evidence."

'In reply the sheriff stated that evidence was led for the prosecution from two forensic scientists. The effect of their evidence was that "the active principles of cannabis are three cannabinol drugs, tetrahydro cannabinol, cannabinol and cannabidiol which form an organic compound". The material found in possession of the respondent contained "a combination of drugs similar to the drugs in cannabis resin". There was evidence that as regards cannabis "the three active principles can be synthesised" and "there was no evidence from either of the witnesses which would exclude synthetic production of the material analysed".

'The question for us is, upon the evidence led, was the sheriff bound in law to convict? To prove its case against the respondent the Crown had to prove that he was in possession of "cannabis resin" as defined in section 37 of the

Act, that is, "the separated resin from any plant of the genus *Cannabis*". The learned advocate-depute accepted—rightly in our view—that the onus was upon the Crown to prove that the substance found in possession of the respondent came from "a plant of the genus cannabis" and was not synthetically produced. In our opinion upon the evidence here the sheriff was fully entitled to find that the Crown had failed to discharge that onus and accordingly to acquit the respondent' (*Herron* v *Meiklejohn*, Unreported, High Court of Justiciary, 25th May 1977).

The necessity for the hand of man to be involved before a naturally occurring substance can be held to be a preparation within the meaning of paragraph 5 of Part I of the Schedule was brought home in *Murray* v *MacNaughton*.

'The vegetable material is described by the sheriff as "magic mushrooms" and on the evidence no one could say that they had not been picked from the ground in the very state in which they were found in the bag in the appellant's pocket. In that state of the evidence, however, the sheriff was not dismayed for he went on to find that in spite of the evidence he was of the opinion that the dry "mushrooms", and they might have been picked in that very state, constituted a preparation in the popular sense of the word. What he says about it is this:

'"In order for the 'magic mushrooms' to be prepared, they have to cease to be in their natural growing state and in some way altered by the hand of man to put them into a condition in which they could be used for human consumption. To my mind even the picking of sun-and-air-dried 'magic mushrooms' from a field in autumn, then not bothering to chop or powder them or to separate the long bits of grass from them, followed by storing them in a plastic bag in a pocket where they remain until the following January, constitutes 'preparation' in the popular sense of 'making them ready for use.'"

'In effect the sheriff is telling us that because the appellant had merely picked dry "mushrooms" and had kept them in a bag without having done anything whatever to them, he had converted the "mushrooms" into a "preparation" containing psilocin within the meaning of the second Schedule to the Act.

'Now the first question we have to ask is whether the sheriff's reasoning in support of his finding that the appellant possessed the relevant "preparation" can bear close examination. The answer is plainly no. There was no evidence that the dry "mushrooms" had not been picked in the very condition in which they were found and the sheriff appreciated that before he could hold that the appellant was in possession of a preparation containing psilocin he had to be satisfied that the dry "mushrooms" had "in some way been altered by the hand of man to put them in a condition in which they could be used for human consumption". It is perfectly plain, however, that the sheriff reached the conclusion that the dry "mushrooms" were a preparation within the meaning of the second Schedule because they had not, on the evidence, been altered in any way by the hand of man. It is not surprising, accordingly, that the learned Lord Advocate who sought to support the result was not prepared to support the sheriff's reasoning. In this situation it would be open to this court to quash the conviction of the appellant on charge (2) simply because it flowed from such a gross error of approach on the part of the sheriff. We do not, however, do so for that reason only but also because the learned Lord Advocate's attempt to justify or support the conviction does not persuade us that the conviction should be allowed to stand. What the learned Lord Advocate said was this: "This was a man who possessed cannabis. He had picked the mushrooms, perhaps in the very condition in which they were found. He had kept them for three months. That is enough to show that he had done enough to them to turn mushrooms, which they still were, into a preparation within the meaning of the Act." We are not disposed to agree with that submission' (*Murray v MacNaughton* 1984 SCCR 361 per Lord Emslie, Lord Justice-General, at p 364).

The human intervention must exceed mere cropping. On very similar initial facts in *R v Stevens* [1981] Crim LR 568, the expert evidence was that the mushrooms, which the appellant had claimed were sun-dried, would have rotted unless dried artifically. Consequently, the resultant powder was a 'preparation'. That word was to be given its ordinary and natural meaning, not a technical one. The mushrooms had to cease to be in their natural growing state and in some way altered by the hand of man to put them into a condition in which they could be used for human consumption. The appellant's conviction was upheld.

APPENDIX I

Misuse of Drugs Act 1971

CHAPTER 38

ARRANGEMENT OF SECTIONS

The Advisory Council on the Misuse of Drugs

n Act to make new provision with respect to dangerous or otherwise harmful
drugs and related matters, and for purposes connected therewith.

[27th May 1971]

B E IT ENACTED by the Queen's most Excellent Majesty, by and with the
advice and consent of the Lords Spiritual and Temporal, and
Commons, in this present Parliament assembled, and by the authority
the same, as follows:—

The Advisory Council on the Misuse of Drugs

1.—(1) There shall be constituted in accordance with Schedule 1 to this Act The Advisory
Advisory Council on the Misuse of Drugs (in this Act referred to as "the Council on the
dvisory Council"); and the supplementary provisions contained in that Misuse of Drugs.
:hedule shall have effect in relation to the Council.

(2) It shall be the duty of the Advisory Council to keep under review the
tuation in the United Kingdom with respect to drugs which are being or
)pear to them likely to be misused and of which the misuse is having or
)pears to them capable of having harmful effects sufficient to constitute a
)cial problem, and to give to any one or more of the Ministers, where either
te Council consider it expedient to do so or they are consulted by the Minister
: Ministers in question, advice on measures (whether or not involving
teration of the law) which in the opinion of the Council ought to be taken for
reventing the misuse of such drugs or dealing with social problems connected
ith their misuse, and in particular on measures which in the opinion of the
ouncil, ought to be taken—

(a) for restricting the availability of such drugs or supervising the
arrangements for their supply;

(b) for enabling persons affected by the misuse of such drugs to obtain
proper advice, and for securing the provision of proper facilities and
services for the treatment, rehabilitation and after-care of such
persons;

(c) for promoting co-operation between the various professional and
community services which in the opinion of the Council have a part
to play in dealing with social problems connected with the misuse of
such drugs;

(d) for educating the public (and in particular the young) in the dangers of
misusing such drugs, and for giving publicity to those dangers; and

(e) for promoting research into, or otherwise obtaining information about,
any matter which in the opinion of the Council is of relevance for the
purpose of preventing the misuse of such drugs or dealing with any
social problem connected with their misuse.

(3) It shall also be the duty of the Advisory Council to consider any matter
lating to drug dependence or the misuse of drugs which may be referred to
tem by any one or more of the Ministers and to advise the Minister or
linisters in question thereon, and in particular to consider and advise the

Secretary of State with respect to any communication referred by him to t
Council, being a communication relating to the control of any dangerous
otherwise harmful drug made to Her Majesty's Government in the Unit
Kingdom by any organisation or authority established by or under any trea
convention or other agreement or arrangement to which that Government is f
the time being a party.

(4) In this section "the Ministers" means the Secretary of State for the Hor
Department, the Secretaries of State respectively concerned with health
England, Wales and Scotland, the Secretaries of State respectively concern
with education in England, Wales and Scotland, the Minister of Home Affa
for Northern Ireland, the Minister of Health and Social Services for Northe
Ireland and the Minister of Education for Northern Ireland.

Controlled drugs and their classification

Controlled drugs
and their
classification for
purposes of this
Act.

2.—(1) In this Act—

(a) the expression "controlled drug" means any substance or product f
the time being specified in Part I, II or III of Schedule 2 to this A
and

(b) the expressions "Class A drug", "Class B drug" and "Class C dru
mean any of the substances and products for the time being specifi
respectively in Part I, Part II and Part III of that Schedule;

and the provisions of Part IV of that Schedule shall have effect with respect
the meanings of expressions used in that Schedule.

(2) Her Majesty may by Order in Council make such amendments
Schedule 2 to this Act as may be requisite for the purpose of adding a
substance or product to, or removing any substance or product from, any
Parts I to III of that Schedule, including amendments for securing that
substance or product is for the time being specified in a particular one of tho
Parts or for inserting any substance or product into any of those Parts in whic
no substance or product is for the time being specified.

(3) An Order in Council under this section may amend Part IV of Schedu
2 to this Act, and may do so whether or not it amends any other Part of th
Schedule.

(4) An Order in Council under this section may be varied or revoked by
subsequent Order in Council thereunder.

(5) No recommendation shall be made to Her Majesty in Council to make
Order under this section unless a draft of the Order has been laid befo
Parliament and approved by a resolution of each House of Parliament; and t
Secretary of State shall not lay a draft of such an Order before Parliament exce
after consultation with or on the recommendation of the Advisory Council.

Restriction of
importation and
exportation of
controlled drugs.

Restrictions relating to controlled drugs etc.

3.—(1) Subject to subsection (2) below—

(a) the importation of a controlled drug; and

(*b*) the exportation of a controlled drug,

hereby prohibited.

2) Subsection (1) above does not apply—

(*a*) to the importation or exportation of a controlled drug which is for the time being excepted from paragraph (*a*) or, as the case may be, paragraph (*b*) of subsection (1) above by regulations under section 7 of this Act; or

(*b*) to the importation or exportation of a controlled drug under and in accordance with the terms of a licence issued by the Secretary of State and in compliance with any conditions attached thereto.

4.—(1) Subject to any regulations under section 7 of this Act for the time ing in force, it shall not be lawful for a person— *Restriction of production and supply of controlled drugs.*

(*a*) to produce a controlled drug; or

(*b*) to supply or offer to suply a controlled drug to another.

2) Subject to section 28 of this Act, it is an offence for a person—

(*a*) to produce a controlled drug in contravention of subsection (1) above; or

(*b*) to be concerned in the production of such a drug in contravention of that subsection by another.

3) Subject to section 28 of this Act, it is an offence for a person—

(*a*) to supply or offer to supply a controlled drug to another in contravention of subsection (1) above; or

(*b*) to be concerned in the supplying of such a drug to another in contravention of that subsection; or

(*c*) to be concerned in the making to another in contravention of that subsection of an offer to supply such a drug.

5.—(1) Subject to any regulations under section 7 of this Act for the time ing in force, it shall not be lawful for a person to have a controlled drug in possession. *Restriction of possession of controlled drugs.*

(2) Subject to section 28 of this Act and to subsection (4) below, it is an offence r a person to have a controlled drug in his possession in contravention of bsection (1) above.

(3) Subject to section 28 of this Act, it is an offence for a person to have a ntrolled drug in his possession, whether lawfully or not, with intent to supply to another in contravention of section 4(1) of this Act.

(4) In any proceedings for an offence under subsection (2) above in which it proved that the accused had a controlled drug in his possession, it shall be defence for him to prove—

(*a*) that, knowing or suspecting it to be a controlled drug, he took possession of it for the purpose of preventing another from committing or continuing to commit an offence in connection with that drug and that as soon as possible after taking possession of it he took all such steps are were reasonably open to him to destroy the drug

or to deliver it into the custody of a person lawfully entitled to ta
custody of it; or

(b) that, knowing or suspecting it to be a controlled drug, he to
possession of it for the purpose of delivering it into the custody of
person lawfully entitled to take custody of it and that as soon
possible after taking possession of it he took all such steps as we
reasonably open to him to deliver it into the custody of such a perso

(5) Subsection (4) above shall apply in the case of proceedings for an offen
under section 19(1) of this Act consisting of an attempt to commit an offen
under subsection (2) above as it applies in the case of proceedings for an offen
under subsection (2), subject to the following modifications, that is to say—

(a) for the references to the accused having in his possession, and to h
taking possession of, a controlled drug there shall be substitute
respectively references to his attempting to get, and to his attemptir
to take, possession of such a drug; and

(b) in paragraphs (a) and (b) the words from "and that as soon as possible
onwards shall be omitted.

(6) Nothing in subsection (4) or (5) above shall prejudice any defence whic
it is open to a person charged with an offence under this section to raise apa
from that subsection.

Restriction of cultivation of cannabis plant.	**6.**—(1) Subject to any regulations under section 7 of this Act for the tim being in force, it shall not be lawful for a person to cultivate any plant of th genus *Cannabis*.

(2) Subject to section 28 of this Act, it is an offence to cultivate any such plan
in contravention of subsection (1) above.

Authorisation of activities otherwise unlawful under foregoing provisions.	**7.**—(1) The Secretary of State may by regulations—

(a) except from section 3(1)(a) or (b), 4(1)(a) or (b) or 5(1) of this Act suc
controlled drugs as may be specified in the regulations; and

(b) make such other provision as he thinks fit for the purpose of makin
it lawful for persons to do things which under any of the followin
provisions of this Act, that is to say sections 4(1), 5(1) and 6(1),
would otherwise be unlawful for them to do.

(2) Without prejudice to the generality of paragraph (b) of subsection (
above, regulations under that subsection authorising the doing of any suc
thing as is mentioned in that paragraph may in particular provide for the doin
of that thing to be lawful—

(a) if it is done under and in accordance with the terms of a licence or othe
authority issued by the Secretary of State and in compliance with an
conditions attached thereto; or

(b) if it is done in compliance with such conditions as may be prescribe

(3) Subject to subsection (4) below, the Secretary of State shall so exercise h
power to make regulations under subsection (1) above as to secure—

(*a*) that it is not unlawful under section 4(1) of this Act for a doctor, dentist, veterinary practitioner or veterinary surgeon, acting in his capacity as such, to prescribe, administer, manufacture, compound or supply a controlled drug, or for a pharmacist or a person lawfully conducting a retail pharmacy business, acting in either case in his capacity as such, to manufacture, compound or supply a controlled drug; and

(*b*) that it is not unlawful under section 5(1) of this Act for a doctor, dentist, veterinary practitioner, veterinary surgeon, pharmacist or person lawfully conducting a retail pharmacy business to have a controlled drug in his possession for the purpose of acting in his capacity as such.

(4) If in the case of any controlled drug the Secretary of State is of the opinion that it is in the public interest—

(*a*) for production, supply and possession of that drug to be either wholly unlawful or unlawful except for purposes of research or other special purposes; or

(*b*) for it to be unlawful for practitioners, pharmacists and persons lawfully conducting retail pharmacy businesses to do in relation to that drug any of the things mentioned in subsection (3) above except under a licence or other authority issued by the Secretary of State,

he may by order designate that drug as a drug to which this subsection applies; and while there is in force an order under this subsection designating a controlled drug as one to which this subsection applies, subsection (3) above shall not apply as regards that drug.

(5) Any order under subsection (4) above may be varied or revoked by a subsequent order thereunder.

(6) The power to make orders under subsection (4) above shall be exercisable by statutory instrument, which shall be subject to annulment in pursuance of resolution of either House of Parliament.

(7) The Secretary of State shall not make any order under subsection (4) above except after consultation with or on the recommendation of the Advisory Council.

(8) References in this section to a person's "doing" things include references to his having things in his possession.

(9) In its application to Northern Ireland this section shall have effect as if for references to the Secretary of State there were substituted references to the Ministry of Home Affairs for Northern Ireland and as if for subsection (6) there were substituted—

"(6) Any order made under subsection (4) above by the Ministry of Home Affairs for Northern Ireland shall be subject to negative resolution within the meaning of section 41(6) of the Interpretation Act (Northern Ireland) 1954 c. 33 1954 as if it were a statutory instrument within the meaning of that Act." (N.I.).

Miscellaneous offences involving controlled drugs etc.

Occupiers etc. of
premises to be
punishable for
permitting certain
activities to take
place there.

8. A person commits an offence if, being the occupier or concerned in the management of any premises, he knowingly permits or suffers any of the following activities to take place on those premises, that is to say—

    (*a*) producing or attempting to produce a controlled drug in contravention of section 4(1) of this Act;

    (*b*) supplying or attempting to supply a controlled drug to another contravention of section 4(1) of this Act, or offering to supply controlled drug to another in contravention of section 4(1);

    (*c*) preparing opium for smoking;

    (*d*) smoking cannabis, cannabis resin or prepared opium.

Prohibition of
certain activities
etc. relating to
opium.

9. Subject to section 28 of this Act, it is an offence for a person—

    (*a*) to smoke or otherwise use prepared opium; or

    (*b*) to frequent a place used for the purpose of opium smoking; or

    (*c*) to have in his possession—

        (i) any pipes or other utensils made or adapted for use connection with the smoking of opium, being pipes or utensils which have been used by him or with his knowledge and permission in that connection or which he intends to use or permit others to use in that connection; or

        (ii) any utensils which have been used by him or with his knowledge and permission in connection with the preparation of opium for smoking.

Powers of Secretary of State for preventing misuse of controlled drugs

Power to make
regulations for
preventing misuse
of controlled
drugs.

10.—(1) Subject to the provisions of this Act, the Secretary of State may by regulations make such provision as appears to him necessary or expedient for preventing the misuse of controlled drugs.

(2) Without prejudice to the generality of subsection (1) above, regulations under this section may in particular make provision—

    (*a*) for requiring precautions to be taken for the safe custody of controlled drugs;

    (*b*) for imposing requirements as to the documentation of transactions involving controlled drugs, and for requiring copies of documents relating to such transactions to be furnished to the prescribed authority;

    (*c*) for requiring the keeping of records and the furnishing of information with respect to controlled drugs in such circumstances and in such manner as may be prescribed;

    (*d*) for the inspection of any precautions taken or records kept in pursuance of regulations under this section;

    (*e*) as to the packaging and labelling of controlled drugs;

(*f*) for regulating the transport of controlled drugs and the methods used for destroying or otherwise disposing of such drugs when no longer required;

(*g*) for regulating the issue of prescriptions containing controlled drugs and the supply of controlled drugs on prescriptions, and for requiring persons issuing or dispensing prescriptions containing such drugs to furnish to the prescribed authority such information relating to those prescriptions as may be prescribed;

(*h*) for requiring any doctor who attends a person who he considers, or has reasonable grounds to suspect, is addicted (within the meaning of the regulations) to controlled drugs of any description to furnish to the prescribed authority such particulars with respect to that person as may be prescribed;

(*i*) for prohibiting any doctor from administering, supplying and authorising the administration and supply to persons so addicted, and from prescribing for such persons, such controlled drugs as may be prescribed, except under and in accordance with the terms of a licence issued by the Secretary of State in pursuance of the regulations.

1.—(1) Without prejudice to any requirement imposed by regulations made pursuance of section 10(2)(*a*) of this Act, the Secretary of State may by notice writing served on the occupier of any premises on which controlled drugs or are proposed to be kept give directions as to the taking of precautions or ther precautions for the safe custody of any controlled drugs of a description cified in the notice which are kept on those premises. Power to direct special precautions for safe custody of controlled drugs to be taken at certain premises.

2) It is an offence to contravene any directions given under subsection (1) ve.

2.—(1) Where a person who is a practitioner or pharmacist has after the ning into operation of this subsection been convicted— Directions prohibiting prescribing, supply etc. of controlled drugs by practitioners etc. convicted of certain offences. 1965 c. 15. 1979 c. 2.

(*a*) of an offence under this Act or under the Dangerous Drugs Act 1965 or any enactment repealed by that Act; or

(*b*) of an offence under section 45, 56 or 304 of the Customs and Excise Act 1952, or under section 50, 68 or 170 of the Customs and Excise Management Act 1979, in connection with a prohibition of or restriction on importation or exportation of a controlled drug having effect by virtue of section 3 of this Act or which had effect by virtue of any provision contained in or repealed by the Dangerous Drugs Act 1965,

Secretary of State may give a direction under subsection (2) below in respect that person.

2) A direction under this subsection in respect of a person shall—

(*a*) if that person is a practitioner, be a direction prohibiting him from having in his possession, prescribing, administering, manufacturing, compounding and supplying and from authorising the administration and supply of such controlled drugs as may be specified in the direction;

(*b*) if that person is a pharmacist, be a direction prohibiting him fr
having in his possession, manufacturing, compounding and supply
and from supervising and controlling the manufacture, compound
and supply of such controlled drugs as may be specified in
direction.

(3) The Secretary of State may at any time give a direction cancelling
suspending any direction given by him under subsection (2) above, or cancell
any direction of his under this subsection by which a direction so given
suspended.

(4) The Secretary of State shall cause a copy of any direction given by h
under this section to be served on the person to whom it applies, and shall ca
notice of any such direction to be published in the London, Edinburgh a
Belfast Gazettes.

(5) A direction under this section shall take effect when a copy of it is serv
on the person to whom it applies.

(6) It is an offence to contravene a direction given under subsection (2) abo

1968 c. 67.

(7) In section 80 of the Medicines Act 1968 (under which a body corpor
carrying on a retail pharmacy business may be disqualified for the purposes
Part IV of that Act and have its premises removed from the register kept und
section 75 of that Act, where that body or any member of the board of that bo
or any officer or any employee of that body is convicted of an offence und
any of the relevant Acts as defined in subsection (5)), for the words "and t
Act" in subsection (5) there shall be substituted the words "this Act and
Misuse of Drugs Act 1971".

Directions
prohibiting
prescribing,
supply etc. of
controlled drugs
by practitioners
in other cases.

13.—(1) In the event of a contravention by a doctor of regulations made
pursuance of paragraph (*h*) or (*i*) of section 10(2) of this Act, or of the ter
of a licence issued under regulations made in pursuance of the said paragra
(*i*), the Secretary of State may, subject to and in accordance with section 14
this Act, give a direction in respect of the doctor concerned prohibiting h
from prescribing, administering and supplying and from authorising
administration and supply of such controlled drugs as may be specified in
direction.

(2) If the Secretary of State is of the opinion that a practitioner is or has a
the coming into operation of this subsection been prescribing, administering
supplying or authorising the administration or supply of any controlled dr
in an irresponsible manner, the Secrtary of State may, subject to and
accordance with section 14 or 15 of this Act, give a direction in respect of
practitioner concerned prohibiting him from prescribing, administering a
supplying and from authorising the administration and supply of su
controlled drugs as may be specified in the direction.

(3) A contravention such as is mentioned in subsection (1) above does not
such constitute an offence, but it is an offence to contravene a direction giv
under subsection (1) or (2) above.

4.—(1) If the Secretary of State considers that there are grounds for giving a direction under subsection (1) of section 13 of this Act on account of such a contravention by a doctor as is there mentioned, or for giving a direction under subsection (2) of that section on account of such conduct by a practitioner as mentioned in the said subsection (2), he may refer the case to a tribunal constituted for the purpose in accordance with the following provisions of this ; and it shall be the duty of the tribunal to consider the case and report on to the Secretary of State. Investigation where grounds for a direction under s 13 are considered to exist.

2) In this Act "the respondent", in relation to a reference under this section, ans the doctor or other practitioner in respect of whom the reference is made.

3) Where—

(*a*) in the case of a reference relating to the giving of a direction under the said subsection (1), the tribunal finds that there has been no such contravention as aforesaid by the respondent or finds that there has been such a contravention but does not recommend the giving of a direction under that subsection in respect of the respondent; or

(*b*) in the case of a reference relating to the giving of a direction under the said subsection (2), the tribunal finds that there has been no such conduct as aforesaid by the respondent or finds that there has been such conduct by the respondent but does not recommend the giving of a direction under the said subsection (2) in respect of him,

Secretary of State shall cause notice to that effect to be served on the pondent.

4) Where the tribunal finds—

(*a*) in the case of a reference relating to the giving of a direction under the said subsection (1), that there has been such a contravention as aforesaid by the respondent; or

(*b*) in the case of a reference relating to the giving of a direction under the said subsection (2), that there has been such conduct as aforesaid by the respondent,

l considers that a direction under the subsection in question should be given respect of him, the tribunal shall include in its report a recommendation to t effect indicating the controlled drugs which it considers should be cified in the direction or indicating that the direction should specify all trolled drugs.

5) Where the tribunal makes such a recommendation as aforesaid, the retary of State shall cause a notice to be served on the respondent stating ether or not he proposes to give a direction pursuant thereto, and where he s so propose the notice shall—

(*a*) set out the terms of the proposed direction; and

(*b*) inform the respondent that consideration will be given to any representations relating to the case which are made by him in writing to the Secretary of State within the period of twenty-eight days beginning with the date of service of the notice.

(6) If any such representations are received by the Secretary of State with the period aforesaid, he shall refer the case to an advisory body constituted the purpose in accordance with the following provisions of this Act; and it sh be the duty of the advisory body to consider the case and to advise the Secreta of State as to the exercise of his powers under subsection (7) below.

(7) After the expiration of the said period of twenty-eight days and, in the ca of a reference to an advisory body under subsection (6) above, after consideri the advice of that body, the Secretary of State may either—

> (*a*) give in respect of the respondent a direction under subsection (1) or, the case may be, subsection (2) of section 13 of this Act specifying or any of the controlled drugs indicated in the recommendation of t tribunal; or

> (*b*) order that the case be referred back to the tribunal, or referred to anoth tribunal constituted as aforesaid; or

> (*c*) order that no further proceedings under this section shall be taken the case.

(8) Where a case is referred or referred back to a tribunal in pursuance subsection (7) above, the provisions of subsections (2) to (7) above shall app as if the case had been referred to the tribunal in pursuance of subsection above, and any finding, recommendation or advice previously made or given respect of the case in pursuance of those provisions shall be disregarded.

Temporary
directions under
s. 13(2).

15.—(1) If the Secretary of State considers that there are grounds for givi a direction under subsection (2) of section 13 of this Act in respect of practitioner on account of such conduct by him as is mentioned in t subsection and that the circumstances of the case require such a direction to given with the minimum of delay, he may, subject to the following provisio of this section, give such a direction in respect of him by vitrue of this secti and a direction under section 13(2) given by virtue of this section may spec such controlled drugs as the Secretary of State thinks fit.

(2) Where the Secretary of State proposes to give such a direction as aforesa by virtue of this section, he shall refer the case to a professional pa constituted for the purpose in accordance with the following provisions of t Act; and

> (*a*) it shall be the duty of the panel, after affording the respondent opportunity of appearing before and being heard by the panel, consider the circumstances of the case, so far as known to it, and report to the Secretary of State whether the information before panel appears to it to afford reasonable grounds for thinking that th has been such conduct by the respondent as is mentioned in secti 13(2) of this Act; and

> (*b*) the Secretary of State shall not by virtue of this section give such direction as aforesaid in respect of the respondent unless the pa reports that the information before it appears to it to afford reasona grounds for so thinking.

) In this Act "the respondent", in relation to a reference under subsection
above, means the practitioner in respect of whom the reference is made.

) Where the Secretary of State gives such a direction as aforesaid by virtue
his section he shall, if he has not already done so, forthwith refer the case
tribunal in accordance with section 14(1) of this Act.

) Subject to subsection (6) below, the period of operation of a direction
er section 13(2) of this Act given by virtue of this section shall be a period
ix weeks beginning with the date on which the direction takes effect.

) Where a direction under section 13(2) of this Act has been given in respect
person by virtue of this section and the case has been referred to a tribunal
ccordance with section 14(1), the Secretary of State may from time to time,
otice in writing served on the person to whom the direction applies, extend
urther extend the period of operation of the direction for a further twenty-
t days from the time when that period would otherwise expire, but shall
so extend or further extend that period without the consent of that tribunal,
f the case has been referred to another tribunal in pursuance of section 14(7)
his Act, of that other tribunal.

) A direction under section 13(2) of this Act given in respect of a person
virtue of this section shall (unless previously cancelled under section 16(3)
his Act) cease to have effect on the occurence of any of the following events,
is to say—

(a) the service on that person of a notice under section 14(3) of this Act
relating to his case;

(b) the service on that person of a notice under section 14(5) of this Act
relating to his case stating that the Secretary of State does not propose
to give a direction under section 13(2) of this Act pursuant to a
recommendation of the tribunal that such a direction should be given;

(c) the service on that person of a copy of such a direction given in respect
of him in pursuance of section 14(7) of this Act;

(d) the making of an order by the Secretary of State in pursuance of section
14(7) that no further proceedings under section 14 shall be taken in
the case;

(e) the expiration of the period of operation of the direction under section
13(2) given by virtue of this section.

6.—(1) The provisions of Schedule 3 to this Act shall have effect with respect Provisions
he constitution and procedure of any tribunal, advisory body or professional supplementary to
el appointed for the purposes of section 14 or 15 of this Act, and with ss. 14 and 15.
ect to the other matters there mentioned.

) The Secretary of State shall cause a copy of any order or direction made
iven by him in pursuance of section 14(7) of this Act or any direction given
him by virtue of the said section 15 to be served on the person to whom it
lies and shall cause notice of any such direction, and a copy of any notice
ed under section 15(6) of this Act, to be published in the London,
nburgh and Belfast Gazettes.

(3) The Secretary of State may at any time give a direction—

(*a*) cancelling or suspending any direction given by him in pursuance
section 14(7) of this Act or cancelling any direction of his under
subsection by which a direction so given is suspended; or

(*b*) cancelling any direction given by him by virtue of section 15 of this *A*

and shall cause a copy of any direction of his under this subsection to be ser
on the person to whom it applies and notice of it to be published as aforesa

(4) A direction given under section 13(1) or (2) of this Act or under subsect
(3) above shall take effect when a copy of it is served on the person to wh
it applies.

Power to obtain
information from
doctors,
pharmacists etc.
in certain
circumstances.
1968 c. 67.

17.—(1) If it appears to the Secretary of State that there exists in any are;
Great Britain a social problem caused by the extensive misuse of dangerous
otherwise harmful drugs in that area, he may by notice in writing served
any doctor or pharmacist practising in or in the vicinity of that area, or on
person carrying on a retail pharmacy business within the meaning of
Medicines Act 1968 at any premises situated in or in the vicinity of that a;
require him to furnish to the Secretary of State, with respect to any such dr
specified in the notice and as regards any period so specified, such particul
as may be so specified relating to the quantities in which and the number ;
frequency of the occasions on which those drugs—

(*a*) in the case of a doctor, where prescribed, administered or supplied by h

(*b*) in the case of a pharmacist, were supplied by him; or

(*c*) in the case of a person carrying on a retail pharmacy business, w
supplied in the course of that business at any premises so situa
which may be specified in the notice.

(2) A notice under this section may require any such particulars to
furnished in such a manner and within such a time as may be specified in
notice and, if served on a pharmacist or person carrying on a retail pharm
business, may require him to furnish the names and addresses of doctors
whose prescriptions any dangerous or otherwise harmful drugs to which
notice relates were supplied, but shall not require any person to furnish ;
particulars relating to the identity of any person for or to whom any such d;
has been prescribed, administered or supplied.

(3) A person commits an offence if without resonable excuse (proof of wh
shall lie on him) he fails to comply with any requirement to which he is subj
by virtue of subsection (1) above.

(4) A person commits an offence if in purported compliance with
requirement imposed under this section he gives any information which
knows to be false in a material particular or recklessly gives any informat
which is so false.

(5) In its application to Northern Ireland this section shall have effect a
for the references to Great Britain and the Secretary of State there w
substituted respectively references to Northern Ireland and the Ministry
Home Affairs for Northern Ireland.

Miscellaneous offences and powers

18.—(1) It is an offence for a person to contravene any regulations made under this Act other than regulations made in pursuance of section 10(2)(*h*) or (*i*).

(2) It is an offence for a person to contravene a condition or other term of a licence issued under section 3 of this Act or of a licence or other authority issued under regulations made under this Act, not being a licence issued under regulations made in pursuance of section 10(2)(*i*).

(3) A person commits an offence if, in purported compliance with any obligation to give information to which he is subject under or by virtue of regulations made under this Act, he gives any information which he knows to be false in a material particular or recklessly gives any information which is so false.

(4) A person commits an offence if, for the purpose of obtaining, whether for himself or another, the issue or renewal of a licence or other authority under this Act or under any regulations made under this Act, he—

(*a*) makes any statement or gives any information which he knows to be false in a material particular or recklessly gives any information which is so false; or

(*b*) produces or otherwise makes use of any book, record or other document which to his knowledge contains any statement or information which he knows to be false in a material particular.

19. It is an offence for a person to attempt to commit an offence under any other provision of this Act or to incite or attempt to incite another to commit such an offence.

20. A person commits an offence if in the United Kingdom he assists in or induces the commission in any place outside the United Kingdom of an offence punishable under the provisions of a corresponding law in force in that place.

21. Where any offence under this Act committed by a body corporate is proved to have been committed with the consent or connivance of, or to be attributable to any neglect on the part of, any director, manager, secretary or other similar officer of the body corporate, or any person purporting to act in any such capacity, he as well as the body corporate shall be guilty of that offence and shall be liable to be proceeded against accordingly.

22. The Secretary of State may by regulations make provision—

(*a*) for excluding in such cases as may be prescribed—

(i) the application of any provision of this Act which creates an offence; or

(ii) the application of any of the following provisions of the Customs and Excise Management Act 1979, that is to say, sections 50(1) to (4), 68(2) and (3) and 170, in so far as they apply in relation to a prohibition or restriction on importation or exportation having effect by virtue of section 3 of this Act;

(b) for applying any of the provisions of sections 14 to 16 of this Act a Schedule 3 thereto, with such modifications (if any) as may prescribed—

(i) in relation to any proposal by the Secretary of State to give direction under section 12(2) of this Act; or

(ii) for such purposes of regulations under this Act as may prescribed;

(c) for the application of any of the provisions of this Act or regulations orders thereunder to servants or agents of the Crown, subject to su exceptions, adaptations and modifications as may be prescribed.

Law enforcement and punishment of offences

Powers to search
and obtain
evidence.

23.—(1) A constable or other person authorised in that behalf by a general special order of the Secretary of State (or in Northern Ireland either of t Secretary of State or the Ministry of Home Affairs for Northern Ireland) sha for the purposes of the execution of this Act, have power to enter the premi of a person carrying on business as a producer or supplier of any controll drugs and to demand the production of, and to inspect, any books or docume relating to dealings in any such drugs and to inspect any stocks of any su drugs.

(2) If a constable has reasonable grounds to suspect that any person is possession of a controlled drug in contravention of this Act or of any regulatic made thereunder, the constable may—

(a) search that person, and detain him for the purpose of searching hi

(b) search any vehicle or vessel in which the constable suspects that t drug may be found, and for that purpose require the person in cont of the vehicle or vessel to stop it;

(c) seize and detain, for the purposes of proceedings under this A anything found in the course of the search which appears to t constable to be evidence of an offence under this Act.

1968 c. 59.

In this subsection "vessel" includes a hovercraft within the meaning of t Hovercraft Act 1968; and nothing in this subsection shall prejudice any pow of search or any power to seize or detain property which is exercisable by constable apart from this subsection.

(3) If a justice of the peace (or in Scotland a justice of the peace, a magistr or a sheriff) is satisfied by information on oath that there is reasonable grou for suspecting—

(a) that any controlled drugs are, in contravention of this Act or of a regulations made thereunder, in the possession of a person on a premises; or

(b) that a document directly or indirectly relating to, or connected with transaction or dealing which was, or an intended transaction dealing which would if carried out be, an offence under this Act, in the case of a transaction or dealing carried out or intended to carried out in a place outside the United Kingdom, an offence agai the provisions of a corresponding law in force in that place, is in the possession of a person on any premises,

e may grant a warrant authorising any constable acting for the police area in which the premises are situated at any time or times within one month from ne date of the warrant, to enter, if need be by force, the premises named in the varrant, and to search the premises and any persons found therein and, if there ; reasonable ground for suspecting that an offence under this Act has been ommitted in relation to any controlled drugs found on the premises or in the ossession of any such persons, or that a document so found is such a document ;s is mentioned in paragraph (b) above, to seize and detain those drugs or that ocument, as the case may be.

(4) A person commits an offence if he—

(a) intentionally obstructs a person in the exercise of his powers under this section; or

(b) conceals from a person acting in the exercise of his powers under subsection (1) above any such books, documents, stocks or drugs as are mentioned in that subsection; or

(c) without reasonable excuse (proof of which shall lie on him) fails to produce any such books or documents as are so mentioned where their production is demanded by a person in the exercise of his powers under that subsection.

(5) In its application to Northern Ireland subsection (3) above shall have effect s if the words "acting for the police area in which the premises are situated" vere omitted.

24.—(1) A constable may arrest without warrant a person who has committed, Power of arrest. or whom the constable, with reasonable cause, suspects to have committed, an offence under this Act, if—

(a) he, with reasonable cause, believes that that person will abscond unless arrested; or

(b) the name and address of that person are unknown to, and cannot be ascertained by, him; or

(c) he is not satisfied that a name and address furnished by that person as his name and address are true.

(2) This section shall not prejudice any power of arrest conferred by law apart rom this section.

25.—(1) Schedule 4 to this Act shall have effect, in accordance with subsection Prosecution and 2) below, with respect to the way in which offences under this Act are punishment of punishable on conviction. offences.

(2) In relation to an offence under a provision of this Act specified in the first olumn of the Schedule (the general nature of the offence being described in he second column)—

(a) the third column shows whether the offence is punishable on summary conviction or on indictment or in either way;

(*b*) the fourth, fifth and sixth columns show respectively the punishment which may be imposed on a person convicted of the offence in the way specified in relation thereto in the third column (that is to say summarily or on indictment) according to whether the controlled drug in relation to which the offence was committed was a Class A drug a Class B drug or a Class C drug; and

(*c*) the seventh column shows the punishments which may be imposed on a person convicted of the offence in the way specified in relation thereto in the third column (that is to say, summarily or on indictment), whether or not the offence was committed in relation to a controlled drug and, if it was so committed, irrespective of whether the drug was a Class A drug, a Class B drug or a Class C drug;

and in the fourth, fifth, sixth and seventh columns a reference to a period gives the maximum term of imprisonment and a reference to a sum of money the maximum fine.

(3) An offence under section 19 of this Act shall be punishable on summary conviction, on indictment or in either way according to whether, under Schedule 4 to this Act, the substantive offence is punishable on summary conviction, on indictment or in either way; and the punishments which may be imposed on a person convicted of an offence under that section are the same as those which, under that Schedule, may be imposed on a person convicted of the substantive offence.

In this subsection "the substantive offence" means the offence under this Act to which the attempt or, as the case may be, the incitement or attempted incitement mentioned in section 19 was directed.

<table>
<tr><td>1980 c. 43.</td><td>(4) Notwithstanding anything in [section 127(1) of the Magistrates' Court Act 1980], a magistrates' court in England and Wales may try an information for an offence under this Act if the information was laid at any time within twelve months from the commission of the offence.</td></tr>
<tr><td>1975 c. 21.</td><td>[(5) Notwithstanding anything in section 331 of the Criminal Procedure (Scotland) Act 1975 (limitation of time for proceedings in statutory offences) summary proceedings in Scotland for an offence under this Act may be commenced at any time within twelve months from the time when the offence was committed, and subsection (3) of the said section 331 shall apply for the purposes of this subsection as it applies for the purposes of that section.]</td></tr>
<tr><td>1964 c. 21 (N.I.)</td><td>(6) Notwithstanding anything in section 34 of the Magistrates' Courts Act (Northern Ireland) 1964, a magistrates' court in Northern Ireland may hear and determine a complaint for an offence under this Act if the complaint was made at any time within twelve months from the commission of the offence.</td></tr>
</table>

[Section **26** repealed by the Customs and Excise Management Act 1979 section 177(3) and Schedule 6. Schedule 1 to that Act, which follows hereafter takes the place of section 26.]

Customs and Excise Management Act 1979

Sections 50(5), 68(4) and 170(4)

SCHEDULE 1

CONTROLLED DRUGS: VARIATION OF PUNISHMENTS FOR CERTAIN OFFENCES
UNDER THIS ACT

1. Sections 50(4), 68(3) and 170(3) of this Act shall have effect in a case where the goods in respect of which the offence referred to in that subsection was committed were a Class A drug or a Class B drug as if for the words from "shall be liable" onwards there were substituted the following words, that is to say—

"shall be liable—

(a) on summary conviction, to a penalty of the prescribed sum or of three times the value of the goods, whichever is the greater, or to imprisonment for a term not exceeding 6 months, or to both;

(b) on conviction on indictment, to a penalty of any amount, or to imprisonment for a term not exceeding 14 years, or to both."

2. Sections 50(4), 68(3) and 170(3) of this Act shall have effect in a case where the goods in respect of which the offence referred to in that subsection was committeed were a Class C drug as if for the words from "shall be liable" onwards there were substituted the following words, that is to say—

"shall be liable—

(a) on summary conviction in Great Britain, to a penalty of three times the value of the goods or £500, whichever is the greater, or to imprisonment for a term not exceeding 3 months, or to both;

(b) on summary conviction in Northern Ireland, to a penalty of three times the value of the goods or £100, whichever is the greater, or to imprisonment for a term not exceeding 6 months, or to both;

(c) on conviction on indictment, to a penalty of any amount, or to imprisonment for a term not exceeding 5 years, or to both."

3. In this Schedule "Class A drug", Cass B drug" and "Class C drug" have the same meanings as in the Misuse of Drugs Act 1971.

27.—(1) Subject to subsection (2) below, the court by or before which a person Forfeiture. is convicted of an offence under this Act may order anything shown to the satisfaction of the court to relate to the offence, to be forfeited and either destroyed or dealt with in such other manner as the court may order.

(2) The court shall not order anything to be forfeited under this section, where a person claiming to be the owner of or otherwise interested in it applies to be heard by the court, unless an opportunity has been given to him to show cause why the order should not be made.

Miscellaneous and supplementary provisions

Proof of lack of knowledge etc. to be a defence in proceedings for certain offences.

28.—(1) This section applies to offences under any of the following provision of this Act, that is to say section 4(2) and (3), section 5(2) and (3), section 6(2 and section 9.

(2) Subject to subsection (3) below, in any proceedings for an offence to whic this section applies it shall be a defence for the accused to prove that he neithe knew of nor suspected nor had any reason to suspect the existence of some fac alleged by the prosecution which it is necessary for the prosecution to prove he is to be convicted of the offence charged.

(3) Where in any proceedings for an offence to which this section applies is necessary, if the accused is to be convicted of the offence charged, for th prosecution to prove that some substance or product involved in the allege offence was the controlled drug which the prosecution alleges it to have beer and it is proved that the substance or product in question was that controlle drug, the accused—

(*a*) shall not be acquitted of the offence charged by reason only of provin that he neither knew nor suspected nor had reason to suspect that th substance or product in question was the particular controlled dru alleged; but

(*b*) shall be acquitted thereof—

(i) if he proves that he neither believed nor suspected nor had reason to suspect that the substance or product in question was controlled drug; or

(ii) if he proves that he believed the substance or product i question to be a controlled drug, or a controlled drug of description, such that, if it had in fact been that controlled drug o a controlled drug of that description, he would not at the materia time have been committing any offence to which this section applies.

(4) Nothing in this section shall prejudice any defence which it is open to person charged with an offence to which this section applies to raise apart from this section.

Service of documents.

29.—(1) Any notice or other document required or authorised by any provision of this Act to be served on any person may be served on him either by delivering it to him or by leaving it at his proper address or by sending i by post.

(2) Any notice or other document so required or authorised to be served on a body corporate shall be duly served if it is served on the secretary or clerk of that body.

1978 c. 30.

(3) For the purposes of this section, and of [section 7 of the Interpretation Act 1978] in its application to this section, the proper address of any person shall, in the case of the secretary or clerk of a body corporate, be that of the registered or principal office of that body, and in any other case shall be the last address of the person to be served which is known to the Secretary of State.

(4) Where any of the following documents, that is to say—

    (*a*) a notice under section 11(1) or section 15(6) of this Act; or

    (*b*) a copy of a direction given under section 12(2), section 13(1) or (2) or section 16(3) of this Act,

 served by sending it by registered post or by the recorded delivery service, ervice thereof shall be deemed to have been effected at the time when the letter ontaining it would be delivered in the ordinary course of post; and so much f [section 7 of the Interpretation Act 1978] as relates to the time when service y post is deemed to have been effected shall not apply to such a document if is served by so sending it.

30. A licence or other authority issued by the Secretary of State for purposes Licences and f this Act or of regulations made under this Act may be, to any degree, general authorities. r specific, may be issued on such terms and subject to such conditions ncluding, in the case of a licence, the payment of a prescribed fee) as the ecretary of State thinks proper, and may be modified or revoked by him at any me.

31.—(1) Regulations made by the Secretary of State under any provision of General
iis Act— provisions as to

    (*a*) may make different provision in relation to different controlled drugs, regulations. different classes of persons, different provisions of this Act or other different cases or circumstances; and

    (*b*) may make the opinion, consent or approval of a prescribed authority or of any person authorised in a prescribed manner material for purposes of any provision of the regulations; and

    (*c*) may contain such supplementary, incidental and transitional provisions as appear expedient to the Secretary of State.

(2) Any power of the Secretary of State to make regulations under this Act hall be exercisable by statutory instrument, which shall be subject to nnulment in pursuance of a resolution of either House of Parliament.

(3) The Secretary of State shall not make any regulations under this Act except fter consultation with the Advisory Council.

(4) In its application to Northern Ireland this section shall have effect as if r references to the Secretary of State there were substituted references to the 1inistry of Home Affairs for Northern Ireland and as if for subsection (2) ere were substituted—

    "(2) Any regulations made under this Act by the Ministry of Home Affairs for Northern Ireland shall be subject to negative resolution within the meaning of section 41(6) of the Interpretation Act (Northern Ireland) 1954 c. 33 1954 as if they were a statutory instrument within the meaning of that Act." (N.I.).

32. The Secretary of State may conduct or assist in conducting research into Research. ny matter relating to the misuse of dangerous or otherwise harmful drugs.

Amendment of
Extradition Act
1870.
1870 c. 52.

33. The Extradition Act 1870 shall have effect as if conspiring to commit an offence against any enactment for the time being in force relating to dangerou drugs were included in the list of crimes in Schedule 1 to that Act.

34. [Repealed.]

Financial
provisions.

35. There shall be defrayed out of moneys provided by Parliament—

> (*a*) any expenses incurred by the Secretary of State under or in consequenc of the provisions of this Act other than section 32; and

> (*b*) any expenses incurred by the Secretary of State with the consent of th Treasury for the purposes of his functions under that section.

Meaning of
"corresponding
law", and
evidence of
certain matters by
certificate.

36.—(1) In this Act the expression "corresponding law" means a law state in a certificate purporting to be issued by or on behalf of the government o a country outside the United Kingdom to be a law providing for the control an regulation in that country of the production, supply, use, export and import o drugs and other substances in accordance with the provisions of the Singl Convention on Narcotic Drugs signed at New York on 30th March 1961 or law providing for the control and regulation in that country of the production supply, use, export and import of dangerous or otherwise harmful drugs i pursuance of any treaty, convention or other agreement or arrangement t which the government of that country and Her Majesty's Government in th United Kingdom are for the time being parties.

(2) A statement in any such certificate as aforesaid to the effect that any fact constitute an offence against the law mentioned in the certificate shall b evidence, and in Scotland sufficient evidence, of the matters stated.

Interpretation.

37.—(1) In this Act, except in so far as the context otherwise requires, th following expressions have the meanings thereby assigned to them respectively that is to say—

> "the Advisory Council" means the Advisory Council on the Misuse o Drugs established under this Act;

> "cannabis" (except in the expression "cannabis resin") means any plant o the genus *Cannabis* or any part of any such plant (by whatever nam designated) except that it does not include cannabis resin or any of th following products after separation from the rest of the plant, namely–
> (*a*) mature stalk of any such plant,
> (*b*) fibre produced from mature stalk of any such plant, and
> (*c*) seed of any such plant;

> "cannabis resin" means the separated resin, whether crude or purified obtained from any plant of the genus *Cannabis*;

> "contravention" includes failure to comply, and "contravene" has corresponding meaning;

> "controlled drug" has the meaning assigned by section 2 of this Act;

> "corresponding law" has the meaning assigned by section 36(1) of this Act

> "dentist" means a person registered in the dentists register under th Dentists Act 1957;

1957 c. 28.

"doctor" means a fully registered person within the meaning of the Medical Acts 1956 to 1969;

"enactment" includes an enactment of the Parliament of Northern Ireland;

"person lawfully conducting a retail pharmacy business", subject to subsection (5) below, means a person lawfully conducting such a business in accordance with section 69 of the Medicines Act 1968;   1968 c. 67.

"pharmacist" has the same meaning as in the Medicines Act 1968;

"practitioner" (except in the expression "veterinary practitioner") means a doctor, dentist, veterinary practitioner or veterinary surgeon;

"prepared opium" means opium prepared for smoking and includes dross and any other residues remaining after opium has been smoked;

"prescribed" means prescribed by regulations made by the Secretary of State under this Act;

"produce", where the reference is to producing a controlled drug, means producing it by manufacture, cultivation or any other method, and "production" has a corresponding meaning;

"supplying" includes distributing;

"veterinary practitioner" means a person registered in the supplementary veterinary register kept under section 8 of the Veterinary Surgeons Act 1966;   1966 c. 36.

"veterinary surgeon" means a person registered in the register of veterinary surgeons kept under section 2 of the Veterinary Surgeons Act 1966.

(2) References in this Act to misusing a drug are references to misusing it by taking it; and the reference in the foregoing provision to the taking of a drug is a reference to the taking of it by a human being by way of any form of self-administration, whether or not involving assistance by another.

(3) For the purposes of this Act the things which a person has in his possession shall be taken to include any thing subject to his control which is in the custody of another.

(4) Except in so far as the context otherwise requires, any reference in this Act to an enactment shall be construed as a reference to that enactment as amended or extended by or under any other enactment.

(5) So long as sections 8 to 10 of the Pharmacy and Poisons Act 1933 remain 1933 c. 25. in force, this Act in its application to Great Britain shall have effect as if for the definition of "person lawfully conducting a retail pharmacy business" in subsection (1) above there were substituted—

" 'person lawfully conducting a retail pharmacy business' means an authorised seller of poisons within the meaning of the Pharmacy and Poisons Act 1933;"

38.—(1) In the application of this Act to Northern Ireland, for any reference to the Secretary of State (except in sections 1, 2, 7, 17, 23(1), 31, 35, 39(3) and 40(3) and Schedules 1 and 3) there shall be substituted a reference to the Ministry of Home Affairs for Northern Ireland. Special provisions as to Northern Ireland.

(2) Nothing in this Act shall authorise any department of the Government of Northern Ireland to incur any expenses attributable to the provisions of this Act until provision has been made by the Parliament of Northern Ireland for those expenses to be defrayed out of moneys provided by that Parliament; and no expenditure shall be incurred by the Ministry of Home Affairs for Northern Ireland for the purposes of its functions under section 32 of this Act except with the consent of the Ministry of Finance for Northern Ireland.

(3) [Repealed.]

(4) Without prejudice to section 37(4) of this Act, any reference in this Act to an enactment of the Parliament of Northern Ireland includes a reference to any enactment re-enacting it with or without modifications.

Savings and transitional provisions, repeals, and power to amend local enactments.

39.—(1) The savings and transitional provisions contained in Schedule 5 to this Act shall have effect.

(2) The enactments mentioned in Schedule 6 to this Act are hereby repealed to the extent specified in the third column of that Schedule.

(3) The Secretary of State may by order made by statutory instrument subject to annulment in pursuance of a resolution of either House of Parliament repeal or amend any provision in any local Act, including an Act confirming a provisional order, or in any instrument in the nature of a local enactment under any Act, where it appears to him that that provision is inconsistent with, or has become unnecessary or requires modification in consequence of, any provision of this Act.

Short title, extent and commencement.

40.—(1) This Act may be cited as the Misuse of Drugs Act 1971.

(2) This Act extends to Northern Ireland.

(3) This Act shall come into operation on such day as the Secretary of State may by order made by statutory instrument appoint, and different dates may be appointed under this subsection for different purposes.

SCHEDULES

Section 1.

SCHEDULE 1

CONSTITUTION ETC. OF ADVISORY COUNCIL ON THE MISUSE OF DRUGS

1.—(1) The members of the Advisory Council, of whom there shall be not less than twenty, shall be appointed by the Secretary of State after consultation with such organisations as he considers appropriate, and shall include—

    (*a*) in relation to each of the activities specified in sub-paragraph (2) below, at least one person appearing to the Secretary of State to have wide and recent experience of that activity; and

    (*b*) persons appearing to the Secretary of State to have wide and recent experience of social problems connected with the misuse of drugs.

(2) The activities referred to in sub-paragraph (1)(a) above are—
   (a) the practice of medicine (other than veterinary medicine);
   (b) the practice of dentistry;
   (c) the practice of veterinary medicine;
   (d) the practice of pharmacy;
   (e) the pharmaceutical industry;
   (f) chemistry other than pharmaceutical chemistry.

(3) The Secretary of State shall appoint one of the members of the Advisory Council to be chairman of the Council.

2. The Advisory Council may appoint committees, which may consist in part of persons who are not members of the Council, to consider and report to the Council on any matter referred to them by the Council.

3. At meetings of the Advisory Council the quorum shall be seven, and subject to that the Council may determine their own procedure.

4. The Secretary of State may pay to the members of the Advisory Council such remuneration (if any) and such travelling and other allowances as may be determined by him with the consent of the Minister for the Civil Service.

5. Any expenses incurred by the Advisory Council with the approval of the Secretary of State shall be defrayed by the Secretary of State.

SCHEDULE 2   Section 2.

CONTROLLED DRUGS

Part I

CLASS A DRUGS

1. The following substances and products, namely—

Acetorphine.	Benzethidine.
Alfentanil.	Benzylmorphine (3-benzylmorphine).
Allylprodine.	Betacetylmethadol.
Alphacetylmethadol.	Betameprodine.
Alphameprodine.	Betamethadol.
Alphamethadol.	Betaprodine.
Alphaprodine.	Bezitramide.
Anileridine.	Bufotenine.

Cannabinol, except where contained in cannabis or cannabis resin.
Cannabinol derivatives.
Clonitazene.
Coca leaf.
Cocaine.

Desomorphine.
Dextromoramide.
Diamorphine.
Diampromide.
Diethylthiambutene.
Difenoxin (1-(3-cyano-3,3-diphenylpropyl)-4-phenylpiperidine-4-carboxylic acid).
Dihydrocodeinone O-carboxymethyloxime.
Dihydromorphine.
Dimenoxadole.
Dimepheptanol.
Dimethylthiambutene.
Dioxaphetyl butyrate.
Diphenoxylate.
Dipipanone.
Drotebanol (3,4-dimethoxy-17-methylmorphinan-6β,14-diol).

Ecgonine, and any derivative of ecgonine which is convertible to ecgonine or to cocaine.
Ethylmethylthiambutene.
Eticyclidine.
Etonitazene.
Etorphine.
Etoxeridine.

Fentanyl.
Furethidine.

Hydrocodone.
Hydromorphinol..
Hydromorphone.
Hydroxypethidine.

Isomethadone.

Ketobemidone.

Levomethorphan.
Levomoramide.
Levophenacylmorphan.
Levorphanol.
Lysergamide.

Lysergide and other N-alkyl derivatives of lysergamide.

Mescaline.
Metazocine.
Methadone.
Methadyl acetate.
Methyldesorphine.
Methyldihydromorphine (6-methyldihydromorphine).
Metopon.
Morpheridine.
Morphine.
Morphine methobromide, morph N-oxide and other pentavalen nitrogen morphine derivatives
Myrophine.

Nicomorphine (3,6-dinicotinoyl-morphine).
Noracymethadol.
Norlevorphanol.
Normethadone.
Normorphine.
Norpipanone.

Opium, whether raw, prepared medicinal.
Oxycodone.
Oxymorphone.

Pethidine.
Phenadoxone.
Phenampromide.
Phenazocine.
Phencyclidine.
Phenomorphan.
Phenoperidine.
Piminodine.
Piritramide.
Poppy-straw and concentrate of poppy-straw.
Proheptazine.
Properidine (1-methyl-4-phenyl-piperidine-4-carboxylic acid isopropyl ester).
Psilocin.

Racemethorphan.
Racemoramide.

Racemorphan.
Rolicyclidine.
Sufentanil.
Tenocyclidine.
Thebacon.
Thebaine.
Tilidate.
Trimeperidine.
4-Bromo-2,5-dimethoxy-α-
  methylphenethylamine.
4-Cyano-2-dimethylamino-4,
  4-diphenylbutane.

4-Cyano-1-methyl-4-phenyl-
  piperidine.
N,N-Diethyltryptamine.
N,N-Dimethyltryptamine.
2,5-Dimethoxy-α,4-dimethyl-
  phenethylamine.
1-Methyl-4-phenylpiperidine-4-
  carboxylic acid.
2-Methyl-3-morpholino-1,
  1-diphenylpropanecarboxylic acid.
4-Phenylpiperidine-4-carboxylic acid
  ethyl ester.

b) Any compound (not being a compound for the time being specified in sub-paragraph (*a*) above) structurally derived from tryptamine or from a ring-hydroxy tryptamine by substitution at the nitrogen atom of the sidechain with one or more alkyl substituents but no other substituent.

c) Any compound (not being methoxyphenamine or a compound for the time being specified in sub-paragraph (*a*) above) structurally derived from phenethylamine, an N-alkylphenethylamine, α-methylphenethylamine, an N-alkyl-α-methylphenethylamine, α-ethylphenethylamine, or an N-alkyl-α-ethylphenethylamine by substitution in the ring to any extent with alkyl, alkoxy, alkylenedioxy or halide substituents, whether or not further substituted in the ring by one or more other univalent substituents.

2. Any stereoisomeric form of a substance for the time being specified in paragraph 1 above not being dextromethorphan or dextrorphan.

3. Any ester or ether of a substance for the time being specified in paragraph 1 or 2 above, not being a substance for the time being specified in Part II of this Schedule.

4. Any salt of a substance for the time being specified in any of paragraphs 1 to 3 above.

5. Any preparation or other product containing a substance or product for the time being specified in any of paragraphs 1 to 4 above.

6. Any preparation designed for administration by injection which includes a substance or product for the time being specified in any of paragraphs 1 to 3 of Part II of this Schedule.

Part II

CLASS B DRUGS

1. The following substances and products, namely:—

(*a*) Acetyldihydrocodeine.   Methylphenidate.
    Amphetamine.   Methylphenobarbitone.
    Cannabis and cannabis resin.   Nicocodine.
    Codeine.   Nicodicodine (6-nicotinoyldihydro
    Dexamphetamine.   codeine).
    Dihydrocodeine.   Norcodeine.
    Ethylmorphine (3-ethylmorphine).   Phenmetrazine.
    Mecloqualone.   Pholcodine.
    Methaqualone.   Propiram.
    Methylamphetamine.

(*b*) Any 5,5 disubstituted barbituric acid.

2. Any stereoisomeric form of a substance for the time being specified in paragraph 1 of this Part of this Schedule.

3. Any salt of a substance for the time being specified in paragraph 1 or 2 of this Part of this Schedule.

4. Any preparation or other product containing a substance or product for the time being specified in any of paragraphs 1 to 3 of this Part of this Schedule, not being a preparation falling within paragraph 6 of Part I of this Schedule.

Part III

CLASS C DRUGS

1. The following substances, namely:—

Benzphetamine.   Mephentermine.
Chlorphentermine.   Phendimetrazine.
Dextropropoxyphene.   Pipradol.
Diethylpropion.

2. Any stereoisomeric form of a substance for the time being specified in paragraph 1 of this Part of this Schedule.

3. Any salt of a substance for the time being specified in paragraph 1 or 2 of this Part of this Schedule.

4. Any preparation or other product containing a substance for the time being specified in any of paragraphs 1 to 3 of this Part of this Schedule.

MEANING OF CERTAIN EXPRESSIONS USED IN THIS SCHEDULE

For the purposes of this Schedule the following expressions (which are not among those defined in section 37(1) of this Act) have the meanings hereby assigned to them respectively, that is to say—

"cannabinol derivatives" means the following substances, except where contained in cannabis or cannabis resin, namely tetrahydro derivatives of cannabinol and 3-alkyl homologues of cannabinol or of its tetrahydro derivatives;

"coca leaf" means the leaf of any plant of the genus *Erythroxylon* from whose leaves cocaine can be extracted either directly or by chemical transformation;

"concentrate of poppy-straw" means the material produced when poppy-straw has entered into a process for the concentration of its alkaloids;

"medicinal opium" means raw opium which has undergone the process necessary to adapt it for medicinal use in accordance with the requirements of the British Pharmacopoeia, whether it is in the form of powder or is granulated or is in any other form, and whether it is or is not mixed with neutral substances;

"opium poppy" means the plant of the species *Papaver somniferum* L;

"poppy straw" means all parts, except the seeds, of the opium poppy, after mowing;

"raw opium" includes powdered or granulated opium but does not include medicinal opium.

SCHEDULE 3

Section 16.

TRIBUNALS, ADVISORY BODIES AND PROFESSIONAL PANELS

PART I

TRIBUNALS

Membership

1.—(1) A tribunal shall consist of five persons of whom—

(a) one shall be a barrister, advocate or solicitor of not less than seven years' standing appointed by the Lord Chancellor to be the chairman of the tribunal; and

(b) the other four shall be persons appointed by the Secretary of State from among members of the respondent's profession nominated for the purposes of this Schedule by any of the relevant bodies mentioned in sub-paragraph (2) below.

(2) The relevant bodies aforesaid are—

(a) where the respondent is a doctor, the General Medical Council, the Royal Colleges of Physicians of London and Edinburgh, the Royal Colleges of Surgeons of England and Edinburgh, the Royal College of Physicians and Surgeons (Glasgow), the Royal College of Obstetricians and Gynaecologists, the Royal College of General Practitioners, the Royal Medico-Psychological Association and the British Medical Association;

(b) where the respondent is a dentist, the General Dental Council and the British Dental Association;

(c) where the respondent is a veterinary practitioner or veterinary surgeon, the Royal College of Veterinary Surgeons and the British Veterinary Association.

(3) Sub-paragraph (1) above shall have effect in relation to a tribunal in Scotland as if for the reference to the Lord Chancellor there were substituted a reference to the Lord President of the Court of Session.

Procedure

2. The quorum of a tribunal shall be the chairman and two other members of the tribunal.

3. Proceedings before a tribunal shall be held in private unless the respondent requests otherwise and the tribunal accedes to the request.

4.—(1) Subject to paragraph 5 below, the Lord Chancellor may make rules as to the procedure to be followed, and the rules of evidence to be observed, in proceedings before tribunals, and in particular—

(a) for securing that notice that the proceedings are to be brought shall be given to the respondent at such time and in such manner as may be specified by the rules;

(b) for determining who, in addition to the respondent, shall be a party to the proceedings;

(c) for securing that any party to the proceedings shall, if he so requires, be entitled to be heard by the tribunal;

(d) for enabling any party to the proceedings to be represented by counsel or solicitor.

(2) Sub-paragraph (1) above shall have effect in relation to a tribunal in Scotland as if for the reference to the Lord Chancellor there were substituted a reference to the Secretary of State.

(3) The power to make rules under this paragraph shall be exercisable by statutory instrument, which shall be subject to annulment in pursuance of a resolution of either House of Parliament.

5.—(1) For the purpose of any proceedings before a tribunal in England or Wales or Northern Ireland the tribunal may administer oaths and any party to the proceedings may sue out writs of subpoena ad testificandum and duces tecum, but no person shall be compelled under any such writ to give any evidence or produce any document which he could not be compelled to give or produce on the trial of an action.

(2) The provisions of section [36 of the Supreme Court Act 1981, of section 67 of the Judicature (Northern Ireland) Act 1978], or of the Attendance of Witnesses Act 1854 (which provide special procedures for the issue of such writs so as to be in force throughout the United Kingdom) shall apply in relation to any proceedings before a tribunal in England or Wales, or, as the case may be, in Northern Ireland as those provisions apply in relation to causes or matters in the High Court or actions or suits pending in the High Court of Justice in Northern Ireland.

(3) For the purpose of any proceedings before a tribunal in Scotland, the tribunal may administer oaths and the Court of Session shall on the application of any party to the proceedings have the like power as in any action in that court to grant warrant for the citation of witnesses and havers to give evidence or to produce documents before the tribunal.

6. Subject to the foregoing provisions of this Schedule, a tribunal may regulate its own procedure.

7. The validity of the proceedings of a tribunal shall not be affected by any defect in the appointment of a member of the tribunal or by reason of the fact that a person not entitled to do so took part in the proceedings.

Financial provisions

8. The Secretary of State may pay to any member of a tribunal fees and travelling and other allowances in respect of his services in accordance with such scales and subject to such conditions as the Secretary of State may determine with the approval of the Treasury.

9. The Secretary of State may pay to any person who attends as a witness before the tribunal sums by way of compensation for the loss of his time and travelling and other allowances in accordance with such scales and subject to such conditions as may be determined as aforesaid.

10. If a tribunal recommends to the Secretary of State that the whole or part of the expenses properly incurred by the respondent for the purposes of proceedings before the tribunal should be defrayed out of public funds, the Secretary of State may if he thinks fit make to the respondent such payments in respect of those expenses as the Secretary of State considers appropriate.

11. Any expenses incurred by a tribunal with the approval of the Secretary of State shall be defrayed by the Secretary of State.

Supplemental

12. The Secretary of State shall make available to a tribunal such accommodation, the services of such officers and such other facilities as he considers appropriate for the purpose of enabling the tribunal to perform its functions.

PART II

ADVISORY BODIES

Membership

13.—(1) An advisory body shall consist of three persons of whom—

    (*a*) one shall be a person who is of counsel to Her Majesty and is appointed by the Lord Chancellor to be chairman of the advisory body; and

    (*b*) another shall be a person appointed by the Secretary of State, being a member of the respondent's profession who is an officer of a department of the Government of the United Kingdom; and

    (*c*) the other shall be a person appointed by the Secretary of State from among the members of the respondent's profession nominated as mentioned in paragraph 1 above.

(2) Sub-paragraph (1) above shall have effect in relation to an advisory body in Scotland as if for the reference to the Lord Chancellor there were substituted a reference to the Lord President of the Court of Session.

Procedure

14. The respondent shall be entitled to appear before and be heard by the advisory body either in person or by counsel or solicitor.

15. Subject to the provisions of this Part of this Schedule, an advisory body may regulate its own procedure.

Application of provisions of Part I

16. Paragraphs 3, 7, 8 and 10 to 12 of this Schedule shall apply in relation to an advisory body as they apply in relation to a tribunal.

PART III

PROFESSIONAL PANELS

Membership

17. A professional panel shall consist of a chairman and two other persons appointed by the Secretary of State from among the members of the respondent's profession after consultation with such one or more of the relevant bodies mentioned in paragraph 1(2) above as the Secretary of State considers appropriate.

18. The respondent shall be entitled to appear before, and be heard by, the professional panel either in person or by counsel or solicitor.

19. Subject to the provisions of this Part of this Schedule, a professional panel may regulate its own procedure.

Application of provisions of Part I

20. Paragraphs 3, 7 and 8 of this Schedule shall apply in relation to a professional panel as they apply in relation to a tribunal.

PART IV

APPLICATION OF PARTS I TO III TO NORTHERN IRELAND

21. In the application of Parts I to III of this Schedule to Northern Ireland the provisions specified in the first column of the following Table shall have effect subject to the modifications specified in relation thereto in the second column of that Table.

TABLE

Provision of this Schedule	Modification
Paragraph 1	In sub-paragraph (1), for the references to the Lord Chancellor and the Secretary of State there shall be substituted respectively references to the Lord Chief Justice of Northern Ireland and the Minister of Home Affairs for Northern Ireland.
Paragraph 4	In sub-paragraph (1), for the reference to the Lord Chancellor there shall be substituted a reference to the Ministry of Home Affairs for Northern Ireland.
	For sub-paragraph (3) there shall be substituted—
	"(3) Any rules made under this paragraph by the Ministry of Home Affairs for Northern Ireland shall be subject to negative resolution within the meaning of section 41(6) of the Interpretation Act (Northern Ireland) 1954 as if they were a statutory instrument within the meaning of that Act."
Paragraphs 8 to 12 ...	For the references to the Secretary of State and the Treasury there shall be substituted respectively references to the Ministry of Home Affairs for Northern Ireland and the Department of Finance for Northern Ireland.

1954 c. 33
(N.I.).

Provision of this Schedule	*Modification*

Paragraph 13	In sub-paragraph (1)—
	  (a) for the references to the Lord Chancellor an Secretary of State there shall be substitute respectively references to the Lord Chi Justice of Northern Ireland and th Minister of Home Affairs for Northe Ireland; and
	  (b) for the reference to a department of th Government of the United Kingdom the shall be substituted a reference to department of the Government of Northe Ireland.

Paragraph 16	The references to paragraphs 8 and 10 to 12 shall construed as references to those paragraphs modified by this Part of this Schedule.
Paragraph 17	For the reference to the Secretary of State there sha be substituted a reference to the Minister of Hom Affairs for Northern Ireland.
Paragraph 20	The reference to paragraph 8 shall be construed as reference to that paragraph as modified by this Pa of this Schedule.

SCHEDULE 4

Section 25.

PROSECUTION AND PUNISHMENT OF OFFENCES

Section Creating Offence	General Nature of Offence	Mode of Prosecution	Punishment			
			Class A drug involved	Class B drug involved	Class C drug involved	General
Section 4(2)...	Production, or being concerned in the production, of a controlled drug.	(a) Summary ...	6 months or £2000, or both.	6 months or £2000, or both.	3 months or £500, or both.	
		(b) On indictment	Life or a fine, or both.	14 years or a fine, or both.	5 years or a fine, or both.	
Section 4(3)...	Supplying or offering to supply a controlled drug or being concerned in the doing of either activity by another.	(a) Summary ...	6 months or £2000, or both.	6 months or £2000, or both.	3 months or £500, or both.	
		(b) On indictment	Life or a fine, or both.	14 years or a fine, or both.	5 years or a fine, or both.	
Section 5(2)...	Having possession of a controlled drug.	(a) Summary ...	6 months or £2000, or both.	3 months or £500, or both.	3 months or £200, or both.	
		(b) On indictment	7 years or a fine, or both.	5 years or a fine, or both.	2 years or a fine, or both.	
Section 5(3)...	Having possession of a controlled drug with intent to supply it to another.	(a) Summary ...	6 months or £2000, or both.	6 months or £2000, or both.	3 months or £500, or both.	
		(b) On indictment	Life or a fine, or both.	14 years or a fine, or both.	5 years or a fine, or both.	
Section 6(2)...	Cultivation of cannabis plant ...	(a) Summary ...	—	—	—	6 months or £2000, or both.
		(b) On indictment	—	—	—	14 years or a fine, or both.

Section Creating Offence	General Nature of Offence	Mode of Prosecution	Punishment			
			Class A drug involved	Class B drug involved	Class C drug involved	General
Section 8 ...	Being the occupier, or concerned in the management, of premises and permitting or suffering certain activities to take place there.	(a) Summary ... (b) On indictment	6 months or £2000, or both. 14 years or a fine, or both.	6 months or £2000, or both. 14 years or a fine, or both.	3 months or £500, or both. 5 years or a fine, or both.	
Section 9 ...	Offences relating to opium ...	(a) Summary ... (a) On indictment	—	—	—	6 months or £2000, or both. 14 years or a fine, or both.
Section 11(2)	Contravention of directions relating to safe custody of controlled drugs.	(a) Summary ... (b) On indictment	—	—	—	6 months or £2000, or both. 2 years or a fine, or both.
Section 12(6)	Contravention of direction prohibiting practitioner etc. from possessing, supplying etc. controlled drugs.	(a) Summary ... (b) On indictment	6 months or £2000, or both. 14 years or a fine, or both.	6 months or £2000, or both. 14 years or a fine, or both.	3 months or £500, or both. 5 years or a fine, or both.	
Section 13(3)	Contravention of direction prohibiting practitioner etc. from prescribing, supplying etc. controlled drugs.	(a) Summary ... (b) On indictment	6 months or £2000, or both. 14 years or a fine, or both.	6 months or £2000, or both. 14 years or a fine, or both.	3 months or £500, or both. 5 years or a fine, or both.	
Section 17(3)	Failure to comply with notice requiring information relating to prescribing, supply etc. of drugs.	Summary ...	—	—	—	£400.

Section creating offence	General nature of offence	Mode of prosecution				Punishment
Section 17(4)	compliance with notice requiring information relating to prescribing, supply etc. of drugs.	*(b)* On indictment	—	—	—	2 years or a fine, or both.
Section 18(1)	Contravention of regulations (other than regulations relating to addicts).	*(a)* Summary ...	—	—	—	6 months or £2000, or both.
		(b) On indictment	—	—	—	2 years or a fine, or both.
Section 18(2)	Contravention of terms of licence or other authority (other than licence issued under regulations relating to addicts).	*(a)* Summary ...	—	—	—	6 months or £2000, or both.
		(b) On indictment	—	—	—	2 years or a fine, or both.
Section 18(3)	Giving false information in purported compliance with obligation to give information imposed under or by virtue of regulations.	*(a)* Summary ...	—	—	—	6 months or £2000, or both.
		(b) On indictment	—	—	—	2 years or a fine, or both.
Section 18(4)	Giving false information, or producing document etc. containing false statement etc., for purposes of obtaining issue or renewal of a licence or other authority.	*(a)* Summary ...	—	—	—	6 months or £2000, or both.
		(b) On indictment	—	—	—	2 years or a fine, or both.
Section 20	Assisting in or inducing commission outside United Kingdom of an offence punishable under a corresponding law.	*(a)* Summary ...	—	—	—	12 months or £2000, or both.
		(b) On indictment	—	—	—	14 years or a fine, or both.
Section 23(4)	Obstructing exercise of powers of search etc. or concealing books, drugs etc.	*(a)* Summary ...	—	—	—	6 months or £2000, or both.
		(c) On indictment	—	—	—	2 years or a fine, or both.

SCHEDULE 5

SAVINGS AND TRANSITIONAL PROVISIONS

1.—(1) Any addiction regulations which could have been made under this A
shall not be invalidated by any repeal effected by this Act but shall have eff
as if made under the provisions of this Act which correspond to the provisio
under which the regulations were made; and the validity of any licence issu
under any such addiction regulations shall not be affected by any such repe:

(2) Any order, rule or other instrument or document whatsoever made
issued, any direction given, and any other thing done, under or by virtue of a
1967 c. 82.   of the following provisions of the Dangerous Drugs Act 1967, that is to s
section 1(2), 2 or 3 or the Schedule, shall be deemed for the purposes of t
Act to have been made, issued or done, as the case may be, under t
corresponding provisions of this Act; and anything begun under any of the sa
provisions of that Act may be continued under this Act as if begun under t
Act.

(3) In this paragraph "addiction regulations" means any regulations ma
1965 c. 15.   under section 11 of the Dangerous Drugs Act 1965 which include provision f
any of the matters for which regulations may be so made by virtue of secti
1(1) of the Dangerous Drugs Act 1967.

2. As from the coming into operation of section 3 of this Act any licen
1964 c. 64.   granted for the purpose of section 5 of the Drugs (Prevention of Misuse) A
1964 or sections 2, 3 or 10 of the Dangerous Drugs Act 1965 shall have effe
as if granted for the purposes of section 3(2) of this Act.

3.—(1) The Secretary of State may at any time before the coming in
operation of section 12 of this Act give a direction under subsection (2) of th
section in respect of any practitioner or pharmacist whose general authori
under the Dangerous Drugs Regulations is for the time being withdrawn; b
a direction given by virtue of this sub-paragraph shall not take effect un
section 12 comes into operation, and shall not take effect at all if the gener
authority of the person concerned is restored before that section comes in
operation.

(2) No direction under section 12(2) of this Act shall be given by virtue
sub-paragraph (1) above in respect of a person while the withdrawal of h
general authority under the Dangerous Drugs Regulations is suspended; b
where, in the case of any practitioner or pharmacist whose general authority h
been withdrawn, the withdrawal is suspended at the time when section 1
comes into operation, the Secretary of State may at any time give a directic
under section 12(2) in respect of him by virtue of this sub-paragraph unless t
Secretary of State has previously caused to be served on him a notice stating th:
he is no longer liable to have such a direction given in respect of him by virtu
of this sub-paragraph.

(3) In this paragraph "the Dangerous Drugs Regulations" means, as regarc
Great Britain, the Dangerous Drugs (No. 2) Regulations 1964 or, as regarc
Northern Ireland, the Dangerous Drugs Regulations (Northern Ireland) 196:

. Subject to paragraphs 1 to 3 above, and without prejudice to the generality   SCH. 5
section 31(1)(*c*) of this Act, regulations made by the Secretary of State under
 provision of this Act may include such provision as the Secretary of State
nks fit for effecting the transition from any provision made by or by virtue
any of the enactments repealed by this Act to any provision made by or by
tue of this Act, and in particular may provide for the continuation in force,
h or without modifications, of any licence or other authority issued or
ving effect as if issued under or by virtue of any of those enactments.

. For purposes of the enforcement of the enactments repealed by this Act
 regards anything done or omitted before their repeal, any powers of search,
try, inspection, seizure or detention conferred by those enactments shall
ntinue to be exercisable as if those enactments were still in force.

. The mention of particular matters in this Schedule shall not prejudice the   1978 c. 30.
neral application of [section 16 of the Interpretation Act 1978] with regard to
 effect of repeals.

SCHEDULE 6   Section 39.

REPEALS

Chapter	Short Title	Extent of Repeal
064 c. 64.	The Drugs (Prevention of Misuse) Act 1964.	The whole Act.
065 c. 15.	The Dangerous Drugs Act 1965.	The whole Act.
067 c. 82.	The Dangerous Drugs Act 1967.	The whole Act.
068 c. 59.	The Hovercraft Act 1968.	Paragraph 6 of the Schedule.
068 c. 67.	The Medicines Act 1968.	In Schedule 5, paragraphs 14 and 15.

APPENDIX II

STATUTORY INSTRUMENTS

1973 No. 797

DANGEROUS DRUGS

The Misuse of Drugs Regulations 1973

Made - - - -	*19th April* 1973
Laid before Parliament	*7th May* 1973
Coming into Operation	*1st July* 1973

ARRANGEMENT OF REGULATIONS

PART I

GENERAL

1. Citation and commencement.
2. Interpretation.
3. Metric system and imperial system.

PART II

EXEMPTIONS FROM CERTAIN PROVISIONS OF THE MISUSE OF DRUGS ACT 1971

4. Exceptions for drugs in Schedule 1 and poppy-straw.
5. Licences to produce etc. controlled drugs.
6. General authority to possess.
7. Administration of drugs in Schedules 1, 2 and 3.
8. Production and supply of drugs in Schedules 1 and 2.
9. Production and supply of drugs in Schedule 3.
10. Possession of drugs in Schedules 2 and 3.
11. Exemption for midwives in respect of pethidine.
12. Cultivation under licence of Cannabis plant.
13. Approval of premises for cannabis smoking for research purposes.

PART III

REQUIREMENTS AS TO DOCUMENTATION AND RECORD KEEPING

PART IV

MISCELLANEOUS

SCHEDULES

In pursuance of sections 7, 10, 22(*a*) and 31 of the Misuse of Drugs Act 1971**(a)**, after consultation with the Advisory Council on the Misuse of Drugs, I hereby make the following Regulations:—

(a) 1971 c. 38.

PART I

GENERAL

Citation and commencement

1. These Regulations may be cited as Misuse of Drugs Regulations 1973 and shall come into operation on 1st July 1973.

Interpretation

2.—(1) In these Regulations, unless the context otherwise requires, the expression—

"the Act" means the Misuse of Drugs Act 1971;

"authorised as a member of a group" means authorised by virtue of being a member of a class as respects which the Secretary of State has granted an authority under and for the purposes of Regulations 8(3), 9(3) or 10(3) which is in force, and "his group authority", in relation to a person who is a member of such a class, means the authority so granted to that class;

"cannabis" has the same meaning as in the Act as amended by section 52 of the Criminal Law Act 1977;

"health prescription" means a prescription issued by a doctor or a dentist either under the National Health Service Acts 1946 [to 1973]**(a)**, the National Health Service (Scotland) Acts 1947 [to 1972]**(b)**, the Health Services Act (Northern Ireland) 1971**(c)** or the National Health Service (Isle of Man) Act 1948 (an Act of Tynwald) or upon a form issued by a local authority for use in connection with the health service of that authority.;

"installation manager" and "offshore installation" have the same meanings as in the Mineral Workings (Offshore Installations) Act 1971**(d)**;

"master" has the same meaning as in the Merchant Shipping Act 1894**(e)**;

"matron or acting matron" includes any male nurse occupying a similar position;

"the Merchant Shipping Acts" means the Merchant Shipping Acts 1894 to 1971;

"officer of customs and excise" means an officer within the meaning of the Customs and Excise Act 1952**(f)**;

"prescription" means a prescription issued by a doctor for the medical treatment of a single individual, by a dentist for the dental treatment of a single individual or by a veterinary surgeon or veterinary practitioner for the purposes of animal treatment;

"register" means a bound book and does not include any form of loose leaf register or card index;

"registered pharmacy" has the same meaning as in the Medicines Act 1968**(g)**;

(a) 1946 c. 81; 1973 c. 32.   **(b)** 1947 c. 27; 1972 c. 58.
(c) 1971 c. 1(N.I.).   **(d)** 1971 c. 61.
(e) 1894 c. 60.   **(f)** 1952 c. 44.
(g) 1968 c. 67.

"retail dealer" means a person lawfully conducting a retail pharmacy business or a pharmacist engaged in supplying drugs to the public at a health centre within the meaning of the Medicines Act 1968;

"sister or acting sister" includes any male nurse occupying a similar position;

"wholesale dealer" means a person who carries on the business of selling drugs to persons who buy to sell again.

(2) In these Regulations any reference to a Regulation or Schedule shall be construed as a reference to a Regulation contained in these Regulations or, as the case may be, to a Schedule thereto; and any reference in a Regulation or Schedule to a paragraph shall be construed as a reference to a paragraph of that Regulation or Schedule.

(3). In these Regulations any reference to any enactment shall be construed as a reference to that enactment as amended, and as including a reference thereto as extended or applied, by or under any other enactment.

(4) Nothing in these Regulations shall be construed as derogating from any power or immunity of the Crown, its servants or agents.

(5) The Interpretation Act 1889(a) shall apply for the interpretation of these Regulations as it applies for the interpretation of an Act of Parliament.

Metric system and imperial system

3.—(1) For the purposes of these Regulations—

    (*a*) a controlled drug shall not be regarded as supplied otherwise than on a prescription or other order by reason only that the prescription or order specifies a quantity of the controlled drug in terms of the imperial system and the quantity supplied is the equivalent of that amount in the metric system;

    (*b*) where any person may lawfully be in possession of a quantity of a controlled drug determined by or under these Regulations in terms of the imperial system he shall be deemed not to be in possession of a quantity of that controlled drug in excess of the first-mentioned quantity by reason only that he is in possession of a quantity of that drug which is the equivalent of the first-mentioned quantity in the metric system.

(2) For the purposes of this Regulation the quantity of a controlled drug in the metric system which is the equivalent of a particular quantity in the imperial system shall be taken to be the appropriate quantity ascertained in accordance with the provisions of the Weights and Measures (Equivalents for dealing with drugs) Regulations 1970(b).

PART II

EXEMPTIONS FROM CERTAIN PROVISIONS OF THE MISUSE OF DRUGS ACT 1971

Exceptions for drugs in Schedule 1 and poppy-straw

4.—(1) Sections 3(1) and 5(1) of the Act (which prohibit the importation, exportation

---

    (a) 1889 c. 63.   **(b)** S.I. 1970/1897 (1970 III, p. 6242).

and possession of controlled drugs) shall not have effect in relation to the controlled drugs specified in Schedule 1.

(2) Sections 4(1) (which prohibits the production and supply of controlled drugs) and 5(1) of the Act shall not have effect in relation to poppy-straw.

Licences to produce etc. controlled drugs

5. Where any person is authorised by a licence of the Secretary of State issued under this Regulation and for the time being in force to produce, supply, offer to supply or have in his possession any controlled drug, it shall not by virtue of section 4(1) or 5(1) of the Act be unlawful for that person to produce, supply, offer to supply or have in his possession that drug in accordance with the terms of the licence and in compliance with any conditions attached to the licence.

General authority to possess

6. Any of the following persons may, notwithstanding the provisions of section 5(1) of the Act, have any controlled drug in his possession, that is to say—

(*a*) a constable when acting in the course of his duty as such;

(*b*) a person engaged in the business of a carrier when acting in the course of that business;

(*c*) a person engaged in the business of the Post Office when acting in the course of that business;

(*d*) an officer of customs and excise when acting in the course of his duty as such;

(*e*) a person engaged in the work of any laboratory to which the drug has been sent for forensic examination when acting in the course of his duty as a person so engaged;

(*f*) a person engaged in conveying the drug to a person authorised by these Regulations to have it in his possession.

Administration of drugs in Schedules 1, 2 and 3

7.—(1) Any person may administer to another any drug specified in Schedule 1.

(2) A doctor or dentist may administer to a patient any drug specified in Schedule 2 or 3.

(3) Any person other than a doctor or dentist may administer to a patient, in accordance with the directions of a doctor or dentist, any drug specified in Schedule 2 or 3.

Production and supply of drugs in Schedules 1 and 2

8.—(1) Notwithstanding the provisions of section 4(1)(*a*) of the Act—

(*a*) a practitioner or pharmacist, acting in his capacity as such, may manufacture or compound any drug specified in Schedule 1 or 2;

(*b*) a person lawfully conducting a retail pharmacy business and acting in his capacity as such may, at the registered pharmacy at which he carries on that business, manufacture or compound any drug specified in Schedule 1 or 2.

(2) Notwithstanding the provisions of section 4(1)(*b*) of the Act any of the following persons, that is to say—

(*a*) a practitioner;

(*b*) a pharmacist;

(*c*) a person lawfully conducting a retail pharmacy business;

(*d*) the matron or acting matron of a hospital or nursing home which is wholly or mainly maintained by a public authority out of public funds or by a charity or by voluntary subscriptions;

(*e*) in the case of such a drug supplied to her by a person responsible for the dispensing and supply of medicines at the hospital or nursing home, the sister or acting sister for the time being in charge of a ward, theatre or other department in such a hospital or nursing home as aforesaid;

(*f*) a person who is in charge of a laboratory the recognized activities of which consist in, or include, the conduct of scientific education or research and which is attached to a university, university college or such a hospital as aforesaid or to any other institution approved for the purpose by the Secretary of State;

(*g*) a public analyst appointed under section 89 of the Food and Drugs Act 1955**(a)** or section 27 of the Food and Drugs (Scotland) Act 1956**(b)**;

(*h*) a sampling officer within the meaning of the Food and Drugs Act 1955 or the Food and Drugs (Scotland) Act 1956;

(*i*) a sampling officer within the meaning of Schedule 3 to the Medicines Act 1968;

(*j*) a person employed or engaged in connection with a scheme for testing the quality or amount of the drugs, preparations and appliances supplied under the National Health Service Acts 1946 to 1973 or the National Health Service (Scotland) Acts 1947 to 1973 and the Regulations made thereunder;

(*k*) an inspector appointed by the Pharmaceutical Society of Great Britain under section 25 of the Pharmacy and Poisons Act 1933**(c)**,

may, when acting in his capacity as such, supply or offer to supply any drug specified in Schedule 1 or 2 to any person who may lawfully have that drug in his possession:

Provided that nothing in this paragraph authorises—

(i) the matron or acting matron of a hospital or nursing home, having a pharmacist responsible for the dispensing and supply of medicines, to supply or offer to supply any drug;

(ii) a sister or acting sister for the time being in charge of a ward, theatre or other department to supply any drug otherwise than for administration to a patient in that ward, theatre or department in accordance with the directions of a doctor or dentist.

(3) Notwithstanding the provisions of section 4(1)(*b*) of the Act, a person who is authorised as a member of a group may, under and in accordance with the terms of his group authority and in compliance with any conditions attached thereto, supply or offer

---

(a) 1955 c. 16 (4 & 5 Eliz. 2).   **(b)** 1956 c. 30.
(c) 1933 c. 25.

to supply any drug specified in Schedule 1 or 2 to any person who may lawfully have that drug in his possession.

(4) Notwithstanding the provisions of section 4(1)(*b*) of the Act, a person who is authorised by a written authority issued by the Secretary of State under and for the purposes of this paragraph and for the time being in force may, at the premises specified in that authority and in compliance with any conditions so specified, supply or offer to supply any drug specified in Schedule 1 to any person who may lawfully have that drug in his possession.

(5) Notwithstanding the provisions of section 4(1)(*b*) of the Act—

(*a*) the owner of a ship, or the master of a ship which does not carry a doctor on board as part of her complement, may supply or offer to supply any drug specified in Schedule 1 or 2—

(i) to any member of the crew;

(ii) to any person who may lawfully supply that drug; or

(iii) to any constable for the purpose of destruction;

(*b*) the installation manager of an offshore installation may supply or offer to supply any drug specified in Schedule 1 or 2—

(i) to any person on that installation, whether present in the course of his employment or not;

(ii) to any person who may lawfully supply that drug; or

(iii) to any constable for the purpose of destruction.

Production and supply of drugs in Schedule 3

9.—(1) Notwithstanding the provisions of section 4(1)(*a*) of the Act—

(*a*) a practitioner or pharmacist, acting in his capacity as such, may manufacture or compound any drug specified in Schedule 3;

(*b*) a person lawfully conducting a retail pharmacy business and acting in his capacity as such may, at the registered pharmacy at which he carries on that business, manufacture or compound any drug specified in Schedule 3;

(*c*) a person who is authorised by a written authority issued by the Secretary of State under and for the purposes of this sub-paragraph and for the time being in force may, at the premises specified in that authority and in compliance with any conditions so specified, produce any drug specified in Schedule 3.

(2) Notwithstanding the provisions of section 4(1)(*b*) of the Act, any of the following persons, that is to say—

(*a*) a practitioner;

(*b*) a pharmacist;

(*c*) a person lawfully conducting a retail pharmacy business;

(*d*) the matron or acting matron of a hospital or nursing home;

(*e*) in the case of such a drug supplied to her by a person responsible for the dispensing and supply of medicines at the hospital or nursing home, the sister or acting sister for the time being in charge of a ward, theatre or other department in a hospital or nursing home;

(*f*) a person in charge of a laboratory the recognized activities of which consist in, or include, the conduct of scientific education or research;

(*ff*) in the case of such a drug required for use as a buffering agent in chemical analysis, a person in charge of a laboratory;

(*g*) a public analyst appointed under section 89 of the Food and Drugs Act 1955 or section 27 of the Food and Drugs (Scotland) Act 1956;

(*h*) a sampling officer within the meaning of the Food and Drugs Act 1955 or the Food and Drugs (Scotland) Act 1956;

(*i*) a sampling officer within the meaning of Schedule 3 to the Medicines Act 1968;

(*j*) a person employed or engaged in connection with a scheme for testing the quality or amount of the drugs, preparations and appliances supplied under the National Health Service Acts 1946 to 1973 or the National Health Service (Scotland) Acts 1947 to 1973 and the Regulations made thereunder;

(*k*) an inspector appointed by the Pharmaceutical Society of Great Britain under section 25 of the Pharmacy and Poisons Act 1933,

may, when acting in his capacity as such, supply or offer to supply any drug specified in Schedule 3 to any person who may lawfully have that drug in his possession:

Provided that nothing in this paragraph authorises—

(i) the matron or acting matron of a hospital or nursing home, having a pharmacist responsible for the dispensing and supply of medicines, to supply or offer to supply any drug;

(ii) a sister or acting sister for the time being in charge of a ward, theatre or other department to supply any drug otherwise than for administration to a patient in that ward, theatre or department in accordance with the directions of a doctor or dentist.

(3) Notwithstanding the provisions of section 4(1)(*b*) of the Act, a person who is authorised as a member of a group may, under and in accordance with the terms of his group authority and in compliance with any conditions attached thereto, supply or offer to supply any drug specified in Schedule 3 to any person who may lawfully have that drug in his possession.

(4) Notwithstanding the provisions of section 4(1)(*b*) of the Act—

(*a*) a person who is authorised by a written authority issued by the Secretary of State under and for the purposes of this sub-paragraph and for the time being in force may, at the premises specified in that authority and in compliance with any conditions so specified, supply or offer to supply any drug specified in Schedule 3 to any person who may lawfully have that drug in his possession;

(*b*) a person who is authorised under paragraph (1)(*c*) may supply or offer to supply any drug which he may, by virtue of being so authorised, lawfully produce to any person who may lawfully have that drug in his possession.

(5) Notwithstanding the provisions of section 4(1)(*b*) of the Act—

(*a*) the owner of a ship, or the master of a ship which does not carry a doctor on board as part of her complement, may supply or offer to supply any drug specified in Schedule 3—

(i) to any member of the crew; or

(ii) to any person who may lawfully supply that drug;

(b) the installation manager of an offshore installation may supply or offer to supply any drug specified in Schedule 3—

(i) to any person on that installation, whether present in the course of his employment or not; or

(ii) to any person who may lawfully supply that drug.

Possession of drugs in Schedules 2 and 3

(1) Notwithstanding the provisions of section 5(1) of the Act—

(a) a person specified in one of sub-paragraphs (a) to (k) of Regulation 8(2) may have in his possession any drug specified in Schedule 2;

(c) a person specified in one of sub-paragraphs (a) to (k) (including sub-paragraph (ff)) of Regulation 9(2) may have in his possession any drug specified in Schedule 3,

for the purpose of acting in his capacity as such a person:

Provided that nothing in this paragraph authorises—

(i) a person specified in sub-paragraph (e) of Regulation 8(2); or

(ii) a person specified in sub-paragraph (e) or (ff) of Regulation 9(2),

to have in his possession any drug other than such a drug as is mentioned in the sub-paragraph in question specifying him.

(2) Notwithstanding the provisions of section 5(1) of the Act a person may have in his possession any drug specified in Schedule 2 or 3 for administration for medical, dental or veterinary purposes in accordance with the directions of a practitioner:

Provided that this paragraph shall not have effect in the case of a person to whom the drug has been supplied by or on the prescription of a doctor if—

(a) that person was then being supplied with any controlled drug by or on the prescription of another doctor and failed to disclose that fact to the first mentioned doctor before the supply by him or on his prescription; or

(b) that or any other person on his behalf made a declaration or statement, which was false in any particular, for the purpose of obtaining the supply or prescription.

(3) Notwithstanding the provisions of section 5(1) of the Act, a person who is authorised as a member of a group may, under and in accordance with the terms of his group authority and in compliance with any conditions attached thereto, have any drug specified in Schedule 2 or 3 in his possession.

(4) Notwithstanding the provisions of section 5(1) of the Act—

(a) a person who is authorised by a written authority issued by the Secretary of State under and for the purposes of this sub-paragraph and for the time being in force may, at the premises specified in that authority and in compliance with any conditions so specified, have in his possession any drug specified in Schedule 3;

(b) a person who is authorised under Regulation 9(1)(c) may have in his possession any drug which he may, by virtue of being so authorised, lawfully produce;

(c) a person who is authorised under Regulation 9(4)(a) may have in his possession any drug which he may, by virtue of being so authorised, lawfully supply or offer to supply.

(5) Notwithstanding the provisions of section 5(1) of the Act—

  (*a*) the owner of a ship, or the master of a ship which does not carry a doctor on board as part of her complement, may have in his possession any drug specified in Schedule 2 or 3 so far as necessary for the purpose of compliance with the Merchant Shipping Acts;

  (*b*) the master of a foreign ship which is in a port in Great Britain may have in his possession any drug specified in Schedule 2 or 3 so far as necessary for the equipment of the ship;

  (*c*) the installation manager of an offshore installation may have in his possession any drug specified in Schedule 2 or 3 so far as necessary for the purpose of compliance with the Mineral Workings (Offshore Installations) Act 1971.

Exemption for midwives in respect of pethidine

11.—(1) Notwithstanding the provisions of sections 4(1)(*b*) and 5(1) of the Act, a certified midwife, who has in accordance with the provisions of the Midwives Act 1951**(a)**, or the Midwives (Scotland) Act 1951**(b)**, notified to the local supervising authority her intention to practise, may, subject to the provisions of this Regulation—

  (*a*) so far as necessary for the practice of her profession or employment as a midwife, have pethidine in her possession;

  (*b*) so far as necessary as aforesaid, administer pethidine; and

  (*c*) surrender to the appropriate medical officer any stocks of pethidine in her possession which are no longer required by her.

(2) Nothing in paragraph (1) authorises a midwife to have in her possession pethidine which has been obtained otherwise than on a midwife's supply order signed by the appropriate medical officer.

(3) In this Regulation, the expression—

  "appropriate medical officer" means—

  (*a*) a doctor who is for the time being authorised in writing for the purposes of this Regulation by the local supervising authority for the region or area in which the pethidine was, or is to be, obtained; or

  (*c*) for the purposes of paragraph (2), a person appointed under section 17 of the Midwives Act 1951, or, as the case may be, section 18 of the Midwives (Scotland) Act 1951, by that authority to exercise supervision over certified midwives within their area, who is for the time being authorised aforesaid;

  "certified midwife" and "local supervising authority" have the same meanings as in the Midwives Act 1951 or, in Scotland, the Midwives (Scotland) Act 1951, as amended by the National Health Service Reorganisation Act 1973 and the National Health Service (Scotland) Act 1972, respectively.

  "midwife's supply order" means an order in writing specifying the name and occupation of the midwife obtaining the pethidine, the purpose for which it is required and the total quantity to be obtained.

  (a) 1951 c. 53.   **(b)** 1951 c. 54.

Cultivation under licence of Cannabis plant

12. Where any person is authorised by a licence of the Secretary of State issued under this Regulation and for the time being in force to cultivate plants of the genus *Cannabis*, it shall not by virtue of section 6 of the Act be unlawful for that person to cultivate any such plant in accordance with the terms of the licence and in compliance with any conditions attached to the licence.

Approval of premises for cannabis smoking for research purposes

13. Section 8 of the Act (which makes it an offence for the occupier of premises to permit certain activities there) shall not have effect in relation to the smoking of cannabis or cannabis resin for the purposes of research on any premises for the time being approved for the purpose by the Secretary of State.

PART III

REQUIREMENTS AS TO DOCUMENTATION AND RECORD KEEPING

Documents to be obtained by supplier of controlled drugs

14.—(1) Where a person (hereafter in this paragraph referred to as "the supplier"), not being a practitioner, supplies a controlled drug otherwise than on a prescription, the supplier shall not deliver the drug to a person who—

(a) purports to be sent by or on behalf of the person to whom it is supplied (hereafter in this paragraph referred to as "the recipient"); and

(b) is not authorised by any provision of these Regulations other than the provisions of Regulation 6(f) to have that drug in his possession,

unless that person produces to the supplier a statement in writing signed by the recipient to the effect that he is empowered by the recipient to receive that drug on behalf of the recipient, and the supplier is reasonably satisfied that the document is a genuine document.

(2) Where a person (hereafter in this paragraph referred to as "the supplier") supplies a controlled drug, otherwise than on a prescription or by way of administration, to any of the persons specified in paragraph (4), the supplier shall not deliver the drug—

(a) until he has obtained a requisition in writing which—

   (i) is signed by the person to whom the drug is supplied (hereafter in this paragraph referred to as "the recipient");

  (ii) states the name, address and profession or occupation of the recipient;

 (iii) specifies the purpose for which the drug supplied is required and the total quantity to be supplied; and

 (iv) where appropriate, satisfies the requirements of paragraph (5);

(b) unless he is reasonably satisfied that the signature is that of the person purporting to have signed the requisition and that that person is engaged in the profession or occupation specified in the requisition:

Provided that where the recipient is a practitioner and he represents that he urgently requires a controlled drug for the purpose of his profesion, the supplier may, if he is reasonably satisfied that the recipient so requires the drug and is, by reason of some emergency, unable before delivery to furnish to the supplier a requisition in writing duly signed, deliver the drug to the recipient on an undertaking by the recipient to furnish such a requisition within the twenty-four hours next following.

(3) A person who has given such an undertaking as aforesaid shall deliver to the person by whom the controlled drug was supplied a signed requisition in accordance with the undertaking.

(4) The persons referred to in paragraph (2) are—

(a) a practitioner;

(b) the matron or acting matron of a hospital or nursing home;

(c) a person who is in charge of a laboratory;

(d) the owner of a ship, or the master of a ship which does not carry a doctor on board as part of her complement;

(e) the master of a foreign ship in a port in Great Britain;

(f) the installation manager of an offshore installation.

(5) A requisition furnished for the purposes of paragraph (2) shall—

(a) where furnished by the matron or acting matron of a hospital or nursing home, be signed by a doctor or dentist employed or engaged in that hospital or nursing home;

(b) where furnished by the master of a foreign ship, contain a statement signed by the proper officer of the port health authority, or, in Scotland, the medical officer designated under section 21 of the National Health Service (Scotland) Act 1972 by the Health Board, within whose jurisdiction the ship is, that the quantity of the drug to be supplied is the quantity necessary for the equipment of the ship.

(6) Where the person responsible for the dispensing and supply of medicines at any hospital or nursing home supplies a controlled drug to the sister or acting sister for the time being in charge of any ward, theatre or other department in that hospital or nursing home (hereafter in this paragraph referred to as "the recipient") he shall—

(a) obtain a requisition in writing, signed by the recipient, which specifies the total quantity of the drug to be supplied; and

(b) mark the requisition in such manner as to show that it has been complied with, and any requisition obtained for the purposes of this paragraph shall be retained in the dispensary at which the drug was supplied and a copy of the requisition or a note of it shall be retained or kept by the recipient.

(7) Nothing in this Regulation shall have effect in relation to the drugs specified in Schedule 1 or poppy-straw.

Form of prescriptions

15.—(1) Subject to the provisions of this Regulation, a person shall not issue a prescription containing a controlled drug other than a drug specified in Schedule 1 unless the prescription complies with the following requirements, that is to say, it shall—

(a) be in ink or otherwise so as to be indelible and be signed by the person issuing it with his usual signature and dated by him;

(*b*) insofar as it specifies the information required by sub-paragraphs (*e*) and (*f*) below to be specified, be written by the person issuing it in his own handwriting;

(*c*) except in the case of a health prescription, specify the address of the person issuing it;

(*d*) have written thereon, if issued by a dentist, the words "for dental treatment only" and, if issued by a veterinary surgeon or a veterinary practitioner, the words "for animal treatment only";

(*e*) specify the name and address of the person for whose treatment it is issued or, if it is issued by a veterinary surgeon or veterinary practitioner, of the person to whom the controlled drug prescribed is to be delivered;

(*f*) specify the dose to be taken and—

    (i) in the case of a prescription containing a controlled drug which is a preparation, the form and, where appropriate, the strength of the preparation, and either the total quantity (in both words and figures) of the preparation or the number (in both words and figures) of dosage units, as appropriate, to be supplied;

    (ii) in any other case, the total quantity (in both words and figures) of the controlled drug to be supplied;

(*g*) in the case of a prescription for a total quantity intended to be dispensed by instalments, contain a direction specifying the amount of the instalments of the total amount which may be dispensed and the intervals to be observed when dispensing.

(2) Paragraph (1)(*b*) shall not have effect in relation to a prescription issued by a person approved (whether personally or as a member of a class) for the purposes of this paragraph by the Secretary of State.

(2A) Paragraph (1)(*b*) shall not have effect in relation to a prescription containing no controlled drug other than—

(*a*) phenobarbitone;

(*b*) phenobarbitone sodium;

(*c*) a preparation containing a drug specified in sub-paragraph (*a*) or (*b*) above; or

(*d*) a drug specified in Schedule 1.

(3) In the case of a prescription issued for the treatment of a patient in a hospital or nursing home, it shall be a sufficient compliance with paragraph (1)(*e*) if the prescription is written on the patient's bed card or case sheet.

Provisions as to supply on prescription

16.—(1) A person shall not supply a controlled drug other than a drug specified in Schedule 1 on a prescription—

(*a*) unless the prescription complies with the provisions of Regulation 15;

(*b*) unless the address specified in the prescription as the address of the person issuing it is an address within the United Kingdom;

(*c*) unless he either is acquainted with the signature of the person by whom it purports to be issued and has no reason to suppose that it is not genuine, or has taken reasonably sufficient steps to satisfy himself that it is genuine;

(*d*) before the date specified in the prescription;

(*e*) subject to paragraph (3), later than thirteen weeks after the date specified in the prescription.

(2) Subject to paragraph (3), a person dispensing a prescription containing a controlled drug other than a drug specified in Schedule 1 shall, at the time of dispensing it, mark thereon the date on which it is dispensed and, unless it is a health prescription, shall retain it on the premises on which it was dispensed.

(3) In the case of a prescription containing a controlled drug other than a drug specified in Schedule 1, which contains a direction that specified instalments of the total amount may be dispensed at stated intervals, the person dispensing it shall not supply the drug otherwise than in accordance with that direction and—

(*a*) paragraph (1) shall have effect as if for the requirement contained in sub-paragraph (*e*) thereof there were substituted a requirement that the occasion on which the first instalment is dispensed shall not be later than thirteen weeks after the date specified in the prescription;

(*b*) paragraph (2) shall have effect as if for the words "at the time of dispensing it" there were substituted the words "on each occasion on which an instalment is dispensed".

Exemption for certain prescriptions

17. Nothing in Regulations 15 and 16 shall have effect in relation to a prescription issued for the purposes of a scheme for testing the quality and amount of the drugs, preparations and appliances supplied under the National Health Service Acts 1946 to 1973 or the National Health Service (Scotland) Acts 1947 to 1973 and the Regulations made thereunder or to any prescriptions issued for the purposes of the Food and Drugs Act 1955 or, in Scotland, the Food and Drugs (Scotland) Act 1956 to a sampling officer within the meaning of those Acts or for the purposes of the Medicines Act 1968 to a sampling officer within the meaning of that Act.

Marking of bottles and other containers

18.—(1) Subject to paragraph (2), no person shall supply a controlled drug otherwise than in a bottle, package or other container which is plainly marked—

(*a*) in the case of a controlled drug other than a preparation, with the amount of the drug contained therein;

(*b*) in the case of a controlled drug which is a preparation—

(i) made up into tablets, capsules or other dosage units, with the amount of each component (being a controlled drug) of the preparation in each dosage unit and the number of dosage units in the bottle, package or other container;

(ii) not made up as aforesaid, with the total amount of the preparation in the bottle, package or other container and the percentage of each of its components which is a controlled drug.

(2) Nothing in this Regulation shall have effect in relation to the drugs specified in Schedule 1 or poppy-straw or in relation to the supply of a controlled drug by or on the prescription of a practitioner.

Keeping of registers

19.—(1) Subject to paragraph (3) and Regulation 21, every person authorised by or under Regulation 5 or 8 to supply any drug specified in Schedule 2 or 4 shall comply with the following requirements, that is to say—

(a) he shall, in accordance with the provisions of this Regulation and of Regulation 20, keep a register and shall enter therein in chronological sequence in the form specified in Part I or Part II of Schedule 5, as the case may require, particulars of every quantity of a drug specified in Schedule 2 or 4 obtained by him and of every quantity of such a drug supplied (whether by way of administration or otherwise) by him whether to persons within or outside Great Britain;

(b) he shall use a separate register or separate part of the register for entries made in respect of each class of drugs, and each of the drugs specified in paragraphs 1, and 6 of Schedule 2 and paragraphs 1 and 3 of Schedule 4 together with its salts and any preparation or other product containing it or any of its salts shall be treated as a separate class, so however that any stereoisomeric form of a drug or its salt shall be classed with that drug.

(2) Nothing in paragraph (1) shall be taken as preventing the use of a separate section within a register or separate part of a register in respect of different drugs or strengths of drugs comprised within the class of drugs to which that register or separate part relates.

(3) The foregoing provisions of this Regulation shall not have effect in relation to—

(a) a person licensed under Regulation 5 to supply any drug, where the licence so directs; or

(b) the sister or acting sister for the time being in charge of a ward, theatre or other department in a hospital or nursing home.

Requirements as to registers

20. Any person required to keep a register under Regulation 19 shall comply with the following requirements, that is to say—

(a) the class of drugs to which the entries on any page of any such register relate shall be specified at the head of that page;

(b) every entry required to be made under Regulation 19 in such a register shall be made on the day on which the drug is obtained or, as the case may be, on which the transaction in respect of the supply of the drug by the person required to make the entry takes place or, if that is not reasonably practicable, on the day next following that day;

(c) no cancellation, obliteration or alteration of any such entry shall be made, and a correction of such an entry shall be made only by way of marginal note or footnote which shall specify the date on which the correction is made;

(d) every such entry and every correction of such an entry shall be made in ink or otherwise so as to be indelible;

(e) such a register shall not be used for any purpose other than the purposes of these Regulations;

(f) the person so required to keep such a register shall on demand made by the

Secretary of State or by any person authorised in writing by the Secretary of State in that behalf—

    (i) furnish such particulars as may be requested in respect of the obtaining or supplying by him of any drug specified in Schedule 2 or 4, or in respect of any stock of such drugs in his possession;

    (ii) for the purpose of confirming any such particulars, produce any stock of such drugs in his possession;

    (iii) produce the said register and such other books or documents in his possession relating to any dealings in drugs specified in Schedule 2 or 4 as may be requested;

  (g) a separate register shall be kept in respect of each premises at which the person required to keep the register carries on his business or occupation, but subject to that not more than one register shall be kept at one time in respect of each class of drug in respect of which he is required to keep a separate register, so, however, that a separate register may, with the approval of the Secretary of State, be kept in respect of each department of the business carried on by him;

  (h) every such register in which entries are currently being made shall be kept at the premises to which it relates.

Record-keeping requirements in particular cases

21.—(1) Where a drug specified in Schedule 2 is supplied in accordance with Regulation 8(5)(a)(i) to a member of the crew of a ship, an entry in the official log book required to be kept under the Merchant Shipping Acts or, in the case of a ship which is not required to carry such an official log book, a report signed by the master of the ship, shall, notwithstanding anything in these Regulations, be a sufficient record of the supply if the entry or report specifies the drug supplied and, in the case of a report, it is delivered as soon as may be to the superintendent of a mercantile marine office established and maintained under the Merchant Shipping Acts.

(2) Where a drug specified in Schedule 2 is supplied in accordance with Regulation 8(5)(b)(i) to a person on an offshore installation, an entry in the installation log book required to be maintained under the Offshore Installations (Logbooks and Registration of Death) Regulations 1972**(a)** which specifies the drug supplied shall, notwithstanding anything in these Regulations, be a sufficient record of the supply.

(3) A midwife authorised by Regulation 11(1) to have pethidine in her possession shall—

  (a) on each occasion on which she obtains a supply of pethidine, enter in a book kept by her and used solely for the purposes of this paragraph the date, the name and address of the person from whom the drug was obtained, the amount obtained and the form in which it was obtained; and

  (b) on administering pethidine to a patient, enter in the said book as soon as practicable the name and address of the patient, the amount administered and the form in which it was administered.

(a) S.I. 1972/1542 (1972 III, p. 4532).

Preservation of registers, books and other documents

22.—(1) All registers and books kept in pursuance of Regulation 19 or 21(3) shall be preserved for a period of two years from the date on which the last entry therein is made.

(2) Every requisition, order or prescription (other than a health prescription) on which a controlled drug is supplied in pursuance of these Regulations shall be preserved for a period of two years from the date on which the last delivery under it was made.

Preservation of records relating to drugs in Schedule 1

23.—(1) A producer of any drug specified in Schedule 1 and a wholesale dealer in any such drug shall keep every invoice or other like record issued in respect of each quantity of such a drug obtained by him and in respect of each quantity of such a drug supplied by him.

(2) A retail dealer in any drug specified in Schedule 1 shall keep every invoice or other like record issued in respect of each quantity of such a drug obtained by him.

(3) Every document kept in pursuance of this Regulation shall be preserved for a period of two years from the date on which it is issued:

Provided that the keeping of a copy of the document made at any time during the said period of two years shall be treated for the purposes of this paragraph as if it were the keeping of the original document.

PART IV

MISCELLANEOUS

Destruction of controlled drugs

24.—(1) No person who is required by any provision of, or by any term or condition of a licence having effect under, these Regulations to keep records with respect to a drug specified in Schedule 2 or 4 shall destroy such a drug or cause such a drug to be destroyed except in the presence of and in accordance with any directions given by a person authorised (whether personally or as a member of a class) for the purposes of this paragraph by the Secretary of State (hereafter in this Regulation referred to as an "authorised person").

(2) An authorised person may, for the purpose of analysis, take a sample of a drug specified in Schedule 2 or 4 which is to be destroyed.

(3) Where a drug specified in Schedule 2 or 4 is destroyed in pursuance of paragraph (1) by or at the instance of a person who is required by any provision of, or by any term or condition of a licence having effect under, these Regulations to keep a record in respect of the obtaining or supply of that drug, that record shall include particulars of the date of destruction and the quantity destroyed and shall be signed by the authorised person in whose presence the drug is destroyed.

(4) Where the master or owner of a ship or installation manager of an offshore installation has in his possession a drug specified in Schedule 2 which he no longer requires, he shall not destroy the drug or cause it to be destroyed but shall dispose of it to a constable or to a person who may lawfully supply it.

Transitional provisions

25.—(1) Any licence issued for the purposes of section 6(1) of the Dangerous Drugs Act 1965**(a)** (which makes it an offence to cultivate any cannabis plant except under licence) and in force immediately before the repeal of that Act shall continue in force for the same period of time as if that Act had not been repealed and shall have effect as if it had been issued for the purposes of Regulation 12.

(2) Any licence issued for the purposes of any provision of the Dangerous Drugs (No. 2) Regulations 1964**(b)** and in force immediately before the repeal of the said Act of 1965 shall, insofar as it authorises any person to do anything which could be authorised by a licence issued under Regulation 5, continue in force for the same period of time as if that Act had not been repealed and shall have effect as if it had been issued for the purposes of Regulation 5.

(3) Any authority granted in respect of any class for the purposes of any provision of the said Regulations of 1964 and in force immediately before the repeal of the said Act of 1965 shall, insofar as it authorises any class of persons to do anything which could be authorised by an authority granted for the purposes of Regulation 8(3) or 10(3), continue in force as if that Act had not been repealed and shall have effect as if granted for the purposes of Regulation 8(3) or 10(3) as the case may be.

(4) Any register, record, book, prescription or other document required to be preserved under Regulation 26 of the said Regulations of 1964 shall, notwithstanding the repeal of the said Act of 1965, be preserved for the same period of time as if that Act had not been repealed.

(5) In the case of a prescription issued before the coming into operation of these Regulations, Regulation 16(1) shall have effect as if—

(*a*) in the case of a prescription containing a controlled drug specified in the Schedule to the Drugs (Prevention of Misuse) Act 1964**(c)** immediately before the repeal of that Act, sub-paragraphs (*a*) and (*b*) of that paragraph were omitted; and

(*b*) in any other case, for the said sub-paragraphs (*a*) and (*b*) there were substituted the words "unless the prescription complies with the provisions of the Dangerous Drugs (No. 2) Regulations 1964 relating to prescriptions".

(6) In this Regulation, any reference to the repeal of the Dangerous Drugs Act 1965 or the Drugs (Prevention of Misuse) Act 1964 shall be construed as a reference to its repeal by section 39(2) of and Schedule 6 to the Act.

Robert Carr,
One of Her Majesty's Principal
Secretaries of State.

Home Office,
 Whitehall.
19th April 1973.

(a) 1965 c. 15.   **(b)** S.I. 1964/1811 (1964 III, p. 3942).
(c) 1964 c. 64.

SCHEDULE 1   *Regulations 4, 7, 8, 14*

15, 16, 18 and 23

CONTROLLED DRUGS EXCEPTED FROM THE PROHIBITION ON IMPORTATION,
EXPORTATION AND POSSESSION AND SUBJECT TO THE REQUIREMENTS OF
REGULATION 23

1.—(1) Any preparation of one or more of the substances to which this paragraph applies, not being a preparation designed for administration by injection, when compounded with one or more other active or inert ingredients and containing a total of not more than 100 milligrammes of the substance or substances (calculated as base) per dosage unit or with a total concentration of not more than 2.5 per cent. (calculated as base) in undivided preparations.

(2) The substances to which this paragraph applies are acetyldihydrocodeine, codeine, dihydrocodeine, ethylmorphine, nicocodine, nicodicodine (6-nicotinoyldihydrocodeine), norcodeine, pholcodine and their respective salts.

2. Any preparation of cocaine containing not more than 0.1 per cent. of cocaine calculated as cocaine base, being a preparation compounded with one or more other active or inert ingredients in such a way that the cocaine cannot be recovered by readily applicable means or in a yield which would constitute a risk to health.

3. Any preparation of medicinal opium or of morphine containing (in either case) not more than 0.2 per cent. of morphine calculated as anhydrous morphine base, being a preparation compounded with one or more other active or inert ingredients in such a way that the opium or, as the case may be, the morphine, cannot be recovered by readily applicable means or in a yield which would constitute a risk to health.

4. Any preparation of dextropropoxyphene, being a preparation designed for oral administration, containing not more than 135 milligrammes of dextropropoxyphene (calculated as base) per dosage unit or with a total concentration of not more than 2.5 per cent. (calculated as base) in undivided preparations.

4A. Any preparation of propiram containing, per dosage unit, not more than 100 milligrammes or propiram calculated as base and compounded with at least the same amount (by weight) of methylcellulose.

5. Any preparation of difenoxin (1-(3-cyano-3,3-diphenylpropyl)-4-phenylpiperidine-4-carboxylic acid) containing, per dosage unit, not more than 0.5 milligrammes of difenoxin and a quantity of atropine sulphate equivalent to at least 5 per cent. of the dose difenoxin.

6. Any preparation of diphenoxylate containing, per dosage unit, not more than 2.5 milligrammes of diphenoxylate calculated as base, and a quantity of atropine sulphate equivalent to at least 1 per cent. of the dose of diphenoxylate.

7. Any preparation of propiram containing, per dosage unit, not more than 100 milligrammes of propiram calculated as base and compounded with at least the same amount (by weight) of methylcellulose.

8. Any powder of ipecacuanha and opium comprising—

          10 per cent. opium, in powder,

          10 per cent. ipecacuanha root, in powder, well mixed with

          80 per cent. of any other powdered ingredient containing no controlled drug.

9. Any mixture containing one or more of the preparations specified in paragraphs 1 to 8, being a mixture of which none of the other ingredients is a controlled drug.

SCHEDULE 2

CONTROLLED DRUGS SUBJECT TO THE REQUIREMENTS OF
REGULATIONS 14, 15, 16, 18, 19, 20, 21 and 24

1. The following substances and products, namely:—

Acetorphine.
Alfentanil.
Allylprodine.
Alphacetylmethadol.
Alphameprodine.
Alphamethadol.
Alphaprodine.
Anileridine.
Benzethidine.
Benzylmorphine (3-benzylmorphine).
Betacetylmethadol.
Betameprodine.
Betamethadol.
Betaprodine.
Bezitramide.
Clonitazene.
Cocaine.
Desomorphine.
Dextromoramide.
Diamorphine.
Diampromide.
Diethylthiambutene.
Difenoxin (1-(3-cyano-3,3-diphenylpropyl)-
    4-phenylpiperidine-4-carboxylic acid).
Dihydrocodeinone *O*-carboxymethyloxime.
Dihydromorphine.
Dimenoxadole.
Dimepheptanol.
Dimethylthiambutene.
Dioxaphetyl butyrate.
Diphenoxylate.
Dipipanone.
Drotebanol (3,4-dimethoxy-17-methyl-
    morphinan-6β,14-diol).

Ecgonine, and any derivative of ecgonine
    which is convertible to ecgonine or to
    cocaine.
Ethylmethylthiambutene.
Etonitazene.
Etorphine.
Etoxeridine.
Fentanyl.
Furethidine.
Hydrocodone.
Hydromorphinol.
Hydromorphone.
Hydroxypethidine.
Isomethadone.
Ketobemidone.
Levomethorphan.
Levomoramide.
Levophenacylmorphan.
Levorphanol.
Medicinal opium.
Metazocine.
Methadone.
Methadyl acetate.
Methyldesorphine.
Methyldihydromorphine.
    (6-methyldihydromorphine).
Metopon.
Morpheridine.
Morphine.
Morphine methobromide, morphine *N*-
    oxide and other pentavalent nitrogen
    morphine derivatives.
Myrophine.
Nicomorphine.

Noracymethadol.
Norlevorphanol.
Normethadone.
Normorphine.
Norpipanone.
Oxycodone.
Oxymorphone.
Pethidine.
Phenadoxone.
Phenampromide.
Phenazocine.
Phencyclidine.
Phenomorphan.
Phenoperidine.
Piminodine.
Piritramide.
Proheptazine.
Properidine.

Racemethorphan.
Racemoramide.
Racemorphan.
Sufentanil.
Thebacon.
Thebaine.
Tilidate.
Trimeperidine.
4-Cyano-2-dimethylamino-4, 4-diphenylbutane.
4-Cyano-1-methyl-4-phenylpiperidine.
1-Methyl-4-phenylpiperidine-4-carboxylic acid.
2-Methyl-3-morpholino-1, 1-diphenylpropanecarboxylic acid.
4-Phenylpiperidine-4-carboxylic acid ethyl ester.

2. Any stereoisomeric form of a substance specified in paragraph 1 not being dextromethorphan or dextrorphan.

3. Any ester or ether of a substance specified in paragraph 1 or 2, not being a substance specified in paragraph 6.

4. Any salt of a substance specified in any of paragraphs 1 to 3.

5. Any preparation or other product containing a substance or product specified in any of paragraphs 1 to 4, not being a preparation specified in Schedule 1.

6. The following substances and products, namely—

Acetyldihydrocodeine.
Amphetamine.
Codeine
Dexamphetamine.
Dextropropoxyphene
Dihydrocodeine.
Ethylmorphine (3-ethylmorphine).
Mecloqualone.
Methaqualone.

Methylamphetamine.
Methylphenidate.
Nicocodine.
Nicodicodine (6-nicotinoyldihydro-codeine).
Norcodeine.
Phenmetrazine.
Pholcodine.
Propiram.

7. Any stereoisomeric form of a substance specified in paragraph 6.

8. Any salt of a substance specified in paragraph 6 or 7.

9. Any preparation or other product containing a substance or product specified in any of paragraphs 6 to 8, not being a preparation specified in Schedule 1.

SCHEDULE 3 *Regulations 7, 9 and 10*

CONTROLLED DRUGS SUBJECT TO THE REQUIREMENTS OF
REGULATIONS 14, 15, 16 AND 18

1. The following substances, namely:—

(*a*) Benzphetamine.
Chlorphentermine.
Diethylpropion.
Mephentermine.

Methylphenobarbitone.
Phendimetrazine.
Pipradrol.

(*b*) Any 5,5 disubstituted barbituric acid.

2. Any stereoisomeric form of a substance specified in paragraph 1.

3. Any salt of a substance specified in paragraph 1 or 2.

4. Any preparation or other product containing a substance specified in any of
paragraphs 1 to 3, not being a preparation specified in Schedule 1.

SCHEDULE 4

CONTROLLED DRUGS SUBJECT TO THE REQUIREMENTS OF
REGULATIONS 14, 15, 16, 18, 19, 20 and 24

1. The following substances and products, namely:—

(*a*) Bufotenine
Cannabinol
Cannabinol derivatives
Cannabis and cannabis resin
Coca leaf
Concentrate of poppy-straw
Eticyclidine
Lysergamide.
Lysergide and other *N*-alkyl derivatives of lysergamide
Mescaline
Psilocin
Raw opium
Rolicyclidine
Tenocyclidine
4-Bromo-2,5-dimethoxy-*α*-methylphenethylamine
N,*N*-Diethyltryptamine
N,*N*-Dimethyltryptamine
2,5-Dimethoxy-*α*,4-dimethylphenethylamine

(*a*) any compound (not being a compound for the time being specified in sub-
paragraph (*a*) above) structurally derived from tryptamine or from a ring-hydroxy

tryptamine by substitution at the nitrogen atom of the sidechain with one or more alkyl substituents but no other substituent;

(b) any compound (not being methoxyphenamine or a compound for the time being specified in sub-paragraph (a) above) structurally derived from phenethylamine, an N-alkylphenethylamine, α-methylphenethylamine, an N-alkyl-α-methyl-phenethylamine, α-ethylphenethylamine, or an N-alkyl-α-ethylphenethylamine by substitution in the ring to any extent with alkyl, alkoxy, alkylenedioxy or halide substituents, whether or not further substituted in the ring by one or more other univalent substituents.

2. Any stereoisomeric form of a substance specified in paragraph 1.

3. Any ester or ether of a substance specified in paragraph 1 or 2.

4. Any salt of a substance specified in any of paragraphs 1 to 3.

5. Any preparation or other product containing a substance or product specified in any of paragraphs 1 to 4, not being a preparation specified in Schedule 1.

Regulation 19

SCHEDULE 5

FORM OF REGISTER

PART I

Entries to be made in case of obtaining

Date on which supply received	NAME	ADDRESS	Amount obtained	Form in which obtained
	Of person or firm from whom obtained			

Part II

Entries to be made in case of supply

Date on which the transaction was effected	NAME	ADDRESS	Particulars as to licence or authority of person or firm supplied to be in possession	Amount supplied	Form in which supplied
	Of person or firm supplied				

APPENDIX III

STATUTORY INSTRUMENTS

1973 No. 798

DANGEROUS DRUGS

The Misuse of Drugs (Safe Custody) Regulations 1973

Made - - - -	19*th April* 1973
Laid before Parliament	7*th May* 1973
Coming into Operation—	
Regulations 1, 2, 5 and	
Schedule 1	1*st July* 1973
Remainder	1*st October* 1974

In pursuance of sections 10(2)(*a*) and 31 of the Misuse of Drugs Act 1971(**a**), after consultation with the Advisory Council on the Misuse of Drugs, I hereby make the following Regulations:—

1. These Regulations may be cited as the Misuse of Drugs (Safe Custody) Regulations 1973 and (with the exception of Regulations 3 and 4 and Schedule 2 which shall come into operation on 1st April 1975) shall come into operation on 1st July 1973.

2.—(1) In these Regulations, unless the context otherwise requires, the expression—

"the Act" means the Misuse of Drugs Act 1971;

"retail dealer" means a person lawfully conducting a retail pharmacy business or a pharmacist engaged in supplying drugs to the public at a health centre within the meaning of the Medicines Act 1968(**b**).

(2) In these Regulations any reference to any enactment shall be construed as a reference to that enactment as amended, and as including a reference thereto as extended or applied, by or under any other enactment.

(3) The Interpretation Act 1889(**c**) shall apply for the interpretation of these Regulations as it applies for the interpretation of an Act of Parliament.

3. —(1) This Regulation applies to the following premises, that is to say:—

(*a*) any premises occupied by a retail dealer for the purposes of his business;

(**a**) 1971 c. 38.   (**b**) 1968 c. 67.   (**c**) 1889 c. 63

(*b*) any nursing home within the meaning of Part VI of the Public Health Act 1936**(a)** or the Nursing Homes Registration (Scotland) Act 1938**(b)**;

(*c*) any residential or other establishment provided under or by virtue of section 59 of the Social Work (Scotland) Act 1968**(c)**;

(*d*) any mental nursing home within the meaning of Part III of the Mental Health Act 1959**(d)**;

(*e*) any private hospital within the meaning of the Mental Health (Scotland) Act 1960**(e)**.

(2) Subject to paragraph (4) of this Regulation, the occupier and every person concerned in the management of any premises to which this Regulation applies shall ensure that all controlled drugs (other than those specified in Schedule 1 to these Regulations) on the premises are, so far as circumstances permit, kept in a locked safe, cabinet or room which is so constructed and maintained as to prevent unauthorised access to the drugs.

(3) Subject to Regulation 4 of these Regulations, the relevant requirements of Schedule 2 to these Regulations shall be complied with in relation to every safe, cabinet or room in which controlled drugs are kept in pursuance of paragraph (2) of this Regulation.

(4) It shall not be necessary to comply with the requirements of paragraph (2) of this Regulation in respect of any controlled drug which is for the time being under the direct personal supervision of—

(*a*) in the case of any premises falling within paragraph (1)(*a*) of this Regulation, a pharmacist in respect of whom no direction under section 12(2) of the Act is for the time being in force; or

(*b*) in the case of premises falling within paragraph (1)(*b*) to (*e*) of this Regulation, the person in charge of the premises or any member of his staff designated by him for the purpose.

4.—(1) Paragraph (3) of Regulation 3 of these Regulations shall not have effect in relation to a safe, cabinet or room situated on any premises occupied for the purposes of his business by a person lawfully conducting a retail pharmacy business (hereafter in this Regulation referred to as "the occupier") if a certificate has been issued in pursuance of paragraph (2) of this Regulation (hereafter in this Regulation referred to as a "certificate") in respect of that safe, cabinet or room and the certificate is for the time being in force.

(2) On receiving written application in that behalf from the occupier, the chief officer of police for the police area in which the premises in question are situated may—

(*a*) cause the said premises and, in particular, any safe, cabinet or room in which controlled drugs are kept, to be inspected; and

(*b*) if satisfied that, in all the circumstances of the case, the safes, cabinets or rooms in which controlled drugs (other than those specified in Schedule 1 to these Regulations) are to be kept provide an adequate degree of security, issue a certificate in respect of those safes, cabinets or rooms.

(3) Every certificate shall specify—

(*a*) every safe, cabinet or room to which the certificate relates; and

---

(a) 1936 c. 49.   **(b)** 1938 c. 73.   **(c)** 1968 c. 49.   **(d)** 1959 c. 72.
(e) 1960 c. 61.

(*b*) any conditions necessary to be observed if the safes, cabinets and rooms to which the certificate relates are to provide an adequate degree of security.

(4) Where a certificate is in force in respect of any safe, cabinet or room on any premises, the chief officer of police may cause the premises to be inspected at any reasonable time for the purpose of ascertaining whether any conditions specified in the certificate are being observed and whether as a result of any change of circumstances the safes, cabinets and rooms to which the certificate relates have ceased to provide an adequate degree of security.

(5) A certificate may be cancelled by the chief officer of police if it appears to him that—

(*a*) there has been a breach of any condition specified in the certificate; or

(*b*) as a result of any change of circumstances, the safes, cabinets and rooms to which the certificate relates no longer provide an adequate degree of security; or

(*c*) the occupier has refused entry to any police officer acting in pursuance of paragraph (4) of this Regulation.

(6) A certificate shall, unless previously cancelled in pursuance of paragraph (5) of this Regulation, remain in force for a period of one year from the date of issue thereof, but may from time to time be renewed for a further period of one year.

5.—(1) Where any controlled drug (other than a drug specified in Schedule 1 to these Regulations) is kept otherwise than in a locked safe, cabinet or room which is so constructed and maintained as to prevent unauthorised access to the drug, any person to whom this Regulation applies having possession of the drug shall ensure that, so far as circumstances permit, it is kept in a locked receptacle which can be opened only by him or by a person authorised by him.

(2) Paragraph (1) of this Regulation applies to any person other than—

(*a*) a person to whom the drug has been supplied by or on the prescription of a practitioner for his own treatment or that of another person or an animal; or

(*b*) a person engaged in the business of a carrier when acting in the course of that business; or

(*c*) a person engaged in the business of the Post Office when acting in the course of that business.

Robert Carr,
One of Her Majesty's Principal
Secretaries of State.

Home Office,
  Whitehall.
19th April 1973.

SCHEDULE 1   *Regulations 3(2), 4(2)(b) and 5.*

EXEMPTED DRUGS

1. Any controlled drug specified in Schedule 1 to the Misuse of Drugs Regulations 1973.

2. Any liquid preparation designed for administration otherwise than by injection which contains any of the following substances and products, that is to say:—

(*a*) Amphetamine; dexamphetamine; levamphetamine
(*b*) Benzphetamine
(*c*) Chlorphentermine
(*d*) Mephentermine
(*e*) Methaqualone
(*f*) Methylamphetamine
(*g*) Methylphenidate
(*h*) Phendimetrazine
(*i*) Phenmetrazine
(*j*) Pipradrol
(*k*) Any stereoisomeric form of a substance specified in any of paragraphs (*b*) to (*j*) above.
(*l*) Any salt of a substance specified in any of paragraphs (*a*) to (*k*) above.

3. Any of the following substances and products, that is to say:—

(*a*) Any 5,5 disubstituted barbituric acid.
(*b*) Methylphenobarbitone.
(*c*) Any stereoisomeric form of a substance specified in paragraph (*a*) or (*b*) above.
(*d*) Any salt of a substance specified in paragraph (*a*), (*b*) or (*c*) above.
(*e*) Any preparation which contains a substance specified in any of paragraphs (*a*) to (*d*) above.

Regulation 3(3)   SCHEDULE 2

STRUCTURAL REQUIREMENTS IN RELATION TO
SAFES, CABINETS AND ROOMS USED FOR KEEPING DRUGS

1. In this Schedule the expression—

"external wall", in relation to any room, means a wall which forms part of the outside of the building in which the room is situated;

"party wall", in relation to any room, means a wall dividing the premises in which the room is situated from other premises under different occupation;

"the Standard of 1963" means the British Standard Specification for Thief Resistant Locks for Hinged Doors B.S. 3621:1963, as published on 6th May 1963;

"two-leaf door" means a door having two leaves which either close on to each other or on to a central pillar, and the two leaves of any such door shall be treated for the purposes of this Schedule as a single door;

"sheet steel" means mild steel sheet being not lighter than 16 gauge.

Safes and Cabinets

2.—(1) A safe or cabinet shall be constructed of—

(*a*) pressed and welded sheet steel; or
(*b*) pressed and welded steel mesh; or

(c) sheet steel or steel mesh welded upon an angle-iron frame of at least 25 millimetres (1 inch) by 25 millimetres (1 inch) section and of at least 5 millimetres ($\frac{3}{16}$ inch) thickness.

(2) The clearance between the door and jamb or, in the case of a two-leaf door, between the two leaves or each leaf and a central pillar shall not be greater than 3 millimetres (⅛ inch).

(3) Each door shall be fitted with an effective lock—

(a) having at least 5 differing levers or, in the case of a pin and tumbler mechanism, at least 6 pins;

(b) designed to permit at least 1000 effective key-differs independent of wards or any other fixed obstruction to the movement of the key; and

(c) provided with a dead-bolt which is either of mild steel of a least 19 millimetres (¾ inch) by 8 millimetres ($\frac{5}{16}$ inch) section or incorporates a suitable anti-cutting device and which has a total throw of at least 12 millimetres (½ inch).

(4) If the length of the vertical closing edge of a door exceeds 914 millimetres (3 feet) and the length of the horizontal edge exceeds 457 millimetres (18 inches) the door shall be fitted with two such locks as are specified in sub-paragraph (3) above, one situated at not more than one third of the length of the vertical closing edge from the top and the other at not more than one third from the bottom, but otherwise the lock required by sub-paragraph (3) above shall be situated in the centre of the vertical closing edge.

(5) If a safe or cabinet is fitted with a two-leaf door, either—

(a) the lock or locks required by sub-paragraphs (3) and (4) above shall be fitted with an integrated espagnolette bolt which is of at least 19 millimetres (¾ inch) by 8 millimetres ($\frac{5}{16}$ inch) section and which has a total throw, at both the top and bottom, of at least 12 millimetres (½ inch); or

(b) the second opening leaf shall be secured at the top and bottom by means of internal bolts of mild steel of at least 6 millimetres (¼ inch) by 6 millimetres (¼ inch) section or 6 millimetres (¼ inch) diameter, each of which has a total throw of at least 12 millimetres (½ inch), the bolt handles being returnable into a holding recess.

(6) A safe or cabinet shall be rigidly and securely fixed to a wall or floor by means of at least two rag-bolts each passing through an internal anchor plate of mild steel which is of at least 3 millimetres (⅛ inch) thickness and which has a surface area of at least 19355 square millimetres (30 square inches).

(7) Nothing shall be displayed outside a safe or cabinet to indicate that drugs are kept inside it.

Rooms

3.—(1) Each wall shall be securely attached to the floor, ceiling and adjacent walls and shall be constructed of—

(a) bricks laid in cement mortar to at least 229 millimetres (9 inches) thickness or, if the joints are reinforced with metal reinforcing ties, to at least 115 millimetres (4½ inches) thickness; or

(b) concrete (being solid concrete, reinforced concrete or dense concrete blocks laid in cement mortar) of at least 152 millimetres (6 inches) thickness, the joints being reinforced with metal reinforcing ties where concrete blocks are used; or

(c) steel mesh fixed externally by welding upon angle-iron frames of at least 50 millimetres (2 inches) by 50 millimetres (2 inches) section and 6 millimetres (¼ inch) thickness, having vertical members not more than 610 millimetres (2 feet) apart and horizontal members not more than 1220 millimetres (4 feet) apart; or

(d) sheet steel fixed externally by welding, or bolting with steel bolts of not less than 12 millimetres (½ inch) diameter and at intervals of not more than 305 millimetres (1 foot), upon either angle-iron frames as specified in (c) above or timber frames of at least 50 millimetres (2 inches) by 100 millimetres (4 inches) section, having vertical and horizontal members spaced as specified in (c) above.

(2) If a party wall or, in the case of a room of which the floor level is less than 2440 millimetres (8 feet) above the external ground level, an external wall is used to form one of the walls of the room, that wall shall be reinforced internally by means of an additional wall which is constructed in accordance with the requirements of sub-paragraph (1) above.

(3) The floor shall be—

(a) constructed of solid concrete or reinforced concrete; or

(b) covered internally with sheet steel or steel mesh, welded at all joints; or

(c) otherwise so constructed that it cannot be readily penetrated from below.

(4) The ceiling shall be constructed of—

(a) solid concrete or reinforced concrete as specified in sub-paragraph (1)(b) above; or

(b) steel mesh fixed externally by welding upon angle-iron frames as specified in sub-paragraph (1)(c) above, the members of which shall not be more than 610 millimetres (2 feet) apart in one direction or more than 1220 millimetres (4 feet) apart in the other; or

(c) sheet steel fixed externally by welding upon angle-iron frames as specified in sub-paragraph (1)(c) above, the members being spaced as specified in (b) above.

(5) Each door or, in the case of a stable-type door, each half-door shall be constructed of—

(a) steel mesh fixed externally by welding upon angle-iron frames as specified in sub-paragraph (1)(c) above; or

(b) sheet steel fixed externally by welding upon angle-iron frames as specified in sub-paragraph (1)(c) above, the members being spaced as specified therein; or

(c) sheet steel fixed externally upon a hardwood frame of at least 50 millimetres (2 inches) by 75 millimetres (3 inches) to stiles, rails and braces or muntins by means of coach bolts at intervals of not more than 305 millimetres (1 foot) (the nuts whereof being on the inside of the door) and with non-withdrawable screws between the bolts at intervals not exceeding 100 millimetres (4 inches), the members of the frame being spaced as specified in sub-paragraph (1)(c) above; or

(d) sheet steel fixed externally upon a solid timber core of at least 50 millimetres (2 inches) thickness.

(6) Each door or, in the case of a stable-type door, each half-door shall be fitted with an effective lock, being a single-sided dead lock having resistance to manipulation and forcing sufficient to comply with the requirements of the Standard of 1963.

(7) If the room is fitted with a two-leaf door, the second opening leaf shall be secured top and bottom by means of—

(a) an espagnolette bolt, operated only from within the room, with vertical fastening rods of mild steel of at least 16 millimetres (⅝ inch) by 16 millimetres (⅝ inch) section or 16 millimetres (⅝ inch) diameter; or

(b) at least two internal tower bolts of mild steel of at least 16 millimetres (⅝ inch) diameter, designed to swivel into a secure holding recess when in the thrown position,

and in either case the bolt shall have a total throw at least 25 millimetres (1 inch) greater than the clearance between the door and the floor or lintel, as the case may be, the lower shooting hole being kept at all times free from obstruction.

(8) The closing frame of each doorway shall be constructed of—

(a) an angle-iron frame as specified in sub-paragraph (1)(c) above; or

(b) hardwood of at least 50 millimetres (2 inches) by 100 millimetres (4 inches) section, covered by sheet steel bolted through the timber at intervals not exceeding 457 millimetres (18 inches) by means of coach bolts (the nuts whereof not being accessible from outside the room); or

(c) pressed steel not lighter than 10 gauge welded at all joints.

(9) Each section of the closing frame of each doorway shall be fixed to the adjoining wall at intervals not exceeding 457 millimetres (18 inches) by means of—

(a) where the wall is constructed of bricks, bent and tanged straps of wrought-iron, screwed or bolted to the frame and built into the brickwork;

(b) where the wall is constructed of concrete, rag-bolts; or

(c) where the wall is constructed of steel mesh or sheet steel, steel bolts or dowels of at least 12 millimetres (½ inch) diameter or welding to the framework or cladding of the room.

(10) Each glass window shall either be constructed of glass blocks not larger than 190 millimetres (7½ inches) by 190 millimetres (7½ inches) and of at least 80 millimetres (3⅛ inches) thickness, set in a reinforced concrete frame having a reinforcing bar between every block, or be guarded by a grille consisting of—

(a) panels of steel mesh fixed on angle-iron frames as specified in sub-paragraph (1)(c) above and fixed—

(i) where the surrounding wall or ceiling is constructed of sheet steel on angle-iron frames, by welding to the sheet steel or framework at intervals not exceeding 305 millimetres (1 foot); or

(ii) where the surrounding wall is constructed of sheet steel on timber frames, by means of steel bolts of at least 12 millimetres (½ inch) diameter, bolted through the timber at intevals not exceeding 457 millimetres (18 inches); or

(iii) where the surrounding wall is constructed of bricks, by means of bent and tanged straps of wrought-iron screwed or bolted to the frame and built into the brickwork at intervals not exceeding 457 millimetres (18 inches); or

(iv) where the surrounding wall or ceiling is constructed of concrete, by means of rag-bolts at intervals not exceeding 457 millimetres (18 inches); or

(b) vertical bars of solid mild steel of at least 25 millimetres (1 inch) by 25 millimetres

(1 inch) square section, having one of their diagonal axes in a plane parallel to that of the window aperture, spaced not more than 127 millimetres (5 inches) apart centre to centre with the outer bars not more than 75 millimetres (3 inches) from the reveals of the window, and running through and welded to flat mild steel horizontal guard-bars which—

   (i) are of at least 62 millimetres (2½ inches) width and 9 millimetres (⅜ inch) thickness;

   (ii) are spaced not more than 762 millimetres (2½ feet) apart, the upper and lower guard-bars being at a distance not exceeding 100 millimetres (4 inches) from the ends of the vertical bars and not exceeding 75 millimetres (3 inches) from the head and sill of the window;

   (iii) are welded at each end to steel brackets of at least 152 millimetres (6 inches) length, 62 millimetres (2½ inches) width and 12 millimetres (½ inch) thickness fixed to the surrounding wall or ceiling, as the case may be, in the manner required by (*a*) above at a distance of at least 152 millimetres (6 inches) from the reveals of the window;

   (iv) if more than 1830 millimetres (6 feet) in length, have the uppermost and lowermost of them fixed to the head and sill of the window at intervals not exceeding 1830 millimetres (6 feet), by means of angle-iron fixings of at least 50 millimetres (2 inches) by 50 millimetres (2 inches) section and 6 millimetres (¼ inch) thickness welded to the guard-bars and fixed to the surrounding wall or ceiling, as the case may be, in the manner required by (*a*) above.

(11) Each service-hatch shall be guarded by a grille consisting of—

   (i) panels of steel mesh or sheet steel on angle-iron frames as specified in sub-paragraph (1)(*c*) above; or

   (ii) vertical bars of solid mild steel as specified in sub-paragraph (10)(*b*)(i) and (ii) above,

and the grille shall be secured at all times when the hatch is not in use in such a way as to be secure against removal from outside the room.

(12) Each aperture other than a window or service-hatch shall be guarded by a grille which satisfies the requirements of sub-paragraph (10)(*a*) or (*b*) above.

(13) Each shelf in a room shall be so situated as to prevent drugs placed upon it from being extracted from outside through any aperture.

(14) Nothing shall be displayed outside a room to indicate that drugs are kept in the room.

General

4.—(1) Subject to sub-paragraph (1A) below, where sheet steel is used in the construction of a safe, cabinet or room, its edges shall be lapped inwards around the margins of apertures and around the edges of doors and service-hatch covers in such manner as to be inaccessible from the outside; and where sheet steel is fixed on a framework, it shall be so fixed as to prevent removal from outside the safe, cabinet or room of which the framework forms part.

(1A) Where sheet steel is used in the construction of the door or the leaf of a door of a safe or cabinet, its edges need not be lapped inwards as required by sub-paragraph (1) above if the sheet steel used is not lighter than 10 gauge and the door or leaf of a door fits flush, or is recessed, so that no edge protrudes when the door is closed.

(2) Any steel mesh used in the construction of a safe, cabinet or room shall be—

(a) welded steel mesh not lighter than 10 standard wire gauge having rectangular apertures not exceeding 75 millimetres (3 inches) by 12 millimetres (½ inch); or

(b) expanded steel not lighter than 12 gauge having diamond apertures not exceeding 44 millimetres (1¾ inches) by 19 millimetres (¾ inch).

(3) Except where otherwise specified in this Schedule, the edges of each panel of sheet steel or steel mesh used in the construction of a safe, cabinet or room shall be arc-welded to a steel frame along their entire length, or, in the absence of a steel frame, continuously arc-welded along the entire length of all joins.

(4) Each hinged door, half-door or leaf of a two-leaf door in a safe, cabinet or room shall be fitted with at least two hinges.

(5) If any part of the hinges of such a door, half-door or leaf of a two-leaf door is on the outside of the door, it shall be fitted—

(a) in the case of a safe or cabinet, with at least two dog-bolts of mild steel of similar gauge and dimensions to the frame of the safe or cabinet or an internal flange or rebate running the entire length of the door and so fitted as to prevent access without unlocking in the event of damage to the hinges;

(b) in the case of a room, with at least two dog-bolts of mild steel which—

(i) are of similar gauge and dimensions to the jamb and either project at least 16 millimetres (⅝ inch) into the jamb or are attached to the jamb and project to a similar extent into the frame of the door, where the closing frame of the doorway is constructed of angle-iron; or

(ii) are of at least 50 millimetres (2 inches) width and 6 millimetres (¼ inch) thickness and either project at least 16 millimetres (⅝ inch) into the jamb or are attached to the jamb and project to a similar extent into the edge of the door, where the closing frame of the doorway is constructed of timber or pressed steel.

(6) Each bar, grille or service-hatch cover and each lock, bolt assembly and other means of securing doors and service-hatch covers in a safe, cabinet or room shall be fitted internally.

(7) The bolt of each lock and each other bolt or catch securing the cover of any aperture in a safe, cabinet or room shall be protected against cutting or manipulation from outside.

(8) Each screw, bolt or other fixing device used in the construction of a safe, cabinet or room shall be such as to be incapable of being removed from outside and shall be of a strength at least equal to that of the component part which it fixes.

APPENDIX IV

STATUTORY INSTRUMENTS

1973 No. 799

DANGEROUS DRUGS

The Misuse of Drugs (Notification of and Supply to Addicts) Regulations 1973

Made - - - -	19*th April* 1973
Laid before Parliament	7*th May* 1973
Coming into Operation	1*st July* 1973

In pursuance of sections 10(2)(*h*) and (*i*), 22(*c*) and 31 of the Misuse of Drugs Act 1971**(a)**, after consultation with the Advisory Council on the Misuse of Drugs, I hereby make the following Regulations:—

1. These Regulations may be cited as the Misuse of Drugs (Notification of and Supply to Addicts) Regulations 1973 and shall come into operation on 1st July 1973.

2.—(1) In these Regulations, the expression—
"drug" means a controlled drug specified in the Schedule to these Regulations;
"hospital"—

(*a*) as respects England and Wales, has the same meaning as in the National Health Service Act 1946**(b)** and includes a nursing home within the meaning of Part VI of the Public Health Act 1936**(c)**, a mental nursing home within the meaning of Part III of the Mental Health Act 1959**(d)** and a special hospital within the meaning of that Act;

(*b*) as respects Scotland, has the same meaning as in the National Health Service (Scotland) Act 1947**(e)** and includes a nursing home within the meaning of the Nursing Homes Registration (Scotland) Act 1938**(f)**, a private hospital within the meaning of the Mental Health (Scotland) Act 1960**(g)** and a state hospital within the meaning of that Act.

(a) 1971 c. 38.   **(b)** 1946 c. 81.   **(c)** 1936 c. 49.   **(d)** 1959 c. 72.
(e) 1947 c. 27.   **(f)** 1938 c. 73.   **(g)** 1960 c. 61.

(2) For the purposes of these Regulations, a person shall be regarded as being addicted to a drug if, and only if, he has as a result of repeated administration become so dependent upon the drug that he has an overpowering desire for the adminstration of it to be continued.

(3) In these Regulations any reference to any enactment shall be construed as a reference to that enactment as amended, and as including a reference thereto as extended or applied, by or under any other enactment.

(4) The Interpretation Act 1889(a) shall apply for the interpretation of these Regulations as it applies for the interpretation of an Act of Parliament.

3.—(1) Subject to paragraph (2) of this Regulation, any doctor who attends a person who he considers, or has reasonable grounds to suspect, is addicted to any drug shall, within seven days of the attendance, furnish in writing to the Chief Medical Officer at the Home Office such of the following particulars with respect to that person as are known to the doctor, that is to say, the name, address, sex, date of birth and national health service number of that person, the date of the attendance and the name of the drug or drugs concerned.

(2) It shall not be necessary for a doctor who attends a person to comply with the provisions of paragraph (1) of this Regulation in respect of that person if—

(*a*) the doctor is of the opinion, formed in good faith, that the continued administration of the drug or drugs concerned is required for the purpose of treating organic disease or injury; or

(*b*) the particulars which, apart from this paragraph, would have been required under those provisions to be furnished have, during the period of twelve months ending with the date of the attendance, been furnished in compliance with those provisions—

  (i) by the doctor; or

  (ii) if the doctor is a partner in or employed by a firm of general practitioners, by a doctor who is a partner in or employed by that firm; or

  (iii) if the attendance is on behalf of another doctor, whether for payment or otherwise, by that doctor; or

  (iv) if the attendance is at a hospital, by a doctor on the staff of that hospital.

4.—(1) Subject to paragraph (2) of this Regulation, a doctor shall not administer or supply to a person who he considers, or has reasonable grounds to suspect, is addicted to any drug, or authorise the administration or supply to such a person of, any substance specified in paragraph (3) below, or prescribe for such a person any such substance, except—

(*a*) for the purpose of treating organic disease or injury; or

(*b*) under and in accordance with the terms of a licence issued by the Secretary of State in pursuance of these Regulations.

(2) Paragraph (1) of this Regulation shall not apply to the administration or supply by a doctor of a substance specified in paragraph (3) below if the administration or supply

---

(a) 1889 c. 63.

is authorised by another doctor under and in accordance with the terms of a licence issued to him in pursuance of these Regulations.

(3) The substances referred to in paragraphs (1) and (2) above are—

    (*a*) cocaine, its salts and any preparation or other product containing cocaine or its salts other than a preparation falling within paragraph 2 of Schedule 1 to the Misuse of Drugs Regulations 1973(**a**);

    (*b*) diamorphine, its salts and any preparation or other product containing diamorphine or its salts;

    (*c*) dipipanone, its salts and any preparation or other product containing dipipanone or its salts.

5. These Regulations and, in relation only to the requirements of these Regulations, sections 13(1) and (3), 14, 16, 19 and 25 of and Schedule 4 to the Misuse of Drugs Act 1971 (which relate to their enforcement) shall apply to servants and agents of the Crown.

6.—(1) The Dangerous Drugs (Notification of Addicts) Regulations 1968(**b**) and the Dangerous Drugs (Supply to Addicts) Regulations 1968(**c**) are hereby revoked.

(2) For the purposes of paragraph 2(*b*) of Regulation 3 of these Regulations, any particulars furnished, before the coming into operation of these Regulations, in compliance with the provisions of paragraph (1) of Regulation 1 of the Dangerous Drugs (Notification of Addicts) Regulations 1968 shall be deemed to have been furnished in compliance with paragraph (1) of Regulation 3 of these Regulations.

(3) Notwithstanding anything in paragraph (1) of this Regulation, any licence issued by the Secretary of State in pursuance of the Dangerous Drugs (Supply to Addicts) Regulations 1968 before the coming into operation of these Regulations shall continue in force for the same time as if these Regulations had not been made and shall be deemed to have been issued in pursuance of these Regulations.

Robert Carr,
One of Her Majesty's Principal
Secretaries of State.

Home Office,
  Whitehall.
19th April 1973.

SCHEDULE   *Regulation 2(1)*

CONTROLLED DRUGS TO WHICH THESE REGULATIONS APPLY

1. The following substances and products, namely:—

Cocaine	Hydromorphone	Oxycodone
Dextromoramide	Levorphanol	Pethidine

(**a**) S.I. 1973/797.   (**b**) S.I. 1968/136 (1968 I, p. 375).
(**c**) S.I. 1968/416 (1968 I, p. 1093).

Diamorphine	Methadone	Phenazocine
Dipipanone	Morphine	Piritramide
Hydrocodone	Opium	

2. Any stereoisomeric form of a substance specified in paragraph 1 above, not being dextrorphan.

3. Any ester or ether of a substance specified in paragraph 1 or 2 above not being a substance for the time being specified in Part II of Schedule 2 to the Misuse of Drugs Act 1971.

4. Any salt of a substance specified in any of paragraphs 1 to 3 above.

5. Any preparation or other product containing a substance or product specified in any of paragraphs 1 to 4 above.

APPENDIX V

1977 No. 1379

DANGEROUS DRUGS

The Misuse of Drugs (Designation) Order 1977

Made - - - -	*8th August* 1977
Laid before Parliament	*16th August* 1977
Coming into Operation—	
Articles 1 and 2	*8th September* 1977
Remainder	*20th September* 1977

In pursuance of section 7(4), (5) and (7) of the Misuse of Drugs Act 1971**(a)**, on the recommendation of the Advisory Council on the Misuse of Drugs, I hereby make the following Order:—

1.—(1) This Order may be cited as the Misuse of Drugs (Designation) Order 1977, and (with the exception of Articles 3 and 4 and the Schedule which shall come into operation on 20th September 1977) shall come into operation on 8th September 1977.

(2) The Interpretation Act 1889**(b)** shall apply for the interpretation of this Order as it applies for the interpretation of an Act of Parliament, and as if any Orders revoked by this Order were Acts of Parliament repealed by an Act of Parliament.

2. During the period beginning with 8th September 1977 and ending with 19th September 1977, the Misuse of Drugs (Designation) Order 1973**(c)**, as amended **(d)**, shall have effect as if in Article 2 thereof there were added at the end the following paragraph:—

'(2) In that Schedule, "cannabis" has the same meaning as in the Misuse of Drugs Act 1971 as amended by section 52 of the Criminal Law Act 1977**(e)**.'

3.—(1) The controlled drugs specified in the Schedule hereto are hereby designated as drugs to which section 7(4) of the Misuse of Drugs Act 1971 applies.

(2) In that Schedule, "cannabis" has the same meaning as in the Misuse of Drugs Act 1971 as amended by section 52 of the Criminal Law Act 1977.

4. The Misuse of Drugs (Designation) Order 1973 and the Misuse of Drugs (Designation) (Amendment) Order 1975**(d)** are hereby revoked.

Merlyn Rees,
One of Her Majesty's Principal
Secretaries of State.

Home Office.
8th August 1977.

(a) 1971 c. 38. **(b)** 1889 c. 63.
(c) S.I. 1973/796 (1973 I, p. 2547). **(d)** S.I. 1975/498 (1975 I, p. 1652).
(e) 1977 c. 45.

SCHEDULE

CONTROLLED DRUGS TO WHICH SECTION 7(4) OF THE
MISUSE OF DRUGS ACT 1971 APPLIES

1. The following substances and products, namely:—

(a)	
Bufotenine	Lysergide and other *N*-alkyl derivatives of lysergamide
Cannabinol	Mescaline
Cannabinol derivatives	Psilocin
Cannabis	Raw opium
Cannabis resin	Rolicyclidine
Coca leaf	Tenocyclidine
Concentrate of	4-Bromo-2,5-dimethoxy-α-methylphenethylamine
poppy-straw	*N,N*-Diethyltryptamine
Eticyclidine	*N,N*-Dimethyltryptamine
Lysergamide	2,5-Dimethoxy-α,4-dimethylphenethylamine

(*b*) any compound (not being a compound for the time being specified in sub-paragraph (*a*) above) structurally derived from tryptamine or from a ring-hydroxy tryptamine by substitution at the nitrogen atom of the sidechain with one or more alkyl substituents but no other substituent;

(*c*) any compound (not being methoxyphenamine or a compound for the time being specified in sub-paragraph (*a*) above) structurally derived from phenethylamine, an *N*-alkylphenethylamine, α-methylphenethylamine, an *N*-alkyl-α-methylphenethylamine, α-ethylphenethylamine, or an *N*-alkyl-α-ethylphenethylamine by substitution in the ring to any extent with alkyl, alkoxy, alkylenedioxy or halide substituents, whether or not further substituted in the ring by one or more other univalent substituents.

2. Any stereoisomeric form of a substance specified in paragraph 1 above.

3. Any ester or ether of a substance specified in paragraph 1 or 2 above.

4. Any salt of a substance specified in any of paragraphs 1 to 3 above.

5. Any preparation or other product containing a substance or product specified in any of paragraphs 1 to 4 above.

GLOSSARY

The glossary which follows is not exhaustive of controlled drugs or of words and phrases which may be encountered in practice. The controlled drugs which are included are the commonest, or those which are designated, notifiable and/or restricted. They appear in block capitals and are cross-referred to their proprietary names. Where the name of a reported case is appended, the drug or other entry can be read about in that context.

Acid Lysergic acid diethylamide. LYSERGAMIDE, LYSERGIDE.

Addict 'A person shall be regarded as being addicted to a drug if, and only if, he has as a result of repeated administration become so dependent upon the drug that he has an overpowering desire for the administration of it to be continued' (reg 2(2)).

ALFENTANIL Class A. Added 1/1/85.

Alkaloid A chemical compound of plant origin, containing nitrogen.

AMPHETAMINE Class B. Stimulant. Slang name: speed.

Barbiturates A large group of sedative and hypnotic drugs, not controlled until 1/1/85. Then 5,5 disubstituted barbituric acids and METHYLPHENOBARBITONE added.

Blow (n) CANNABIS or CANNABIS RESIN.

Bromo-STP A bromine derivative of which 4-BROMO-2,5-DIMETHOXY-α-METHYLPHENETHYLAMINE (Class A) is the active hallucinogen. Designated. Bromo-DOM in chemical literature. (*Mieras* v *Rees*)

BUFOTENINE Class A. Designated. Hallucinogen. (*DPP* v *Goodchild*)

Bush CANNABIS.

Bust (v) To detect (a person) in possession, etc, of a controlled drug.

Cannabidiol One of the CANNABINOL DERIVATIVES.

CANNABINOL Class A. Designated. One of the active principles of CANNABIS and CANNABIS RESIN. Not a Class A drug when contained in either of those.

CANNABINOL DERIVATIVES Class A. Designated. 'The following substances, except where contained in cannabis or cannabis resin, namely tetrahydro derivatives of cannabinol and 3-alkyl homologues of cannabinol or of its tetrahydro derivatives' (Sched 2, Part IV).

CANNABIS Class B. Designated. Mild hallucinogen. Slang names: grass, bush. 'Any plant of the genus *Cannabis* or any part of any such plant (by whatever name designated) except that it does not include cannabis resin or any of the following products after separation from the rest of the plant, namely—

    (*a*) mature stalk of any such plant,

    (*b*) fibre produced from mature stalk of any such plant, and

    (*c*) seed of any such plant' (s 37(1), as amended by the Criminal Law Act 1977, s 52).

Cannabis oil. Purified CANNABIS RESIN.

CANNABIS RESIN Class B. Designated. Mild hallucinogen. Slang names: hash, pot. 'The separated resin, whether crude or purified, obtained from any plant of the genus *Cannabis*' (s 37(1)).

Cannabis seeds Seeds of any plant of the genus *Cannabis*. Not a controlled drug. In use as cagebird food.

Charlie COCAINE. (*R* v *Greensmith*)

Chase the Dragon Sniff (heated or burning) heroin.

Chillum Smoking utensil. (*Allan and Others* v *Milne*)

CLONITAZENE Class A. Designated.

COCA LEAF Class A. Designated. 'The leaf of any plant of the genus *Erythroxylon* from whose leaves cocaine can be extracted either directly or by chemical transformation' (Sched 2, Part IV).

COCAINE Class A. Notifiable. Restricted. Slang names: charlie, coke, snow. Drug of addiction. Sniffed. (*R* v *Greensmith*)

CODEINE Class B. Narcotic analgesic used in mild to moderate pain. An alkaloid of opium.

Coke COCAINE. (*R* v *Greensmith*)

CONCENTRATE OF POPPY-STRAW Class A. (Listed under POPPY-STRAW.) Designated. 'The material produced when poppy-straw has entered into a process for the concentration of its alkaloids' (Sched 2, Part IV).

Controlled drug 'Any substance or product for the time being specified in Part I, II or III of Schedule 2' (s 2(1)(*a*)).

Cultivation Included in production (s 37(1)). (*Tudhope* v *Robertson and Another*)

Cut (v) To adulterate.

Daprisal Proprietary name of DEXAMPHETAMINE.

Deal (n) A quantity, generally the smallest conventional quantity in which drugs are sold.

Designated Designated by the Misuse of Drugs (Designation) Order 1977 and listed in Sched 4 to the Misuse of Drugs Regulations 1973, ie, as having no approved medical use and being available under licence only for research.

Designation Order The Misuse of Drugs (Designation) Order 1977 (SI 1977 No 1379), as amended.

DEXAMPHETAMINE Class B. Stimulant. Proprietary names: Daprisal, Dexedrine, Drinamyl, Durophet. Stereoisomer of AMPHETAMINE. (*R* v *Watts*)

Dexedrine Proprietary name of DEXAMPHETAMINE.

Dextromethorphan A stereoisomer of LEVORPHANOL, but excluded by para 2 of Part I of Sched 2.

DEXTROMORAMIDE Class A. Notifiable. Proprietary name: Palfium. Narcotic analgesic used in severe pain but less sedating than morphine.

Dextrorphan A stereoisomer of LEVORPHANOL, but excluded by para 2 of Part I of Sched 2.

DF118 Proprietary name of DIHYDROCODEINE.

DIAMORPHINE Class A. Notifiable. Restricted. A derivative of MORPHINE; known as heroin. Slang names: smack, junk. Powerful analgesic used for severe pain. Drug of addiction. Psychic dependence common. Withdrawal syndrome may be severe.

Diazepam A tranquillising drug, used in anxiety and agitated-depressive states. Not controlled. Proprietary name: Valium.

Diconal Proprietary name of DIPIPANONE.

DIETHYLPROPION Class C. Added 1/1/85.

DIHYDROCODEINE Class B. Proprietary name: DF118. Narcotic analgesic used in mild to moderate pain.

DIPIPANONE Class A. Notifiable. Restricted. Proprietary name: Diconal. Narcotic analgesic used in moderate to severe pain but less sedating than morphine.

Dope CANNABIS RESIN, or any drug.

Draw (n) CANNABIS or CANNABIS RESIN.

Drinamyl Proprietary name of DEXAMPHETAMINE.

Dromoran Proprietary name of LEVORPHANOL.

Drop (v) To take (drugs) orally.

Drug Any substance used as a medicine, or in making medicines (*Webster's New International Dictionary*).

Durophet Proprietary name of DEXAMPHETAMINE.

Ester A characteristic derivative of a drug.

Ether A characteristic derivative of a drug.

ETHYLMORPHINE Class B. Cough suppressant. (*Morrison* v *Smith*)

ETICYCLIDINE Class A. Added 1/1/85.

Filter A plug made of paper torn from a cigarette or cigarette-paper packet and inserted at the mouthpiece of a cannabis cigarette.

Fix (n) Injection (of a drug).

Ganja CANNABIS. India, West Indies.

Gear Drugs.

Grain 0.0648 of a gram.

Grams to an ounce 28.35.

Grass CANNABIS.

Habit Dependence on a drug.

Hash CANNABIS RESIN.

Hash oil Cannabis oil.

Herbal cannabis CANNABIS.

Heroin DIAMORPHINE.

Hit (n) Injection (of a drug).

Homologues Closely related members of a series of chemical compounds having properties similar to those of a parent compound.

Hydrochloride The biologically inactive component of the salt of a drug.

HYDROCODONE Class A. Notifiable.

HYDROMORPHONE Class A. Notifiable. Analgesic.

Indian hemp CANNABIS.

Jack Heroin.

Joint Cigarette containing CANNABIS or CANNABIS RESIN.

Junk Heroin.

Junkie Heroin user.

Kit Drugs.

Levoamphetamine Stereoisomer of AMPHETAMINE. (*R* v *Watts*)

LEVORPHANOL Class A. Notifiable. Proprietary name: Dromoran. Narcotic analgesic used in severe pain. Less sedating than morphine.

LSD LYSERGAMIDE, LYSERGIDE.

LYSERGAMIDE Class A. Designated. Hallucinogen. Known as LSD (from lysergic acid diethylamide).

Lysergic acid diethylamide LYSERGAMIDE, LYSERGIDE.

LYSERGIDE AND OTHER N-ALKYL DERIVATIVES OF LYSERGAMIDE Class A. Designated. Hallucinogens. Known as LSD.

Mandrax Proprietary name of METHAQUALONE.

Marijuana, marihuana CANNABIS. American usage.

MECLOQUALONE Class B. Added 1/1/85.

MEDICINAL OPIUM Class A. (Listed under OPIUM.) Notifiable. 'Raw opium which has undergone the process necessary to adapt it for medicinal use in accordance with the requirements of the British Pharmacopoeia, whether it is in the form of powder or is granulated or is in any other form, and whether it is or is not mixed with neutral substances' (Sched 2, Part IV).

Melsedin Proprietary name of METHAQUALONE.

MESCALINE Class A. Designated. Hallucinogen. Derived from the Mexican peyotl cactus. (*DPP* v *Goodchild*).

METHADONE Class A. Notifiable. Proprietary name: Physeptone. Narcotic analgesic used in severe pain. As Methadone mixture, used in the replacement and maintenance treatment of drug dependence. Two and a half times the strength of Methadone linctus.

METHADONE linctus Class A. Notifiable. Cough suppressant. Proprietary name: Physeptone. Used in the replacement and maintenance treatment of drug dependence.

METHAQUALONE Class C to 1/1/85, thereafter Class B. Proprietary names: Mandrax, Melsedin. Sedative used in insomnia as an alternative to barbiturates.

Methedrine Proprietary name of METHYLAMPHETAMINE.

METHYLAMPHETAMINE Class B. A stimulant similar to AMPHETAMINE. Proprietary name: Methedrine.

METHYLPHENIDATE Class B. Anti-depressant. Proprietary name: Ritalin.

METHYLPHENOBARBITONE Class B. Added 1/1/85. Anti-epileptic.

Mexican magic mushroom Toadstool source of PSILOCIN. (*DPP* v *Goodchild*; *Murray* v *MacNaughton*)

Microdot Single dose of LYSERGAMIDE.

Microgram One-millionth part of a gram (0.000001 gm). Misuse: 'References in this Act to misusing a drug are references to . . . the taking of it by a human being by way of any form of self-administration, whether or not involving assistance by another' (s 37(2)).

Modification Orders The Misuse of Drugs Act 1971 (Modification) Orders 1973 (SI 1973 No 771) and 1984 (SI 1984 No 859).

MORPHINE Class A. Notifiable. Narcotic analgesic used in severe pain. Drug of addiction. The principal alkaloid of OPIUM. Also present in CONCENTRATE OF POPPY-STRAW.

Narcotic (n) A drug which in moderate doses allays sensibility, relieves pain and produces profound sleep, but which in poisonous doses produces stupor, coma or convulsions (*Webster's New International Dictionary*).

Notifiable Notification Regulations apply.

Notification Regulations The Misuse of Drugs (Notification of and Supply to Addicts) Regulations 1973 (SI 1973 No 799), as amended.

Opiate (n) Any medicine containing, or derived from, opium and tending to induce sleep or repose (*Webster's New International Dictionary*).

OPIUM Class A. (Full entry: OPIUM, WHETHER RAW, PREPARED OR MEDICINAL.) Notifiable. Drug of addiction. The dried juice from the capsules of the opium poppy. Contains 10 per cent morphine.

Opium poppy 'The plant of the species *Papaver somniferum* L' (Sched 2, Part IV).

OXYCODONE Class A. Notifiable. Narcotic analgesic.

Palfium Proprietary name of DEXTROMORAMIDE.

PETHIDINE Class A. Notifiable. Narcotic analgesic less potent than morphine. May be lawfully possessed and administered by certified midwives (Principal Regulations, reg 11(1)).

Peyotl, peyote Cactus source of MESCALINE. (*DPP* v *Goodchild*)

PHENAZOCINE Class A. Notifiable. Narcotic analgesic used in severe pain.

Physeptone Proprietary name of METHADONE.

PIRITRAMIDE Class A. Notifiable. Analgesic.

POPPY-STRAW Class A. (Full entry: POPPY-STRAW AND CONCENTRATE OF POPPY-STRAW.) 'All parts, except the seeds, of the opium poppy, after mowing' (Sched 2, Part IV).

Pot CANNABIS RESIN. Journalistic usage.

PREPARED OPIUM Class A (listed under OPIUM). Notifiable. 'Opium prepared for smoking, including dross and any other residues remaining after opium has been smoked' (s 37(1)).

Principal Regulations The Misuse of Drugs Regulations 1973 (SI 1973 No 797), as amended.

Produce (v) 'To produce by manufacture, cultivation or any other method' (s 37(1)). (*DPP* v *Nock and Another*)

PSILOCIN Class A. Designated. Hallucinogen. Derived from the Mexican magic mushroom. (*DPP* v *Goodchild*; *Murray* v *MacNaughton*)

Punt (v) Sell.

RAW OPIUM   Class A (listed under OPIUM). Designated. Notifiable. Includes powdered or granulated opium but does not include medicinal opium (Sched 2, Part IV).

Reefer   Cigarette containing CANNABIS or CANNABIS RESIN.

Restricted   May be administered or supplied to addicts only under licence or for the purpose of treating (including the relief of pain in) organic disease or injury. Applies to COCAINE, DIAMORPHINE and DIPIPANONE (Notification Regulations, reg 4).

Ritalin   Proprietary name of METHYLPHENIDATE.

Roach   The filter and other unsmoked parts of a cannabis cigarette; the stub.

ROLICYLIDINE   Class A. Added 1/1/85.

Safe Custody Regulations   The Misuse of Drugs (Safe Custody) Regulations 1973 (SI 1973 No 798), as amended.

Salt   The salt of a drug may be formed by combining it with an acid, eg, sulphuric acid. Hence MORPHINE sulphate, MORPHINE hydrochloride, etc.

Score (v)   To buy.

Script   Prescription.

Secretary of State   Secretary of State for Home Affairs. Interpretation Act 1889; or Ministry of Home Affairs for Northern Ireland (s 38(1)).

Shit   CANNABIS and CANNABIS RESIN. (*R* v *Blake and Another*)

Skin   Cigarette paper.

Smack   Heroin.

Snort (v)   To sniff (COCAINE, heroin).

Snow   COCAINE.

Speed   AMPHETAMINE.

Stereoisomers   Chemical compounds in which the constituent atoms and the sequence in which they are linked are identical but the spatial arrangements of which differ.

Sulphate   The biologically inactive component of the salt of a drug. In slang, denotes AMPHETAMINE sulphate.

Supply (v)   Includes to distribute (s 37(1)).

Tab of acid   Blotting paper or card impregnated with LYSERGAMIDE or LYSERGIDE.

Tartrate   Combined with tartaric acid.

TENOCYCLIDINE   Class A. Added 1/1/85.

Tetrahydrocannabinol   One of the CANNABINOL DERIVATIVES. Known as THC. (*DPP* v *Goodchild*)

THEBAINE   Class A. An alkaloid of OPIUM. (*DPP* v *Goodchild*)

Valium   Proprietary name of Diazepam.

Works, set of   Hypodermic syringe.

4 - BROMO - 2,5 - DIMETHOXY - α - METHYLPHENETHYLAMINE   Class A. Designated. Known as Bromo-STP. (*Mieras* v *Rees*)

BIBLIOGRAPHY

BARLOW, N. L. A., 'Possession of Minute Quantities of a Drug' [1977] Crim LR 26.

[BOVEY, K. S.] 'Possession of Minute Quantities of a Drug' (1979) 24 JLSS 513.

[BOVEY, K. S.] 'Possession of Minute Quantities of a Drug' (1980) 25 JLSS 330.

[BOVEY, K. S.] 'Possession of Controlled Drugs' (1980) 25 JLSS 360.

BOVEY, K. S., 'Possession of Controlled Drugs with Intent to Supply' (1984) 91 SCOLAG Bul 48.

BOVEY, K. S., 'Misuse of Drugs: Recent Developments' (1985) 30 JLSS 237.

BOVEY, K. S., 'Defences under the 1971 Act' (1985) 30 JLSS 494.

BOVEY, K. S., 'Duplication in Charges under the Misuse of Drugs Act 1971' (1986) 31 JLSS 242.

BUCKNELL, P. and GHODSE, H., *Misuse of Drugs*, Waterlow, 1986.

CARD, R. I. E., 'The Misuse of Drugs Act 1971' [1972] Crim LR 744.

LORD, R., *Controlled Drugs: Law and Practice*, Butterworths, 1984.

LYDIATE, P. W. H., *The Law Relating to the Misuse of Drugs*, Butterworths, 1977.

RIBEIRO, R. and PERRY, J., 'Possession and Section 28 of the Misuse of Drugs Act 1971' [1979] Crim LR 90.

SHIELS, R. S., 'Possession of Controlled Drugs with Intent to Supply' (1984) 89 SCOLAG Bul 23.

SHIELS, R. S., 'Minute Quantities of Drugs', *Scottish Law Gazette*, vol 50, p 32.

SHIELS, R. S., '*R* v *Boyesen*', *Scottish Law Gazette*, vol 50, p 88.

SHIELS, R. S., 'Controlled Drugs and the Power of Forfeiture', *Scottish Law Gazette*, vol 51, p 15.

INDEX